THE AGRICULTURE OF THE WORLD

The Agriculture of the World

ANNA BURGER
Professor of Economic Geography
Attila József University
Szeged, Hungary

Avebury

Aldershot · Brookfield USA · Hong Kong · Singapore · Sydney

© A. Burger 1994

Published by
Avebury
Ashgate Publishing Company
Gower House
Croft Road
Aldershot
Hants GU11 3HR
England

Ashgate Publishing Company
Old Post Road
Brookfield
Vermont 05036
USA

British Library Cataloguing in Publication Data

Burger, Anna
  Agriculture of the World
  I. Title
  338.109
ISBN 1 85628 609 6
Reprinted 1996

Library of Congress Cataloging-in-Publication Data

Burger, Anna.
    The agriculture of the world / Anna Burger.
      p. cm.
    Includes bibliographical references and index. (p.   )
    ISBN 1-85628-609-6 : £35.00 ($59.95 U.S. : est.)
    1. Agricultural geography. 2. Agriculture. 3. Agriculture-
-Economic aspects. 4. Agricultural ecology. I. Title
S439.B87 1994
338.1'09--dc20   94-26966
                                                 CIP

Typeset by Alan Campbell.

Printed and bound by Athenæum Press Ltd.,
Gateshead, Tyne & Wear.

Contents

List of tables   viii
List of figures   xi
Preface   xiii

Introduction   1

PART I: ECONOMIC DEVELOPMENT, ECONOMIC GROWTH   7

**1 Some major principles of economic growth and
    development**   9

    Measures of development   9
    Economic growth   18
    Indicators and models of economic growth   20
    The historical school of economic growth   28

2 Development of agriculture in different regions   30

    How did the agriculture of the developed countries reach
      its present level of development?   30
    Agriculture in developing countries   37
    The development and growth of agriculture in present
      and former socialist countries   45
    Reforms in socialist countries   52
    Transformation of agriculture in the Central-East
      European former socialist countries and the CIS   54
    The faltering and slowing of growth across the world   58
    World models of growth   63

PART II: AGRICULTURAL TRADE   71

3 Some principles of trade   73

The evolution of trade 73
Thünen's theory of location and rent 74
The development of foreign trade 79
The applicability of Ricardo's principle of comparative
costs 81

4 Agricultural world trade 87

Agricultural protectionism 87
The development of agricultural imports and exports 94
The North-South dilemma and the GATT negotiations 111
The Uruguay Round 112

**5 Regional trade agreements and market regulation
systems** 118

The EC and its agricultural market regulation system 118
Agricultural market regulation in the USA 123
International free trade agreements 127

PART III: NATURAL ENDOWMENT AND FACTORS OF
PRODUCTION 133

6 Agro-ecological conditions 135

Arable land and its agro-ecological characteristics 135
Land area 137
Agro-ecological potential of the world's regions 142
Irrigation 146
Fertilization 150
Agricultural mechanization 154
Environmental damage 156

7 Social and Economic Conditions of Production 160

Agricultural population and workforce 160
Theories of population growth 160
Agricultural population and rural population 167
Vertical integration 170
The mutual substitution of land, labour and means of
production in raising productivity of land, from the
aspect of economic theory 170

PART IV: THE GEOGRAPHICAL LOCATION OF
AGRICULTURAL PRODUCTION 183

8 History of agricultural production 185

9 The regional division of today's agriculture 195

Wet equatorial zone agriculture   199
Agriculture of the savannah zone   199
Agriculture of the tropical monsoon zone   199
Agriculture of zonal deserts and tropical steppelands, and
of middle latitude dry steppelands   200
Agriculture of the wet sub-tropics   201
Agriculture of the dry sub-tropical zone   202
Agriculture of temperate zone   203
Agriculture of the cold climatic zone   205
Agricultural zones changing with altitude   205

PART 5: AGRICULTURAL LAND   213

10 Land tenure and use   215

Size of estates   216
Forms of land tenure   218
Communal land and shifting cultivation   218
Pastoral nomadism   220
State-owned lands   221
State farms   223
Farming cooperatives   224
Socialist production cooperatives   225
New land reforms in former socialist countries   228
Socialist cooperatives outside Europe   233
Production cooperatives in other developing countries   237
Private and individual farming   239
Ranching   240
Plantations   242
The family farm   248
The development of family farming in Europe   251
Family farms in Europe   255
Family farms in North America and Oceania   257

11 Land reforms in the developing world   261

Latin America   263
South and South-East Asia   273
The Near East   277
Africa   280

Closing remarks   286

Bibliography   290

Index   303

Tables

Table 1.1   Comparison of the world's economies (ascending order)   12

Table 1.2   GDP per capita as a percentage of the USA's in 1990 ICP estimates   14

Table 1.3   Level of development in some countries in 1990: Distribution of GDP (per cent)   16

Table 2.1   Annual growth rates for GNP, food production and population   34

Table 2.2   Daily food supply per capita   40

Table 2.3   Countries of lowest and highest per capita animal protein consumption per day in 1989-90 (grams)   40

Table 2.4   Some initial data used by the FAO for its projection for year 2000   41

Table 2.5   Main data for the FAO projection for 1980-2000 (annual per cent)   42

Table 2.6   Percentage of total production by individual producers in the CMEA countries (1980)   50

Table 2.7   Average annual growth rate of gross agricultural output at constant prices   51

Table 4.1   Net percentage PSE of all agricultural products   88

Table 4.2   Average PSE per unit value for some developing countries' agriculture   90

Table 4.3	Nominal protection coefficients 1980-82	92
Table 4.4	Percentage share of developed and developing countries in agricultural world exports in value terms	96
Table 4.5	Exports of agricultural products of major exporting countries and their percentage share in the world's exports (1989-1991 average)	98
Table 4.6	Trade in agricultural products as a percentage of value of total traded products	101
Table 4.7	Level of self-sufficiency in the OECD countries in per cent	103
Table 4.8	The EC countries' and some other developed countries' agricultural balance of trade	104
Table 4.9	Annual percentage change of export and import volumes	105
Table 4.10	Geographical structure of exports in per cent 1989-1992	107
Table 4.11	Self-sufficiency ratios	110
Table 4.12	Percentage structure of Hungarian agricultural export-import in US dollars and changes between 1991 and 1992	111
Table 6.1	Cultivated land area and reserves (million hectares)	139
Table 6.2	Land use in 1990 in percent of land area	142
Table 6.3	Percentage rise in irrigated areas between 1950 and 1985 by world region	148
Table 6.4	Irrigated areas in 1990 and their growth	149
Table 6.5	Fertilizer use	151
Table 6.6	Yields and fertilizer use	152
Table 6.7	Number of tractors and harvester-threshers per 1000 hectare arable land and permanent crop land in 1990	155
Table 7.1	Average annual growth of population	162
Table 7.2	Effect of level of development and population density on yields	166
Table 7.3	Agricultural employment as a percentage of total employed	168

Table 7.4   Percentage rates of national gross added value of the agro-food industry in the European Community economies at 1985 market prices   171

Table 7.5   Percentage share of food processing industry in 1985   171

Table 7.6   Substitution of land by labour   173

Table 7.7   Values and costs of, and income from, producing wheat   176

Table 7.8   Value and costs of, and income from, producing wheat on better land   179

Table 7.9   The rate of substitution of land and fertilizer   181

Table 8.1   Places of origin of domesticated plants   187

Table 9.1   Agriculture typical of climatic zones   207

Table 9.2   Production of the major agricultural products in quantity and percentage of the world's production (1989-91 average)   210

Table 10.1   Proportion of small and large estates in the 1970s, as a percentage of total land area   217

Table 10.2   Size of farms (1987)   250

Figures

Figure 3.1   Thünen's concentric agricultural zones around one or more cities   77

Figure 3.2   Change in the value of exports from the USA and the EC between 1975 and 1989   84

Figure 4.1   Changes in percentage PSE   89

Figure 4.2   The composition of OECD trade in unprocessed agricultural goods in value terms as a percentage share of the world's unprocessed agricultural exports and imports   99

Figure 4.3   Agricultural product trade of some major exporters as a percentage share of total merchandise exports in value terms   102

Figure 4.4   Wallerstein Regions c 1900   113

Figure 4.5   Wallerstein Regions of the world at present   114

Figure 4.6   Budget expenditure for agricultural price and income support in the USA and the EC between 1980 and 1990   115

Figure 4.7   Net total PSE   126

Figure 6.1   Distribution of the world's land area   138

Figure 6.2   Quality of cultivable land in the developing countries   140

Figure 6.3   Cultivated land as a percentage of potentially cultivable land area according to continent or region   141

Figure 6.4   Fertilizer use and yields 1990   153

Figure 7.1   The connection between population density and yields   165

Figure 7.2   Substitution of labour for land   174

Figure 7.3   Value, cost and income of wheat production   175

Figure 7.4   Differential rent   178

Figure 7.5   Substitution of fertilizer for land   180

Figure 8.1   Gene centres of cultivated plants (after Vavilov)   188

Figure 8.2   Main centres of domestication (after Vavilov and
              followers)   190

Figure 9.1   Principal agricultural zones of the world   206

Figure 10.1   Major production areas of Africa   247

Figure 10.2   Decrease in the number of farms from 1970 to 1986   256

Figure 10.3   Main agricultural regions of the United States   259

Preface

There is an enormous literature which deals with the problems of world agriculture. Much has been published about the agriculture of developing and developed countries and regions, about agricultural trade, agricultural economics and policy, natural factors and their distribution, environmental protection etc.

There are, however, few comprehensive works, modern textbooks or handbooks which bring together the above questions in a world context. I have felt the lack of this throughout my time as a university teacher, as a lecturer in agricultural economic geography, and in writing this book I have set out to fill this gap.

In my book I have striven to present side by side the agricultural problems of the developed and developing world, and former and existing socialist or communist countries, demonstrating the interdependencies between them. I have attempted to cover these regions' and countries' economic growth, level of development, trade, production, conditions of production, production environment, technologies and the agricultural produce appropriate to their climate, and their land-use and land-tenure. I have dealt with questions of their economic policy and, where it seemed necessary, with theoretical treatments of these. It has been my particular aim not only to describe the way of doing agriculture in the various parts of the world, but to give an answer as to why it has become the way it is through the processes of development.

In my work I have made great use of international literature and statistics. I would like to acknowledge my debt to all of the authors and compilers of statistics whose results and data I have used in my work and to which I refer.

My thanks are also due to my colleagues in the Economic Geography Department of the Attila József University of Szeged, particularly Professor Rezső Mészáros, and also to József Tóth at the Janus Pannonius University of Pécs for their valuable advice.

I would like to thank my students for their questions and also for their answers – the wrong at least as much as the right – which have helped to clarify the problems and explain them more clearly, and ultimately prompted research.

Thanks also to Katalin Szép, lecturer at the Agricultural University of Budapest, for preparing some of the figures and to Katalin Kasza for drawing all of the figures.

I would especially like to thank Alan Campbell for his help in making the English of this book real, and for preparing it for publication.

Finally my thanks are due to the Hungarian National Research Fund (Országos Kutatási Alap, OTKA) which provided financial support for my research and for the writing and publication of the book.

Anna Burger

Introduction

In the changing economy of our time, the role of agriculture in the world's affairs has – against all expectations – steadily increased. In the earlier part of the 20th century, economists and politicians thought that the significance of agriculture would diminish with industrialization. Today, with the service and information economy developing and indeed already dominating in advanced countries, it has turned out that agricultural production has maintained and even increased its significance. In the less developed and developing countries which make up 4/5 of the world, the meeting of the demand for food is a more basic question than ever. Of the 100 countries registered by the FAO as developing, altogether 15 are capable of supplying themselves with their staple grains. In most less-developed countries food production is still, or in fact is ever more a question of existence, the difference between prosperity and mass starvation.

The developed countries, despite their agricultural workforce's decline to a tiny proportion of the total, are struggling with the problems of agricultural production and trade more now than at any time in history. Agricultural protectionism and subsidy, and the related overproduction, sparks internal political conflict and foreign trade wars leading to serious international strife. Food has become a strategic weapon in the hands of developed countries, which it can use to keep numerous less developed countries under control.

Central to economic decline in former and existing socialist countries has been the chronic lack of food, a result of decades of neglect and deprivation of agricultural interests.

This book is concerned with questions of economics, economic theory and economic policy of the world's agriculture. It analyses the geographical disposition of production, production facilities and the conditions for production. It examines how ways of doing agriculture are determined by

1

factors of the *natural environment*, and how they interrelate with economic and social conditions.

The *natural factors* are the climatic, soil, relief and water conditions governing cultivation.

The various climatic zones and different soil, relief and water conditions determine the forms of natural plant cover found, which kinds of cultivated plants and domesticated animals can be kept, and which modes of cultivation are feasible.

Agricultural production has, of course, absolute limits, but within these there are wide differences, and throughout the world there is a wide variety and interchangeability of forms of cultivation. The absolute limits are: a suitable climate for production, land that can be brought under cultivation, suitable relief for farming and the presence of the required minimum of water for plants.

The absolute northern limit set by climate is 55°N in Labrador and 65°N in Alaska, and in scattered parts of Scandinavia and Siberia as far as 70-71°N. In the south it is 44°S in Chile and 55°S in Patagonia.

The natural vegetation of the climatic zone greatly influences agricultural production, but does not absolutely dictate it. Man's measures of improvement and adaptation serve to push back the limits within which plants and animals can thrive. Of course the tropical and subtropical bananas, tea and coffee cannot be produced in temperate zones, but production of mediterranean wheat and subtropical groundnut and soya beans has been spread far to the north by man. Similarly, temperate-zone plants and fruits have been adapted to the tropics and subtropics. All kinds of domesticated animals can be found far from their places of origin.

Within the climatic limitations, the existence of fertile soil is the most important condition. Sandstone, rocky desert and rocky hill areas are unsuitable for production, as are swamps and moorland, although unproductive land can be partly improved by irrigation, drainage and other measures. Soil, even the worst types, can be improved within wide limits, or brought into use through appropriately adapted plants.

Another important feature of the land is relief, which imposes limits on production partly through altitude and partly through gradient. The limit of altitude differs according to climatic zone. Whereas the limit is 100-200 m near the poles and a few hundred metres in the temperate zones, cultivation is still possible at 3000-4000 m in the tropics.

For plants, the availability of water can also limit production. Natural precipitation does not set an absolute limit on cultivation if there is enough water for irrigation. Swampland can also be brought under cultivation by drainage. Irrigation is of significance in the tropical and subtropical belts and

2

those dry regions in temperate belts with long summers, and drainage in cooler areas of relatively high rainfall.

The requirements of environmental protection also set limits to agricultural production, although their direct effects are not as rigid as those mentioned above. Destroying the rainforest can provide more industrial, residential and agricultural land, capturing wild animals more fur, and fertilising and using pesticides higher yields. Such activities – if they are undertaken without the appropriate care and consideration – only show the negative, ally harmful effects over the long term. Cutting down forests can lead to soil erosion, flooding, drying out, desertification, destruction of wildlife and vegetation to diminution and extinction of living species and upset of the ecological balance, and use of artificial fertilizers to nitrogenation of soil and water. If all of these are not taken into account relative to the immediate gains, and future interests are not safeguarded by good practice (careful and restrained use of dangerous materials, replanting of forests and trees and forest plants, hunting within quotas etc.) future production will itself be endangered.

Social and economic factors determine the level of production in a given natural environment. Among these, population and population growth are important, as well as economic development and the form it takes. Connected with the latter is the technical level and sophistication of agriculture, input and output relations, as well as the skill and knowledge of the workforce. Forms of land ownership and the farming systems fitting into the economic and environmental conditions affect the farming methods as well. Further determining factors are the development of market and trade.

There is a mutual effect between population density and growth on one side and standards of farming on the other. Low population density and slow population growth commonly accompany a satisfactory standard of production and food supply even with extensive cultivation methods. If, however, population is high and it is growing rapidly, an insufficient rate of agricultural intensification results in insufficient production and famine. Rapid economic development is as a rule associated with simultaneous reduction of population growth.

A country's economic and industrial development usually determines the level of agricultural development too. Developed countries use, for example, on average 117 kg of fertilizer per permanently cultivated hectare, less developed countries, with the exception of India and China, less than 10 kg. In developed countries the number of people living and working in the agricultural sector is very small and reducing, with machines progressively taking their place. Mechanization and the large proportion of industrial materials (fertilizer and pesticides) make possible further improvement of their high yields. Agriculture in general constitutes an ever decreasing proportion of the national product due to the growth of the industrial and service sectors.

3

In a significant proportion of developing countries those employed in agriculture make up the majority of the economic workforce – in many countries 70-75% – and despite the relatively low productivity, the share of agriculture in the national product is high.

Among developing countries those developing rapidly in the industrial sphere are usually successful in agriculture too, as are those who have achieved significant results from the green revolutions (India, Pakistan, Sri Lanka, Philippines) with the considerable use of fertilizer and irrigation.

In developed countries agriculture is well integrated into the national economy, and the chain of production, processing and trade is well established and organized. In less developed countries there is a high proportion of subsistence production, and the market is weak. In most cases the infrastructure is also undeveloped (roads, transport, cooling, storing, etc.), which also limits the building of the trade network.

In the same way the developed countries control the international market. They are responsible for more than 70 per cent of the world's food exports, and 90 per cent of those of agricultural raw materials. Most developed countries are obliged to import food, and have serious problems with basic agricultural production.

In the face of developed countries' protectionist and support policies, production in developing countries is seriously depressed through low domestic prices. Overproduction and oversupply in developed countries depresses prices on the world market, further reducing the opportunities for the less developed to export.

Disputes between North and South (developed and developing countries) have so far met with little result. The countries of the South have hardly managed to wring any concessions from the North in giving up or reducing protectionism or in treating Southern exports favourably.

The farming systems of today have taken shape as a result of the prevailing environment, population density, economic development and land tenure and their mutual interdependence. In sparsely populated parts of the most backward and least developed countries, it is still common to find shifting cultivation in tropical and subtropical regions, and nomadism in dry grassland areas. In the tropics and subtropics the privately, state- or cooperatively owned monocultural plantations originally established by settlers are often the most developed plant-growing forms. In dry grassland areas the developed farming type is extensive ranch farming. Mixed farming in large and small holdings is spread throughout the world, with a special form being irrigated farming in tropical and subtropical regions and in dry areas with long summers. A special case of irrigated farming is rice production in monsoon regions.

Shifting cultivation and nomadism goes with common ownership of land. In densely populated regions the dominant form of ownership is usually the

4

intensively farmed smallholding. In sparsely populated former settler countries, depending on traditions, large family holdings are typical as in North America and New Zealand, and large estates together with share tenants and smallholders in South America.

Since the Second World War there have been numerous land reform schemes in many lesser and medium developed countries with the result that, except for a few, mainly large, sparsely populated countries, small and medium holdings have become the norm at the expense of large estates.

The creation of cooperative and state farms was a component of socialist aims. In some developing countries aspiring to socialism the movement for cooperative production in many cases met with setbacks and in some, especially in latter times, was completely dismantled. At the same time procurement, sales, processing and service cooperatives managed to thrive. State farms in many places became showplaces for demonstrating developed techniques, technology and the results of biological development, and at the same time producing commodities for the market.

In socialist, or communist, countries cooperative farming exist in a state of crisis. A few of the developing socialist countries, such as China and Vietnam, reorganized their unsuccessful large farms into family holdings. In the former socialist countries of Europe, collective farms are awaiting their fate in impending privatization.

Part I
ECONOMIC DEVELOPMENT, ECONOMIC GROWTH

1 Some major principles of economic growth and development

Measures of development

Among the countries of the world there is an enormous range in the standard of economic development.

In order to assess economic development most common systems of statistics use some measure of national income per capita. This is also used for purposes of international comparison, usually transposed into a single currency unit at some rate, usually the official one.

There are two generally accepted ways of measuring national product. The former Council of Mutual Economic Aid (CMEA or Comecon) countries' system measured the total material product and the national product from material services in the various national accounts, and the national income deriving from them, as well as the use to which it is put. They are now switching over to the method below.

Other countries usually measure national product using the System of National Accounts (SNA). As well as material product, this system takes account of the complete range of services in such a way as to deduct services expenditure as well as material expenditures from the total product value so that 'net result' represents not only the material product but also the final use of services. There are several different measures within this scheme, the best-known and most used being the gross and net national products (GNP and NNP) and the gross domestic product (GDP).

In the last few years, several former CMEA countries have used both schemes to measure national income, not least to ensure the comparability with other countries. In Hungary this began in the early 1970s.

GDP is based on added value, that is the total final value of the product minus current expenditures. The figure for GDP represents the added value of all products produced over a year through material and non-material activities.. From the consumption side, the added value is equal to the total final consumption together with the gross investment, including the difference between exports and imports. The added value differs from the net national product in including the depreciation of fixed assets and their replacement values.

GDP is a similar measure to GNP. The two differ in that GNP includes income from abroad and deducts outflow (e.g. minus capital outflow, transport out of the country, insurance costs abroad etc., plus profit from foreign investments, inward freight and inward tourism by foreigners etc.), while GDP only counts income generated within the country. Both deduct production costs and include depreciation. NNP deducts depreciation from production, hence use contains net investment along with total final consumption.

The comparison of development levels by national product is often criticized. It meets with objections first of all because of the effects of aggregation, which obscures differences in standard of living, standards of culture and health, social security, lifestyle and quality of life. In addition many economists feel that the national product is only a reliable overall index in the developed countries, since in less developed countries they have to make use of unreliable estimates of the value of subsistence production. In less developed countries a large part of the population lives by subsistence agriculture and handicrafts, the value of which might be underestimated in the national product.

But the amount of national production is not a straightforward measure of a country's economic standards even in developed countries, since there is a wide variation in the proportions of use and consumption depending on how much a country spends on military purposes and administration etc. Average figures hide large inequalities depending on the distribution of income. It does not show whether the differences in income are large or small. Such inequalities are particularly wide in the less developed countries. For countries with equal national products, those with unequal income distribution can contain starving masses alongside the strikingly rich, while more equal distribution allows everybody bread, even if not much of it.

Some ways of comparative accounting, for instance that of F. Jánossy (Jánossy, 1963) and É. Ehrlich (Ehrlich, 1991) have attempted to get over the errors of aggregation by including more factors (the per capita production of a few important goods, the number of doctors, hospital beds, teachers, the amount of living space per capita etc.) Such schemes are useful but too complicated to be used systematically in the way that the UN and other international organizations produce annual aggregated indexes. In any case the results of comparisons involving more human factors usually correlate with those using indices of national product.

Other errors in comparison arise form the uncertainty of currency exchange rates. The official rates are accepted to be the least appropriate for comparison, since they usually express the purchasing power of foreign rather than domestic trade. So it does not express how many foreign exchange units (usually dollars, due to that currency's international status) the domestic money corresponds to in the course of domestic purchasing, but how much it is worth for exports and imports. Even the latter is not certain, since a country's currency can be over- or under-valued. Another problem is that the structure of production varies considerably between different countries. For example, the mass of the Indian population depends for its nutrition on various grains. They grind their own grain which they have either bought or grown themselves into flour which the then cook into chapatis or porridge. In Kenya the most important source of nutrition is cooked corn cobs. In developed countries such goods appear on the market not as food ready to eat, but as raw materials for food processing, industrial material or fodder. These goods are therefore not comparable at prices of grain consumed as food. Thus there are problems of comparison arising from different patterns of consumption, variable purchasing power of the local currency for different goods, and differing proportions of unprocessed consumption.

Some approaches attempt to avoid errors of comparison arising from the official exchange rates by calculating purchasing-power parities. These compare prices of equivalent goods and services and calculate weighted averages. The weights are the amounts of consumption of certain products in one or other of the countries. Such purchasing-power parity comparisons have been carried out by, for example, the United Nations Development Program, UNDP. This organization also worked out the Human Development Index (HDI) which, as well as a figure for GDP calculated according to purchasing-power parity, includes the factors of life expectancy and literacy rates.

For each of these three factors in their index, the UN experts determined the 'minimum', and the 'desirable' figures. In each case the minimum figures were considered as the lowest actually experienced in the world. These were: for life expectancy 42 years (Afghanistan, Ethiopia and Sierra Leone); literacy 12 per cent (Somalia); annual per capita GDP on the basis of purchasing power parity $220 (Zaire). The desirable, i.e. high, figures were for life expectancy 78 years (equal to Japan's); literacy 100 per cent, and per capita GDP $4,861, which corresponded to the average poverty line in the nine most developed countries. The simple average of the three indexes is the 'level of human development' index, which is shown on the fourth column of table 1.1. The countries are listed in ascending order: number 1 is the worst, number 130 the best. The same ordering applies to per capita GDP (Nagy, 1990).

Table 1.1
Comparison of the world's economies (ascending order)

Country	Life expectancy at birth	Literacy rate % (1985)	GDP per capita at purchasing power US$ (1987)	Human Development Index (HDI)	Ranking according to per capita GDP at purchasing power	GNP per capita at official exchange rates (1987)
Niger	45	14	452	0.116	20	260
Mali	45	17	543	0.143	15	210
Burkina Faso	48	14	500	0.150	13	190
Sierra Leone	42	30	480	0.150	27	300
Chad	46	26	400	0.157	4	150
Guinea	43	29	500	0.162	31	..
Somalia	46	12	1,000	0.200	23	290
Mauritania	47	17	840	0.208	40	440
Afghanistan	42	24	1,000	0.212	17	..
Benin	47	27	665	0.224	28	310
Hungary	71	98	4,500	0.915	87	2,240
Uruguay	71	95	5,063	0.916	86	2,190
Costa Rica	75	93	3,760	0.916	77	1,610
Bulgaria	72	93	4,750	0.918	99	..
Soviet Union	70	99	6,000	0.920	101	..
Czechoslovakia	72	98	7,750	0.931	102	..
Chile	72	98	4,862	0.931	73	1,310
Hong Kong	79	88	13,906	0.936	111	8,070
Greece	76	93	5,500	0.949	98	4,020
GDR	74	99	8,000	0.953	115	..
Israel	76	95	9,182	0.957	108	6,800
USA	76	96	17,615	0.961	129	18,530
Austria	74	99	12,386	0.961	118	11,980
Ireland	74	99	8,566	0.961	106	6,120
Spain	77	95	8,989	0.965	105	6,010
Belgium	75	99	13,140	0.966	116	11,480
Italy	76	97	10,682	0.966	112	10,350
New Zealand	75	99	10,541	0.966	109	7,750
FRG	75	99	14,730	0.967	120	14,400
Finland	75	99	12,795	0.967	121	14,470
Great Britain	76	99	12,270	0.970	113	15,830
Denmark	76	99	15,119	0.971	123	14,930

Table 1.1 contd.

Country	Life expect-ancy at birth	Literacy rate % (1985)	GDP per capita at purchas-ing power US$ (1987)	Human Develop-ment Index (HDI)	Ranking according to per capita GDP at purchas-ing power	GNP per capita at official exchange rates (1987)
France	76	99	13,961	0.974	119	12,790
Australia	76	99	11,782	0.978	114	11,100
Norway	77	99	15,940	0.983	128	17,190
Canada	77	99	16,375	0.983	124	15,160
Netherlands	77	99	12,661	0.984	117	11,860
Switzerland	77	99	15,403	0.986	130	21,330
Sweden	77	99	13,780	0.987	125	15,550
Japan	78	99	13,135	0.996	126	15,760

Source: Human Development Indices (Nagy, 1990)

Table 1.1 shows the clear difference of GDP order from that of the HDI, and that of the GNP calculated by the International Bank for Reconstruction and Development, or World Bank, although in this case there are significant differences only between GDP and GNP of those countries where there is a large international circulation of capital and services. A feature of the figures calculated by purchasing power parity is that they tend to show a higher GDP for the poorer countries relative to those derived using the official exchange rate, and a lower GDP for some richer countries. The differences indicate the under- or over-valuations of the currency relative to actual internal purchasing power.

From time to time the UN International Comparison Program, ICP, also carries out a comparison based on actual purchasing power. Table 1.2 shows the per capita GDP for each country as a percentage that of the USA.

This comparison also gives a higher figure for the national product of the poorer countries relative to that using the official exchange rate, and there is downvaluing for the developed countries according to the internal purchasing power of their currencies. If we express the figures as a percentage of the USA GNP, those using the official exchange rate, in 1990, were for Ethiopia 0.6, Nigeria 1.3, Thailand 6.5 and Hungary 12.8, whereas for the Netherlands it was 79.4, Sweden 108.8 and Japan 116.7 (see table 1.3). The ICP comparison of GDPs for the same year gave figures of 1.5, 6.6, 21.6, 29.0, and 68.3, 74.9 and 79.4 respectively.

The International Monetary Fund has recently decided to switch over to purchasing power parities in national product comparisons. Its latest World Economic Outlook already includes such a comparison.

Table 1.2
GDP per capita as a percentage of the USA's in 1990
ICP estimates

Ethiopia	1.5	Republic of Korea	33.7
Zambia	3.8	Greece	34.4
Kenya	5.4	United Kingdom	70.0
India	5.2	Netherlands	68.3
Nigeria	6.6	Austria	69.1
Egypt	14.5	Sweden	74.9
Botswana	20.1	Australia	75.1
Thailand	21.6	Japan	79.4
Hungary	29.4	USA	100.0

Source: World Development Report, 1992

The World Bank divides developing countries into those of low and middle income, and within the middle, lower and upper.

The high-income group is made up of the 24 developed industrial market economies belonging to the OECD (Organization of Economic Cooperation and Development), and the high-income oil producing countries.

In 1990 countries with incomes of between $80 per person (Mozambique) and $600 per person (Egypt) appeared in the low-income category. The lower-middle income group was between $630 (Bolivia) and $2,370 (Argentina). The upper-middle group's income was between $2,490 (Iran and Mexico) and $7,050 (Saudi Arabia).

The high-income group varied between 9,950 USD (Ireland) and 32,680 USD (Switzerland) in 1990.

The sectoral division of GDP also shows the level of development of a country. The main sectors are: agriculture, extracting and manufacturing industries and services .*

---

* Division into sectors I, II and III is also common. Along with agriculture, sector I incorporates extractive industries (mining, natural gas, oil extraction etc., sector II is made up of the more dynamic sectors of manufacturing industry, and sector III includes services and others.

Sometimes the sectoral distribution of GDP better reflects development than the per capita GDP or GNP. The newly rich oil countries, for example, have not had time to develop processing industries at a sufficient level, while lower middle income countries, such as Argentina, Brazil, Czech Republic, Greece, Hungary, Malaysia, Mexico, Portugal, South Africa, South Korea and Thailand, have much more developed and export-capable industries.

Agriculture usually dominates the early stages of development in the economy but nowadays extractive industries can be as important a determining factor for developing countries. The role of manufacturing industry increases with development and that of agriculture falls, at least as a proportion of output. Countries where manufacturing industry represents less than 10-15 per cent of GDP are generally considered to be backward.

Development of service industries normally follows industrial growth. The service sector usually constitutes quite a large proportion in the early and later stages of development. In underdeveloped economies the activity of small traders and personal services (domestic services, night watchmen, hairdressers etc.) hide surplus manpower. As industry develops such services usually decline, unless there is high unemployment, as in Brazil. It should be pointed out that whereas in the past, one of the characteristics of rapid industrialization was that the service sector as a whole was squeezed, this is not found in countries with high industrial growth at present because of the growing significance of financial, trade, transport, travel, information and tourist services. In developed societies, industry as well as agriculture is in proportionate decline as the demand for services rises. In most cases agriculture already accounts for less than 5 to 6 per cent of their GDP, services between 60 and 70 per cent.

Another important index of development is the distribution of labour in the national economy, following laws similar to those for GDP distribution and often expressing the above tendencies even more strongly. In backward countries most of the population, 70 to 75 per cent, live from agriculture, but the percentage reflected in the GDP is normally less than that (in less naturally well-endowed countries much less) because of the low productivity of agricultural labour. In advanced countries the proportion of the total workforce employed in agriculture is 5 to 6 per cent or even less. At the same time 60-70 per cent work in services, compared with 30-40 per cent in the middle of the century.

As mentioned earlier, there are several other indices of development apart from national product and distribution of employment, based on production, investment, infrastructure, consumption, standard of living, health, culture and others. From these, particularly revealing, and strongly correlated with the level of national product, is the expected lifespan at birth, which in underdeveloped countries is less than 50 due to lack of nutrition and health

Table 1.3

Level of development in some countries in 1990 : Distribution of GDP (per cent)

Country	GNP per capita Dollars	Agriculture	Industry	Manufacturing	Services, etc.	Economically active population in agriculture (%)	Life expectancy at birth (years)
Ethiopia	120	41	17	11	42	74.5	48
Bangladesh[a]	210	38	15	9	46	68.5	52
Nigeria	290	36	38	7	25	64.8	52
India	350	31	29	19	40	66.5	59
China[a]	370	27	42	38[b]	31	67.5	70
Kenya	370	28	21	11	51	77.0	59
Zambia[a]	420	17	55	43	29	68.9	50
Egypt	600	17	29	16	53	40.5	60
Syria[a]	1,000	28	22	..	50	24.1	66
Thailand[a]	1,420	12	39	26	48	64.3	66
Botswana[a]	2,040	3	57	6	40	62.8	67
Algeria[a]	2,060	13	47	12	41	24.4	65
Argentina[a]	2,370	13	41	..	45	10.4	71
Brazil	2,680	10	39	26	51	24.3	66
Hungary[a]	2,780	12	32	27	56	11.5	71
Czechoslovakia[a]	3,140	8	56	..	36	9.3	72

Table 1.3 contd.

Country	GNP per capita Dollars	Agriculture	Industry	Manufacturing	Services, etc.	Economically active population in agriculture (%)	Life expectancy at birth (years)
Korea, Rep[a]	5,400	9	45	31	46	24.6	71
Greece	5,990	17	27	14	56	24.2	77
Saudi Arabia[a]	7,050	8	45	9	48	39.0	64
United Kingdom	16,100	2[c]	38[c]	25[c]	60[c]	2.0	76
Australia	17,000	4	31	15	64	5.0	77
Netherlands[a]	17,320	4	31	20	65	3.7	77
Austria[a]	19,060	3	37	27	60	5.7	76
United Arab Emirates	19,860	2	55	9	43	2.5	72
United States[a]	21,790	2[c]	30[c]	20[c]	68[c]	2.3	76
Sweden	23,660	3	35	24	62	3.8	78
Japan	25,430	3	42	29	56	6.4	79

[a] GDP and its components are at purchaser values
[b] World Bank estimate
[c] 1987

Source: World Bank Development Report, 1992 and FAO Production Yearbook, 1992

care, in developed countries over 70. Table 1.3 shows for a few countries the per capita level of national product (by the official exchange rate) and its distribution along with the sectoral distribution of the workforce and the life expectancy. (World Development Report, 1992 and FAO Production Yearbook, 1992).

Economic growth

National product as an overall economic indicator is also used to characterize economic growth. The idea of development is also used in a wider sense and includes not only the growth of national product, but that of standard of living, culture, skills, health care and sometimes qualitative indicators, such as the 'quality of life', which incorporates several non-material factors affecting the people's well-being as, for example, democratic freedom.

Each country has reached its current level of development at its own rate. Development has been slow over most of the few thousand years of recorded history, and in that time agriculture was paramount. Although many ancient nations, among them Phoenicia, the Greek city states and Rome, were well known for their trading activities, and there was a handicraft industry, the sectoral division of labour was never anywhere decisive. Countries maintained self-sufficiency in agriculture, and what little industry and trade there was complemented and enriched the economy but was not an essential element of it.

Agriculture itself hardly developed over the millennia. In ancient times the most advanced regions had iron-bladed wooden ploughs, spades, harrows, hoes, sickles, ancestors of the tools used up to the present day. The techniques of ploughing with oxen, cross-ploughing, fertilization and fallowing were already known. In the middle of the immediately pre-Christian millennium all of the today's crop plants and farm animals were already domesticated.

Tools developed very slowly over the millennia. The coultered iron plough evolved, the scythe replaced the sickle, wind and watermills were invented in the middle ages, three-field system was introduced, followed by crop rotation.

Acceleration of development only started at the end of the 18th and start of the 19th centuries, initiated by the industrial revolution, firstly in the most developed European countries, with other European countries catching up later, along with new settler countries overseas.

Systematic economic development was accompanied by the rise to dominance of the industrial population and the proportionate decline of agriculture.

Growth can be measured by the annual rise in national product. Even in the last century this hardly rose above 1 to 1.5 per cent, and in our own century it was mainly after the Second World War that it reached 4 to 5 per cent, and in

18

some countries even higher (e.g. in Japan above 10 per cent), only to fall again after the 1973 oil shock to 1.5 to 3 per cent in the developed countries.

Even more significant than systematic growth were the structural changes associated with technical developments. In the industrial revolution, the major breakthroughs were in the textile, iron and machinery industries, and in the technical revolution after the Second World War, it was in the motor, chemical, agricultural machinery industries and in production of household machines and products of mass consumption that the greatest changes were felt. The electronic and computer revolutions of the 1970s brought with them the information economy which led to a significant decline of the proportion not only of agriculture but of industry. Quantitative changes were accompanied by qualitative ones which transformed the structure of both production and consumption and were responsible for an even greater contribution to development.

For historical reasons, most former colonial, poor and so-called developing countries (designated as such by a decision of the UN General Assembly at the beginning of the 1960s) have not followed the developed countries' path to economic progress. After achieving independence, it seemed that they would rapidly make good the gap. As well as being set free from colonial exploitation they could benefit from *the principle of uneven growth*, according to which later developing countries can catch up by establishing their new industries with the most modern machinery and technology from developed countries (as, for example, in Germany, Sweden and Japan at the end of the last century, and Norway and Finland in this century). Relatively few developing countries, however, have caught up so far. It turned out that not only did they not have the necessary capital for it, but the whole condition of their economies worked against rapid development: market relations, weakness of trade and infrastructure, lack of expertise and skilled manpower, i.e.. factors which countries capable of rapid development already had when they started to catch up, and have now.

To date the South-East Asian countries (firstly the so-called threshold countries: Taiwan, South Korea, Hong Kong, Singapore, but after these also Malaysia, Thailand, the Philippines and Indonesia, and from some points of view China too) have started on the road to fast modern development. In the last decade India and Sri Lanka have also started to develop rapidly and have set up significant export channels. China has started to develop more rapidly since it began to open up economically in the 1980s and strengthen the private sector in its coastal Special Economic Zones, assisted by the flow of international capital into the area. There are also certain encouraging signs in Vietnam.

19

In the oil-producing regions of the Middle East there has also been investment of petro-dollars in the industrialization and the modernization of agriculture.

In the medium-developed countries of South America (Argentina and Brazil), the rapid development of the 60s and early 70s came to an end through large-scale indebtedness, but has started again recently.

Africa, mostly in the sub-Saharan regions, has shown the slowest progress, with several countries in this part of the world actually falling back in comparison with their previous state.

Thus the most dynamically developing countries are in Asia, but with many exceptions – for example Burma, Nepal, Bhutan, Bangladesh are still among the world's poorest nations. A significant part of the developing world, therefore, has still not properly started on the road to development.

Indicators and models of economic growth

The first theory of growth was elucidated by Marx (Marx, 1965) on the basis of the classical economic principles of Smith and Ricardo. The *two-sector model* which he established divides the economy into a production sector for capital equipment (I) and one for consumer goods (II). The total production in each sector is given by:

$$\text{I. } c_1 + v_1 + m_1$$
$$\text{II. } c_2 + v_2 + m_2$$

where
  c = capital
  v = labour
  m = net income

In the case of increasing production:

$$c_1 + v_1 + m_1 > c_1 + c_2$$

so that

$$v_1 + m_1 > c_2$$

This shows that in the case of an increasing rate of reproduction, more capital equipment is produced than is required to replace the depreciated capital goods of sectors I and II. Its value more than covers both the replacement requirement of the capital producing sector I and that of the consumption producing sector II which in exchange for capital goods satisfies the demand for consumption goods of sector I.

20

Marx considered the systematic accumulation and increase of production an inevitable and intrinsic law of capitalist production. Whereas his great predecessors in economics, Smith and Ricardo, only got as far as the creation of value with their labour theory of value, Marx elucidated the principle of the creation, use and accumulation of surplus value (Burger, 1980 and 1985).

For a hundred years after the appearance of Marxist political economy, neoclassical economists took little interest in questions of macroeconomics and economic growth, dealing rather with more detailed microeconomic questions. The microeconomic theory was essentially static. However it should be pointed out that at the start of this century there were already signs of emergence of a dynamic economics encompassing development. Whereas most economists held the view that economic development was the result of external factors (e.g. discovery of new parts of the world, of new sources of raw materials, conquest of colonies, etc.), Schumpeter (Schumpeter, 1912) asserted that growth is primarily a result of the activities of risk-taking entrepreneurs, who introduce new products and techniques of production and whose innovations cause the structure of the old economy to change.

In the 1930s a new synthesis of the microeconomic theories was put forward. The founder of modern macroeconomics, J.M. Keynes (Keynes, 1936) attributed a fundamental role to investments in promoting or restraining aggregate demand, and through this in determining the upswing or downturn of trade cycles. Most governments of developed countries successfully followed Keynesian policies of investment incentives and other countercyclical intervention measures in the interests of stimulating and restraining demand and tempering trade cycles until the 1973 oil shock and the subsequent recession.

It was the English economist R. Harrod (Harrod, 1948) and the American E.D. Domar (Domar, 1957) who first arrived at dynamic growth models using Keynes' theory, reaching more or less identical results from independent starting points. Domar's model states that in order to consume the extra production from new capacity which investors put in place, the national product has to rise annually by the same amount as this new production. Harrod looked at the question the other way round, asking how much investment is required in the economy for a given steady rate of growth in the national product. The needed new investment will be a constant fraction of the national product divided by the capital-output ratio, presuming that this ratio is constant in the case of neutral technological progress, and also that the population is static. This can be expressed as:

$$\frac{\Delta Y}{Y} = \frac{I}{Y} E$$

where Y =   total (national) income
      ΔY =   annual increase in total (national) income
      I =   annual investment
      E = $\dfrac{1}{\text{capital-output ratio}}$ or efficiency, i.e. productivity of capital.

The capital-output ratio expresses how many units of capital are required to attain one unit of new product. This coefficient also indicates the return of invested capital:

$$\frac{C}{P-c}$$

where P =   total annual product
      c =   annual cost of production
      C =   capital

Therefore, if 25 per cent of the national product is turned to investment, and the capital-output ratio is always 5 – i.e. 5 units of investment results in 1 unit of new product every year (in other words \$5 of investment produces \$1-worth) – then $25 \cdot 1/5 = 5$, or the national product rises by 5 per cent. On the basis of these proportions the 5 per cent annual rise in the volume of investment results in a 5 per cent rise in national product.

Harrod and Domar assumed the constancy of the capital-output ratio and the neutrality of technical progress in their models. However, the use of more modern, more efficient means of production or their better use can diminish the coefficient and conversely worse utilization of existing capacity or the use of less modern, lower quality techniques can lead to capital growing faster than production and a fall in the capital productivity.

It is clear from the formula that if the capital-output ratio falls or rises, a smaller or greater investment fraction can secure the same change in national income; conversely, if the investment ratio remains steady the national product can rise at a greater or lesser rate depending on the change in efficiency. If the capital-output ratio in our previous example falls to 4 then the coefficient becomes 0.25 and the rise in national income is 25 x 0.25=6.25 per cent. It is now sufficient to invest 20 per cent of the national income to maintain an annual growth of national income of 5 per cent.

If the productivity of new investments rises, investment is said to be capital intensive (less capital is required for the same production); if it falls it is capital-extensive (more capital is required).

Harrod and Domar attributed almost exclusive importance to the accumulation of capital in economic growth. Harrod did mention that the growth of national income could also be determined from the viewpoint of labour productivity, but pointed out that in the case of neutral technical development (constant capital-output ratio) the labour productivity grows with that of capital, i.e. as the investment per worker. Expressed as a formula:

$$\frac{\Delta Y}{Y} = \frac{I}{Y} E = \alpha$$

where α =   rise in labour productivity

It can be added that if the capital-output ratio or the capital productivity changes, labour productivity changes at the same rate. Taking the reverse case, if for some reason the labour productivity grows less than the capital per labour – through bad management, lack of skills etc. – then the efficiency of capital also falls.

When the workforce is changing in size, increasing production (national income) is shared between the growth in numbers and growth of productivity.

Putting the expression in another form:
$$\frac{\Delta Y}{Y} = \frac{C + \Delta C}{C} \cdot E : \frac{L + \Delta L}{L}$$

where C =   capital
                  ΔC =   capital growth
                  L =   number of workers
                  ΔL =   growth in number of workers

The formula shows that if the capital productivity and the workforce is constant, a 5 per cent rise in capital per worker implies a 5 per cent rise in labour productivity which, when multiplied by the size of the workforce gives the same 5 per cent rise in income. The same rise in investment accompanied by a 2 per cent rise in the workforce results in the labour productivity per worker growing in the ratio 105:102 = 1.03 per cent, but an unchanged 5 per cent growth in total production.

For the growth of labour productivity to be 5 per cent in the case of a 2 per cent growth in the workforce, the total capital stock (and the production) has to grow by 7 per cent, still assuming an unchanging capital efficiency

(107:102= 1.05). We arrive at a more or less similar result if we add the factors (see the Kalecki-formula below) for productivity growth + workforce rise = production growth (5 + 2 = 7) instead of multiplying them.

Labour productivity – assuming a given capital-labour ratio – can rise with the employment of a more highly skilled and educated workforce, better utilization of working time, more intensive working, better management etc.; and of course in less favourable conditions it can fall.

It follows that the production and the national income can grow up to a certain limit by making better use of existing facilities, using measures such as, for example, shift work. But production can also grow by drawing more workers into production, maybe even if the capital per worker does not grow for a while, because the existing production facilities are better used. New employment can only become significant on the level of the national economy if there are reserves of labour. This assumption holds in developing countries, and in developed countries where unemployment is high.

Labour is therefore as significant in determining growth as capital. In less developed economies the labour productivity, and its growth, tend to be much lower than in more developed countries – even in the case of identical magnitude or growth of capital-labour ratio – because of the differences in the level of skill in the workforce and the standards of management of production. This is experienced in factories with identical equipment in countries at different levels of economic development. A factory employing more skilled labour and with better management than another can, in extreme cases, achieve twice the labour productivity.

The Polish economist M. Kalecki (Kalecki, 1966) represented labour in his growth formula thus:

$$\frac{\Delta Y}{Y} = \frac{I}{Y} . E - d + u = \alpha + \beta + \alpha\beta$$

where d =   depreciation

            u =   coefficient of growth of national income by better use of existing capital (e.g. by improved organization of work and utilization of raw material, elimination of waste, more shift work etc.)

            α =   average rise of labour productivity, i.e. the growth in production due to this.

            β =   rise in the number of workers , i.e. the production growth due to this.

            $\alpha\beta$ =   The rise in productivity of newly employed workers corresponding to the average growth of productivity.

24

It should be pointed out that Kalecki – similarly to Harrod and Domar – also assumed stable population, or rather that the rise in population was so small as to be negligible for his model. Clearly in most developing countries, population increase must be taken into account. The actual growth is therefore given by the per capita growth:

$$\frac{\Delta Y}{Y} : \frac{\Delta Pop}{Pop}$$

where   Pop   =   population
            ΔPop   =   population growth

In the case of significant population growth the per capita growth of national income can be much less than the absolute growth.

Models of growth apply not only to the overall national economy, but to each industry and its branches, and so is can also be applied to agriculture. In developed and rapidly developing countries the agricultural workforce usually is not growing, but falling. The Kalecki-type formula may thus be modified:

$$\frac{\Delta Y}{Y} = \frac{(I+k)}{Y} . E - d + u = \alpha - (\beta + \alpha\beta)$$

where k = the investment replacing workforce decline.

For the labour productivity, α, to rise in agriculture, the departing workers have to be substituted by equipment. In other words, investment has to exceed the rate needed for a steady growth of income at a constant labour level by the capital-labour substitution ratio. The substitution ratio may be constant if the capital-output ratio is constant, but if the latter increases then both **I** and **k** must increase as proportions of national income.

If, for example, the capital-output ratio is 3, then for each unit of new production, capital must rise by 3 units. If at the same time three additional units of capital substitute for one unit of work and the workforce diminishes by one unit, then this must also be substituted by 3 additional units of capital. The required growth of capital is therefore not 3 but 6. The systematic decline in the workforce is one of the main reasons for agriculture having a higher capital-output ratio than other sectors of the economy.

On the other hand, the labour productivity, α, must rise to meet the fall in β + $\alpha\beta$. Let us assume that agricultural labour productivity is rising by an annual 3 per cent with a stable workforce. Production thus grows by 3 per cent too.

25

If, on the other hand, the workforce falls by 1 per cent, then roughly 4 per cent productivity growth is required for the 3 per cent rise in production (1.03:99 = 1.04).

More recent models of growth are usually expressed as production functions. Notable among the first of these are the models of R. Solow (Solow, 1956) and J.E. Maede (Maede, 1962).

The general formula for the production function is

$$Y = f(L, C, S)$$

where
Y = increase in production, and thus national income
L = labour
C = capital
S = land

The function expresses the effect of each factor of production on the increase in national income.

The effect of land has a special significance in agriculture. In some developing countries, where there are still significant reserves of land, agricultural production can be greatly increased by bringing new land under cultivation. Where, however, most cultivable land is already in use, land has to be substituted by capital in the same way as labour.

Other factors can be included in the production function, and the significance for growth of technical progress and increasing skill have been recognized by building them into the later models.

Among others, the Cobb-Douglas function is widely used, which can be written as:

$$Y = b\, L^m C^k S^f,$$

where
m, k, f = parameters representing the marginal productivities of factors of production
b = dummy parameter of the function which expresses the effec of external factors on production.

The Cobb-Douglas is a first-order homogeneous function if the exponents are constant and add up to one, and that the elasticity of substitution* is constant and equal to 1.

---

* The elasticity of substitution is defined on the basis of the formula:

continued on next page

Modifying the Cobb-Douglas function gives other functions which relax the restrictions on the sum of the exponents and the constancy of their ratio (Constant Elasticity of Substitution, CES, and Constant Marginal Shares, CMS).

These models mentioned above measured economic growth in the context of a single-sector model. Increased mathematical knowledge, and not less importantly the use of computers, has allowed the construction of multisectoral models.

Dynamic input-output models are an important subset of the multisectoral category (Leontief, 1970). In contrast to static input-output models, which calculate the production using given quantities, the dynamic models use changes in quantities and their effect on the growth of production. The Leontief dynamic input-output model examines the effect of investment on the growth of gross output.

The basic formula of the static model is:

$$x = Ax + i + f,$$

where $\qquad$ x $\;=\;$ vector of each industry's gross output

---

$$e = \frac{\Delta C}{C} \cdot \frac{L}{\Delta L} = \frac{k}{m}$$

where

e	=	the elasticity of substitution
C	=	capital
ΔC	=	increase in capital
L	=	labour
ΔL	=	increase in labour
k	=	parameter representing marginal productivity of capital
m	=	a parameter representing marginal productivity of labour

i.e. elasticity represents the marginal rate of substitution of factors of production, equal to the reciprocal of the parameters expressed as a percentage. That is, if m = 0.75 and k = 0.25, then

$$e = \frac{0.75}{0.25} = \frac{3}{1}$$

In this case the capital:labour elasticity of substitution is equal to 3:1. Thus for production to rise by 1 per cent, leaving the other factors unchanged, the capital must rise by 4 per cent and the number of workers by 1.33 per cent. The substitution proportion of land and capital may be calculated similarly, as may that of land and labour.

$$A \quad = \quad \text{input-output coefficient matrix}$$
$$i \quad = \quad \text{vector for the output for investment in each industry}$$
$$f \quad = \quad \text{vector for each industry's output for consumption}$$

That of the dynamic model is

$$x = Ax + f + B\Delta x$$

where $\quad B \quad = \quad$ the coefficient matrix showing the required investment for per unit of production growth.

$\quad\quad\quad\quad \Delta x \quad = \quad$ the vector representing the production growth in each industry.

In the model, the maximization of gross output is obtained by maximising investments.

The early mathematical models, using only a few factors for analysis, turned out to be inadequate for the investigation of the many-layered influences affecting growth, but laid down the basic principles which were later fleshed out by more sophisticated models. Economists working on growth and development included in their analysis other features of economic life. They dealt with the history of economic growth (the historical school); social, economic-political, institutional characteristics; sectional characteristics of the national economy, as well as technical development, skill levels, surplus or shortage of labour, the standard of living, income distribution, the roles in growth played by social and cultural provision; one-sided or balanced growth etc.

The historical school of economic growth

There is an important school of economic growth which looks at the historical processes which determine the development and growth of countries. One of the outstanding representatives of this school is W.W. Rostow (Rostow, 1960). In his theory he identifies three major stages in the historical path of economic growth. The first is the pre-conditions, the period following traditional society, when the conditions for industrialization are created. The second is take-off, or the beginning of industrialization, and the third is sustained growth, the period when the economic growth becomes a steady process. The period of sustained growth is divided into two phases: the drive to maturity and the maturity reached in the age of high mass consumption.

During the period when the preconditions are created, the capital required for industrialization is accumulated (trade capital, bank capital etc.), the basic infrastructure (roads, railways etc.) and industry are established, but the proportion of investment in the national economy does not exceed five per cent. At the same time the labour productivity of agriculture increases significantly. According to Rostow, agriculture starts to develop on such a scale that it is capable of satisfying the increased demand for food and loan capital needed for industrialization.

In the take-off period the percentage of investment in the national economy rises from below five to ten. One or more high-growth industrial sectors, the leading sectors, emerge. The political, social and institutional framework takes the appropriate form to take advantage of the impulse provided by these sectors, and to promote further development. Take-off is the explosive, jump-like stage of industrialization, the time of industrial revolution. According to Rostow this stage can be more or less completed in two decades, as in Britain in 1783-1802, France 1830-1860, Belgium 1833-1860, Sweden 1868-1890, Japan 1878-1900, Russia 1890-1914, Canada 1896-1914, Argentina 1935-, Turkey 1937-, India 1952-, China 1952-.

This stage is followed by the stage of steady growth. The ability of the economy to attain a state of constant, self-sustaining growth depends on the magnitude of the push it received during the two decades of rapid industrialization. At this time the invested proportion of national income steadily exceeds the 10 per cent level, and the original leading sector or sectors are joined by new fast-growing industries, so that new leading sectors take shape. Growth is widespread and constant. In this period the technology of production reaches maturity.

S. Kuznets, another major proponent of the historical school (Kuznets, 1966) criticized Rostow's assignment of time periods. He took the view that the stages cannot be sharply delineated. Take-off cannot be clearly associated with a twenty-year period. In addition, for many countries and many cases a significant part of the Rostowian preconditions only materialize in the take-off period (concentration of capital under control of the banks, railway building, rise in agricultural productivity etc.). Conversely, industrialization can begin concurrently with the creation of the pre-conditions, or even before this, (an example of this being England, where the agricultural revolution took place to satisfy demand for raw material of the textile industry, or Japan, where railway building and the industrialization accompanying it was also begun by the transport requirements of the textile industry).

On the basis of Rostow's theory, some South-East Asian countries appear to be going through the take-off stage. Some Latin-American countries have started out on the road to development several times (Argentina, Brazil), and as many times have come to a halt.

2 Development of agriculture in different regions

How did the agriculture of the developed countries reach its present level of development?

A characteristic of the early growth and development of today's developed countries' is that agriculture kept pace with the rise of industry. This was not a continuous or trouble-free process, as the example of the most developed capitalist country of the time shows: England, and more especially the rest of the United Kingdom (for example Ireland in 1845), suffered a series of famines at the beginning of the 19th century. However, from the middle of the 19th century, mostly due to the development of chemical and fertilizer industry, agriculture was capable of satisfying the food and raw material requirements of industry and the cities.

Agriculture contributed to economic growth by providing:
1. Labour to the industrial and service sectors;
2. Food to the growing city population and raw material to industry;
3. Capital and finance for development of industry and services;
4. Foreign currency from agricultural exports or import substitution of food and raw material;
5. A market to take up industrial production;
6. Stimulation to industrialization and to other sectors of the national economy (Lewis, 1963).

Let us examine each of these in order:

1. The ever-increasing demand for labour by the other sectors of the economy has been satisfied by labour migrating from agriculture since the beginnings of industrialization, making possible the rise in the agricultural labour .

In countries only beginning to industrialize the reserve of labour is enormous, and it is still significant in the medium-industrialized countries where 30-40 per cent of the workforce is employed in agriculture, compared with 2-5 per cent in most developed countries. Mobilization of this reserve is partly a function of the stage of development of industry and services, and partly of mechanization of agriculture and the rise of productivity that goes with it.

2. Industrialization, the expanding industrial and service workforce, and the gradual rise in real wages and real incomes demands more and more agricultural produce. Agriculture must keep up with the development of industry and other sectors of the economy, or it will not be able to provide the raw materials for industry or the food requirements of industrial and service sectors, becoming a brake on the growth of their workforces and on industrial development in general. For example in England at the end of the 18th and beginning of the 19th centuries much agricultural land was turned to sheep grazing to satisfy the raw material demands of the wool industry, while cheap food was brought from the colonies.

Greater consumption of food within agriculture puts a further demand on agricultural development. When there is an abrupt structural change in agriculture – such as land reform where large estates are broken up and allotted to peasants – consumption of those living on the land of their own produce can suddenly increase. If the level of agricultural production has been very low before land reform then the peasants (or farm workers), having hitherto scraped along at subsistence level, naturally respond to the end or reduction of exploitation by consuming more food. Since cannot grow in as short a time as the division of the estates and the change of income distribution, the increase in consumption may be at the expense of the surplus previously extracted from the peasantry. This increase in consumption depends firstly on the previous standard of living of the peasantry and whether or not they had an adequate diet, and secondly on the type and quantity of goods industry can offer for food they produce. Industry's capability to exchange is determined by its own level of development. If industry can supply agriculture with the goods it demands in the appropriate quantity, this can in turn affect further development of agriculture; this induces the production and sale of more goods. As its trading activity widens, agriculture's techniques become more modern and industrial and its productivity grows, so that it is able to continuously expand the supply of food for the industrial workers and at the same time gradually free up labour for industry and other parts of the economy. This process, however, takes time.

There can be, and frequently are, periods during the start of industrialization when agriculture does not have enough surplus nor industry the ability to supply enough goods in exchange. In this case the food supply for the rising city population and industrial development is endangered. Such a case can arise if subsistency still prevails in agriculture, the standard of production is low, and industry is insufficiently developed to offer enough goods to agriculture. This problem appears today in most developing countries where the largely subsistence agriculture cannot supply sufficient food to industrially underdeveloped cities with populations of 8-10 million or more.

Permanent shortage of food can be alleviated by systematic imports. This solution was often chosen by colonial countries when they started to industrialize, their position of power allowing them to import a greater value than they exported. Developing countries can also live with systematic imports if they have and can produce sufficient highly-demanded raw materials. If agriculture does not sell enough goods, and industry cannot export enough to cover food imports, then if the country has no access to other external or internal resources, it is usually forced into taking some kind of drastic measures, as history has shown. This happened at the end of the last century in many relatively poor industrializing countries. Governments typically hurried to the aid of the rising industries, and by some means forced agriculture to hand over its "surplus food" to industry. In this case however it was not a matter of exchange between agriculture and industry, but of withdrawal of capital from agriculture.

3. The classical form of withdrawal of capital is taxation. At the end of the last century most newly industrializing countries imposed heavy taxes on agriculture. This taxation was particularly significant in those countries where industrialization was supported by state loans and subsidy (e.g. Japan). Although the financial taxation of underdeveloped agriculture is a heavy burden for it, it also brings advantages. It stimulates the ending of subsistency, connects agriculture to the market system, and ultimately gives an incentive to producers to sell a larger part of their goods. In the interests of having more goods to sell, the agricultural producer strives to increase production and introduces more intensive methods of cultivation. If consequently industrial growth can keep step with the growing purchasing power of agriculture, then agriculture can undergo a rapid phase of development.

Capital can migrate to industry in other ways. As the banking system and industrialization progressed, more and more large landowners become shareholders in large banks and companies, getting onto the boards of banks and large companies and bringing in their property and agricultural income to these institutions. Hungary provides a good example of this at the end of the 19th and beginning of the 20th centuries.

4. Agriculture can also contribute to economic growth through exports, as an important procurer of foreign currency for the national economy. Exports can be agricultural raw materials or processed goods. With the progress of industrialization and economic development the latter becomes the major

source of foreign currency (manufactured woollen, silk and cotton goods, processed meat and milk products, deep frozen food etc.).

Exports of processed agricultural goods in large quantities is a feature of a later stage of development, when connections between agriculture and industry and the integration of agriculture into the national economy are strong enough. Export of such products can play a very important role for already developed countries, indeed in some cases even in the most developed (e.g.. in the Netherlands about 26 per cent, in Denmark about 31 per cent, in Australia 27 per cent and in New Zealand approximately 66 per cent of total merchandise exports are agricultural). For Hungary even today one of the most important sources of convertible currency is the approximately 23-25 per cent of exports represented by agricultural products.

Agricultural and food exports are especially significant in the early industrial development of countries which have few natural resources and industrial raw materials of their own. In addition, with the substitution of agricultural imports – producing substituting goods to a large extent domestically – there can be great savings in foreign currency. In the later stages the higher level of economic development and the rise in significance of foreign trade leads to a decline in the role of this import saving. Comparative advantages of exports and imports become more important.

5. The integration of agriculture into the economy is not just a matter of agriculture supplying food and raw materials to industry, but of industry making a range of exchange goods available to agriculture. Agriculture thus becomes a market for industrial goods. For it to play a full part in the exchange of goods in the economy, not only must industry, trade, and transport reach a standard of development such that they can supply agriculture with goods needed, but a corresponding standard of development is also called for in agriculture. Agriculture can only play a permanent and integral purchasing role in the market, if by regularly selling of some of its products it obtains the money required to buy industrial products. For this, agriculture must abandon subsistence and acquire a permanent and systematic surplus, and its development must keep in step with that of industry. Only thus is it capable of satisfying industry's ever-growing demand for food and raw materials, contributing to the country's exports and at the same time establishing a market for growing industrial production. Agriculture can constitute a market both for consumer goods and capital equipment, helping to widen the range of products of industries.

6. A related effect is the impetus agriculture can give to industrial and general economic development if the means of industrial production are sufficiently developed to respond positively to some outside influence. Thus in the last century the markets opening up to grain exports started railway building in the important grain-producing countries (e.g. the USA, Canada, Russia and

Table 2.1
Annual growth rates for GNP, food production and population

Country	GNP per capita (US$) 1990	Average growth rate of GNP per capita (%) 1965-90	Average index of food production per capita (1979-81=100) 1988-90	Average growth rate of agricultural production (%) 1980-90	Average growth rate of population (%) 1980-90
Ethiopia	120	-0.2	84	-0.1	3.1
Bangladesh	210	0.7	96	2.6[b]	2.3
Nigeria	290	0.1	106	3.3	3.2
India	350	1.9	119	3.1	2.1
China[a]	370	5.8	133	6.1[b]	1.4
Kenya	370	1.9	106	3.3	3.8
Zambia	420	-1.9	103	3.7[b]	3.7
Egypt	600	4.1	118	2.5	2.4
Syria	1,000	2.9	80	-0.6[b]	3.6
Thailand	1,420	4.4	106	4.1[b]	1.8
Botswana	2,040	8.4	75	-4.0[b]	3.3
Algeria	2,060	2.1	96	4.3[b]	3.0
Argentina	2,370	-0.3	93	1.1[b]	1.3
Brazil	2,680	3.3	115	2.8	2.2
Hungary	2,780	..	113	1.6[b]	-0.2
Czechoslovakia	3,140	..	119	0.3[b]	0.3
Korea, Rep	5,400	7.1	106	2.8[b]	1.1
Greece	5,990	2.8	103	0.7	0.4
Saudi Arabia	7,050	2.6	189	14.6[b]	4.7
United Kingdom	16,100	2.0	105	-3.1	0.2
Australia	17,000	1.9	95	3.2[b]	1.5
Netherlands	17,320	1.8	111	3.6[b]	0.5
Austria	19,060	2.9	106	1.0	0.2
United Arab Emirates	19,860	..	..	9.3	4.3
United States	21,790	1.7	92	..	0.9
Sweden	23,660	1.9	99	1.1	0.3
Japan	25,430	4.1	101	1.3[b]	0.6

34

Table 2.1 continued

Country	GNP per capita (US$) 1990	Average growth rate of GNP per capita (%) 1965-90	Average index of food production per capita (1979-81=100) 1988-90	Average growth rate of agricultural production (%) 1980-90	Average growth rate of population (%) 1980-90
Low and middle income economies[a]	840	2.5	115	3.2	2.0
Sub-Saharan Africa[a]	340	0.2	94	2.1	3.1
East asia and Pacific[a]	600	5.3	127	4.8	1.6
South Asia[a]	330	1.9	116	3.0	2.2
Europe[a]	2,400	..	102	1.0	0.1
Middle East and N. Africa[a]	1,790	1.8	101	4.3	3.1
Latin America and Caribbean[a]	2,180	1.8	106	1.9	2.1
High-income economies[a]	19,590	2.4	100	1.7	0.6
OECD members[a]	20,170	2.4	101	1.7	0.6
Other[a]	..	..	80	..	1.8

a) Weighted average
b) Data are at purchaser values

Source: World Development Report, 1992.

Hungary), whereas the demand for railway-, locomotive-, wagon- and rail-building stimulated the iron and steel, vehicle, engineering and many other industries. Similarly it accelerated the development of food-processing and machinery for food processing (e.g. the Hungarian milling and mill-machinery industries at the turn of the century) and many more. Agriculture can give not only the starting impetus to development, but – setting up markets for various industrial products – can encourage later development. A good example of this is the chemical industry, whose development in many countries is due to the rising demand for fertilizers. The rise of the engineering industry in many countries after the second world war – for example in West Germany – was a consequence of the making of agricultural machinery as well as of cars.

⅄ The result of the agricultural development's keeping pace with that of industry and services is the large-scale rise in yields and production. However its growth is usually lower than that of industry and, later, that of services. The result of this and the shift of labour to other industries is the decline in agriculture's share of the national economy (see table 1.3) although the absolute quantity of production increases. After reaching a certain level of development the growth of agriculture slows even more (Burger, 1969).

It can be seen from table 2.1 that food and other agricultural produce in most cases rises less than national product, which is boosted by the above average growth of industry and, occasionally, services. This is even more marked in those highly and medium developed countries well supplied with food, where attempts to avoid overproduction can actually reduce agricultural production.

Of course rising population also affects per capita growth. Faster population growth implies greater demand for food production. If a country's economy cannot keep pace with its population growth, then it falls back, no matter how large the absolute rise in production.

In the developed countries the relatively slow agricultural development arises partly for supply and partly demand reasons. On the supply side, the limited availability of land is a determining factor. Certainly, yields in a given land area can be raised almost indefinitely, but at ever greater cost. Machinery, materials and new production techniques must substitute not only for the declining workforce, but for land too, partly that agricultural land which is withdrawn for industrial, urbanization and infrastructural purposes and partly new virgin land which either does not exist or if it does, and could be brought into production, the expenses of doing so would be extremely high. All the produce from this land has to be substituted, therefore, by the increase of production on existing land. There is however a limit to this increase. This limit depends on prices which have to cover increasing costs. Higher prices allow higher costs to be borne, lower prices lower costs. Since the demand for agricultural goods is usually smaller and grows more slowly than for many industrial goods and services, prices are suppressed – in spite of their being subsidized – and so it is not worth raising production beyond a certain level.

On the demand side, the modest growth in production can be attributed to the relatively small rise in demand for agricultural products. Demand for agricultural products in developed countries does not grow even at the rate that technical developments make possible for production. A significant proportion of raw materials of agricultural origin have now been replaced by industrially-sourced equivalents. Food consumption reaches a level of relative saturation faster then it does for most industrial goods and services. Income and price elasticities of food are low. Within total food consumption, there is a rise of demand for better-quality, more valuable and rarer foods (animal protein, non-mass-produced and exotic fruit and vegetables, sweets and other processed goods etc.). Total food consumption, however, rises less; growth is determined by the relatively slow rise in demand and the extra requirement from the similarly slow rate of population growth.

The fact that agricultural production often grows beyond its natural limits is a result of systems of support for agriculture, which are largely political in origin. Agricultural overproduction is therefore manifested in most developed countries.

Agriculture in developing countries

By contrast with the tendency to overproduce discussed above, developing countries could benefit from a faster rate of agricultural development. This is required partly because of the low level of food consumption and fast population expansion, and partly for the rising need to export. In most developing countries, however, governments pay less attention to agriculture than it deserves, both through its own importance and its weight within the national economy.

After decolonialization, most developing nations set out on a programme of rapid economic growth with the aim of catching up with the developed countries as soon as possible. It is the lesson of history that it is industry that drives rapid economic growth. The rate of industrial growth is usually considerably greater than that of agriculture. It therefore seemed to the newly independent governments that the way to rapid development was the preference for industry over agriculture.

The approach to growth termed the 'industrial fundamentalism model' (Stevens and Jabara, 1988) not only neglected agricultural development, but used every means possible to divert resources from it to industry. Many developing countries took for their example in this area – as in many other areas – the Soviet socialist model. The rapid development in the formerly backward Soviet Union – later to be revealed as merely apparent in many areas – was an attractive example to follow.

In most developing countries – as in the Soviet Union and many other socialist countries – agricultural prices were held low. In this way food prices were also kept down and also subsidized, to make labour cheap and reduce costs to industry. Low food prices were also aimed at politically influencing industrial workers in the cities. Because of the working class's higher level of organization and political mobilization, its dissatisfaction always posed more of a threat to the existing regime than the numerically much larger, but less politically organized and active rural population.

Low agricultural prices were ultimately a device for subsidizing industry. At the same time they reduced the interest of agricultural producers in producing for the market.

Many developing countries introduced a system of compulsory deliveries, maintaining or even extending one imposed by the former colonial power. Deliveries had to be made at centrally-determined, and therefore low, prices. A disincentive to production was provided not only by the low prices but also by the high quotas, which made producers unable to diversify and address demand. Compulsory delivery to the state, or to the parastate trade organizations (the marketing boards), did not create but rather cut the connections to the markets, or at least restricted them to areas of lesser significance such as fruit and vegetables. The will to produce was also lowered in many areas by the imposition of export taxes on many export products. Disincentives led to falling production and a loss of export share in several cases: Ghana and Nigeria, for example, lost their position in cocoa exports compared with the 1960s, Nigeria and Zaire in palm oil, and by the 1980s Egypt's share in world cotton exports had fallen to half of what it had been in the 1960s (despite compulsory delivery of cotton) and Sri Lanka's share of tea exports to a third.

The policy against agriculture had a deleterious effect on both the food supply to the population and the country's ability to export. Food supply problems were aggravated by the rise in population resulting from improving health and falling mortality. Former food-exporting countries became importers. The supply problems of food and agricultural raw materials, the falling export earnings and significant currency demands of food imports naturally had a depressing effect on industrialization and general growth. Attention was drawn to these dangers as early as the 1960s by some authors (Jorgenson, 1961; Ranis and Fei, 1961; Mellor, 1967; Hayami and Ruttan, 1971).

As a result of bad experiences and the recommendations of experts at home and abroad and in international organisations, many governments changed their agricultural policies. In these countries support for agriculture more and more

38

took the place of taxation and obligation. This was felt most especially in South- and South-East Asia where governments supported the incipient green revolution* with seed and fertilizer subsidies, higher agricultural prices and building of irrigation facilities.

Particularly outstanding was the agricultural development in those countries classified as developing but with high earnings from oil (see table 2.1). Saudi Arabia and the United Arab Emirates, for example, have spent enormous amounts on making desert land productive.

In South Asia, both where significant development has taken place (India and Pakistan), and, most especially, where the green revolution has hardly started (African countries), the food supply even today is on a low level. Broad masses of people do not receive the medically-determined minimum of nutrition.

The daily intake of calories in each region is shown in table 2.2 (FAO Production Yearbook, 1992), which shows that every region has experienced an increase in calorie intake, but that there has been a decrease in several sub-Saharan African countries just as their food production has decreased, as shown on table 2.1.

The medically established average normal calorie intake is 2,330 for tropical climates and 2,800 for temperate and cold climates, with the minimum being 1,900 and the lower limit for survival being 1,520. The average for African countries south of the Sahara and South Asia is still below those recommended. Some countries (Comoros 1,760, Mozambique 1,805, Somalia 1,874, Sierra Leone 1,899, Bangladesh 2,037 and India 2,229) barely, if at all, reached the minimum in 1988-90.

Looking at the intake of protein, the situation in certain regions and countries is even worse than indicated on tables 2.2 and 2.3.

The medically recommended minimum of animal protein is 20 g/head/day. This level is not reached in the continents of Africa or Asia and many countries are well below it. The adverse effect of low calorie intake is mainly on the ability to do physical work, and insufficient protein also – especially in childhood – inhibits intellectual development.

---

* The FAO (Food and Agricultural Organization) initiated the biotechnological 'green' revolution in the second half of the 1960's. Its aim was the widespread introduction of a high-yielding variety of wheat suitable for the tropics which had been developed in Mexico (at the International Maize and Wheat Improvement Centre, CIMMYT) and of a high-yielding rice variety, developed in the Philippines (the International Rice Research Institute, IRRI). These varieties only give high yields with suitable fertilizer and irrigation.

Table 2.2
Daily food supply per capita*

Region	Calories 1961-63	Calories 1988-90	Protein (grams) Total 1961-63	Protein (grams) Total 1988-90	Protein (grams) of animal products 1961-63	Protein (grams) of animal products 1988-90
Africa	2,117	2,204	53.9	53.3	10.3	10.6
Latin America	2,363	2,690	61.9	66.8	23.6	28.8
Near East	2,237	2,954	63.8	78.5	14.2	18.0
Far East	1,825	2,442	46.1	59.2	5.8	11.5
Developing All	1,940	2,473	449.7	60.6	8.7	13.8
North America	3,054	3,603	97.1	109.1	64.2	70.2
Europe	3,088	3,452	88.0	102.1	41.8	58.4
Oceania	3,173	3,328	97.7	100.7	65.3	67.8
Former USSR	3,146	3,380	97.6	107.3	38.2	57.1
Developed All	3,031	3,404	90.4	103.5	44.0	59.5

* Provisional

Table 2.3
Countries of lowest and highest per capita animal protein consumption per day in 1989-90 (grams)

Lowest		Highest	
Burundi	3.1	Iceland	91.9
Mozambique	3.7	Ireland	73.5
Bangladesh	4.6	France	73.0
Nigeria	5.6	USA	71.1
Malawi	5.9	New Zealand	69.5
Zaire	6.7	Australia	67.5
		Belgium-	
Sierra Leone	7.5	Luxembourg	65.7
Zimbabwe	7.8	Germany N.L.	64.8
Nepal	7.9	Sweden	63.9
Guatemala	8.0	Germany F.R.	63.4

Source (both tables): FAO Production Yearbook, 1992

The FAO's prognosis for the year 2000 (Agriculture: Towards 2000, 1981) established with the aid of data from 1974-76 for 90 developing and 34 developed countries, that there are 435 million undernourished people in the world. Annually 13-18 million die of starvation. Among the hunger belts, particularly severe is the Sahel-belt, where because of continual drought millions of people and animals are dying. According to the FAO a fifth of humanity are living in below the poverty line.

The initial data used by the FAO for its projection (table 2.4) clearly show the difference between production in developed and developing countries and the consequent levels of consumption.

Table 2.4
Some initial data used by the FAO for its projection for year 2000

Lowest	Units	Developing countries	Developed countries
Distribution of world population	%	67	33
Distribution of world agricultural production	%	38	62
Production per agricultural worker	$ (1970)	550	5,220
Cultivated land area per agricultural worker	ha	1.3	8.9
Fertilizer used per cultivated hectare	kg	9	40
Food consumption per capita	kcal/day	2,180	3,315
	(kJ/day)	(9,156)	(13,924)
Number of seriously malnourished people	million people	435	..

Source: FAO: Agriculture: Toward 2000, Rome, 1981

The projection took as its aim the reduction of differences. Its authors did not want to calculate using present trends of population growth and food production, since they took the view that this would make the future hopeless. On the basis of the current trend the number of malnourished would grow from its 1974 figure of 435 million to 510 million in 1990 and 590 million in 2000. They therefore predicted a population growth lower than the trend and made the calculations associated with their programme according to lower (B) and a higher (A) variants (table 2.5).

The FAO publication did not consider the B variant to be satisfactory, since it implied that production in the developing countries would only grow by 80 per cent between 1980 and 2000, so that the number of malnourished would be 410 million in 1990 and 390 million in 2000. Version A implied a doubling of production by 2000, but even so the number of malnourished would be 345 million in 1990 and 260 million in 2000. 19 countries with a total population of 1 billion in 2000, would not be able to supply themselves with food even with large scale expenditure on production.

Table 2.5
Main data for the FAO projection for 1980-2000 (annual growth in percent)

Region	Gross domestic product version		Gross agricultural product			Population growth
	A	B	Trend between 1961/65 and 1980	version A	B	
9 developing countries	7.0	5.7	2.8	3.7	3.1	2.0
Africa	6.9	5.4	1.8	4.3	3.4	3.0
South-east Asia	6.9	5.8	2.9	3.6	3.0	2.1
Latin America	7.1	6.0	3.0	3.8	3.0	2.6
South-west Asia	7.1	5.4	3.0	3.7	3.0	2.6
Developed countries	3.8	3.2	2.8	3.7	3.1	0.7

Extending the prognosis to 2050, the FAO calculated that between 1980 and 2055 the food production would have to rise by a factor of 5 with population growth held at an average of 0.9 per cent if there is to be sufficient food to feed everybody by the middle of next century. Even so, the food supply in the developing countries will by then be only half of that in the developed countries compared to 32 per cent in 1980 and 36 per cent in 2000.

The FAO document claims that in order to reach this goal, most of the existing land reserves will have to be brought under cultivation by 2000 and the long-term investments made. New workplaces will have to be created, the use of fertilizer and pesticide greatly increased and the use of irrigation widened. There will have to be many institutional as well as land reforms. Exploitative rent systems must be ended, goods and food must be more evenly distributed. Production incentives should be given through higher prices, cheap credit and subsidies. The infrastructure, transport, storage, water-supply, housing etc. must all be improved. Significant investments must be made in the interests of soil and environmental conservation. Science, education and consultancy must be developed. The ability to export must be increased.

All this will require a large amount of assistance from the developed countries, as well as a peaceful environment, avoidance of wars, and political and economic stability.

The likelihood that the above institutional recommendations will be implemented – as usual for such schemes – is of doubtful. It does serve the purpose, however, of bringing to governments' attention the seriousness of the problems and the possibilities for solving them.

The FAO's revised prognosis (World Agriculture: Toward 2000, 1987), taking changes up to 1985 into account, sounded a more optimistic note. Between 1961/63 and 1983/85 the world's per capita calorie intake rose from 2320 to 2660. The greatest changes took place in the 70s and early 80s (mostly in China and India). Whereas in many countries, among them high-population ones, the calorie intake hardly reached the 1900 daily minimum in the early 1970s, by 1983/85 along with China 35 countries of average population 1.86 billion the average surpassed 2500 calories per day.

The report notes that earlier fears of acute food shortage have proved to be unfounded in most parts of the world. Despite this the low-income countries – with the exception of China and India – do not consume more food than 15 years ago. There are varying estimates of the number of seriously malnourished people of between 350 and 510 million. (The World Development Report, 1992 estimated the proportion of people living below the poverty line in developing countries to be 30 per cent. If this line is taken to be an annual income of $420 per capita at the 1990 dollar value, more like 50 per cent of the population in sub-Saharan Africa and South Asia live in poverty.) But with agriculture becoming able to respond dynamically to demand in the developed nations, and increasingly in developing countries, the problem of starvation has been solved in most of the world.

The biotechnological 'green' revolution brought in during the 1960s was the watershed. In developing countries between 1969/71 and 1983/85 the yields of rice and wheat grew by 41 and 77 per cent respectively. Labour productivity grew by 50 per cent in the same time, although it remained a fraction of that of the developed world.

The regional average of agricultural production grew everywhere in the developing world between 1961 and 1985 by about 3 per cent (cf. 2 per cent in the developed countries), except in the crisis-ridden region of Africa south of the Sahara, where weak development in the 1960s was followed over the next two decades by production decrease aggravated by continual drought. In other parts of the world the reasons for improvement were:

- Significant progress in food production in the Middle East, North Africa and China. In Asia production of high-yielding varieties was widened. Contrary to expectations, the area of crisis shifted from Asia to sub-Saharan Africa. The developing world used ten times as much fertilizer in 1983/85 as it did in 1961/63.
- Population grew more slowly than had been predicted.
- Oil producing countries were able to import a large quantity of food. Weaker countries received significant food aid.
- In many countries policies were altered to the benefit of agriculture. The changes were precipitated by the food crisis in the 1970s and later the difficulties of importing caused by balance of payments deficits and indebtedness.
- Rich countries provided more aid to the poor ones.

The later prognosis covers only 15 years rather than 20, and has only one version. It concerns itself with 94 developed and 34 underdeveloped countries. Considering that economic growth slowed down everywhere in the intervening years (the annual growth of GDP between 1980 and 1986 was 3.5 per cent in the developing countries, excluding China, and 3 per cent in the developed), instead of the 7 per cent growth predicted earlier for the developing and 3.8 per cent for the developed countries, figures of 4.9 per cent and 3.4 per cent were used for the calculations, with a world average of 3.7 per cent. This in turn implies a lower demand for agricultural products. Slower population growth is another feature.

According to current trends the developing countries' agriculture would grow at 3.5 per cent between 1983/85 and 2000., compared with the 3.2 per cent of 1961-85. Growth would primarily be due to the rapidly developing countries of Libya, Saudi Arabia, Ivory Coast, Malaysia and China, which carry growing weight in the average.

Because of the slowing economic growth and the slower rise in demand, the new prognosis envisages a growth in agricultural output of only 3.1 per cent, compared with the current trend of 3.5 per cent for the period between 1983/8 and 2000. The annual rise in per capita food production would not be less than the preceding 15 years' average of 1.2 per cent, however, because of slowing population growth.

In Latin America, the Middle East and North Africa, the predicted growth of agriculture is less than before as a result of more slowly rising population and the already relatively high standard of nutrition, as well as the smaller rise in national and personal incomes and indebtedness.

The FAO report predicts an annual rise of 3.4 per cent in production for black Africa following the 1.7 per cent experienced between 1970 and 1985. This is hoped for as a result of political reforms and the more favourable treatment of agriculture in the channelling of resources, but although slightly higher than before, growth in Africa is still tiny, considering the rapidly rising population. In the same continent the number of malnourished is set to rise from 140 to 200 million in 2000; and in the world at large, despite the reduction in Asia, there will be 530 million hungry people in 2000 compared with 510 million in the mid 1980s.

The development and growth of agriculture in present and former socialist countries

The list of former socialist countries contains members from Europe, Asia, Africa and America. Many developing countries have at some time called themselves socialist, but were only regarded as such by the leading Socialist country, the Soviet Union, and also by the capitalist world, if they maintained a one-party system under a communist or near-communist ideology, so that the economy was centrally planned and controlled; industry, trade and services were largely state-owned; and in agriculture the prevailing type of farming was the state-run production cooperative or state farm, at least according to government aspirations. The communist one-party systems in developing countries did not always achieve complete socialization of the economy (Angola, Ethiopia, Mozambique, Tanzania, Laos, Nicaragua) up to the middle of the 1980s, when socialist ideas and practices in developing countries underwent a decline.

Being called socialist was determined according to the fundamental Marxist principles, according to which socialism was the lowest stage of communism, where society, still in a state of transition, did not have all the features of communism, in fact did not even have the main communist characteristics of abundant production from which goods are distributed according to need, and the withering away of the state. Thus rather than ensuring free distribution of goods, commodity production was predominant.

The socialist systems – except in the Soviet Union and Mongolia – were created after the Second World War. The European socialist countries were those brought into the Soviet sphere of influence, along with their economic and agricultural systems, as a result of the victory of the Soviet Union in the World War. Most Asian and African countries became socialist on the coming to power of the communist parties which had been leading forces in the anti-colonial wars of independence. The communist party of Cuba, and later that of

Nicaragua, came to power after wars against repressive dictatorships. Many developing countries, such as Algeria, Ghana, Guinea, Iraq and India, adopted socialist labels and implemented certain elements of the socialist economy: there was widespread nationalization, central planning and attempts at collectivization. In addition there were many examples of nationalization in countries which did not intend to develop along socialist lines.

Outside the Soviet Union, the European socialist countries were: Albania, Bulgaria, Czechoslovakia, Yugoslavia, Poland, German Democratic Republic, Hungary and Romania. The communist one-party systems came to an end in these countries in 1990-91-92 and their foreign policies became independent. The German Democratic Republic was unified with the German Federal Republic. Yugoslavia broke up into several states, among which only Slovenia had become a parliamentary democracy at the time of writing.

The political institutions of the Soviet Union fell apart and left the economic system in a very uncertain state. In 1991 at first Latvia, Lithuania and Estonia (which had become member republics at the beginning of the Second World War) became independent, and then several more republics established their independence, so that ultimately the Soviet Union ceased to exist as a political entity, and each member country broke away. From the former 15 member republics, 11, and later 12, formed a loose association known as the Community of Independent States (CIS).

The former socialist countries in Asia were Afghanistan, South Yemen, North Korea, Laos, Cambodia, China, Mongolia and Vietnam; those in Africa were Angola, Ethiopia, Mozambique, and Tanzania; and in the Caribbean area Cuba and Nicaragua.

Most of the former communist countries of Asia and Africa, as well as Nicaragua, more or less liberalized economically and politically in the second half of the 1980s. South Yemen united with North Yemen. Only China, North Korea, Vietnam and Cuba maintained their one-party socialist systems. China and Vietnam have significantly liberalized economically, if not politically, in the last few years.

Most of the socialist countries – as mentioned above – transformed their agriculture from small to large units after the communists came to power.

The leading ideologues of the workers' movement, Marx and Engels, for a while Kautsky (in his work The Question of Agriculture, Kautsky, 1899), and later Lenin, claimed that the semi-feudal and capitalist large estates should be expropriated in a socialist society, and the peasantry gradually organized by persuasion into cooperatives. As well as freeing the peasants from the exploitation they suffered under the former system of ownership, the transformation of agriculture into a system of large scale units of socialist or communist production would make it more efficient. With the large units, it was claimed, it would be possible to produce the same quantities as the small units with lower costs, less equipment, machinery, and less buildings. (The principle of economy of scale, where productivity is higher in larger scale production units, is also an accepted precept of neoclassical economic theory.)

The example was already there. The large farms of the time – especially the well-equipped farms in England, Germany and Russia – were more productive than the usually backward peasant farms.

The new socialist countries everywhere implemented or tried to implement this principle, even if they did not achieve the total socialization of agriculture. (In Europe, only in Poland and Yugoslavia did private farming remain prevalent.) Peasants often found themselves rapidly and forcibly pressed into work on the large farms, in contrast to the Marxist principle of leading them by gradual persuasion.

Neither was the thesis regarding economies of scale completely borne out. Few large socialist farms worked more efficiently than most family-run small farms in developed and medium-developed countries. It was not the principle that was at fault, however, but the way it was implemented.

The primary cause of the inefficiency was that socialist enterprises – whether they be industrial, service or agricultural – had little incentive to achieve.

The economy, including farms and other enterprises, were controlled by the central and local party and state bureaucracies. The bureaucracy was not directly interested in production as much as in the favourable statistical indicators which would prove their effective control. In the socialist economy, it was most convenient to prove the indicators of growth of production – even of low-quality or unwanted goods – because these best documented the successful working of the economy and proved to the masters of the socialist economy the premise that the economy was growing faster than in capitalist countries, as Stalin claimed and leaders of socialist countries always accepted. The low labour productivity and capital efficiency, the obsolete mode of production unmatched with demand, and the shortages, were eclipsed by the main aim of raising production.

Neither were the leaders of the enterprises interested in the efficiency of production, as much as in serving the local and central bureaucracy. Their titles, jobs, and prospects of promotion depended on its attitude. Good contacts ensured not only the career of the leader of the organization, but state support for the company, exemption from some withdrawals and other advantages. The only achievements demanded in fulfilment of the quantitative requirements of the plan – and frequently not in reality, but as shown by the records.

The support of the middle managers was enlisted in the high officials' seeking of favour with central bureaucracy by bestowing advantages on them.

The workers were at the bottom of this hierarchy. They became interested in doing as little work as possible. The causes of this were firstly that there was no real pressure to achieve; secondly that wages did not or hardly depended on achievement because of the egalitarian principles, and so there incentive was low, and finally there was full employment, partly because of a socialist declaration to that effect, partly because in view of the low level of productivity, it was the only way to attain the desired growth in production. Thus there was no fear of unemployment to encourage hard work.

Bureaucratic overregulation was a further cause of low efficiency. Enterprises' ability to adjust to shifting world-market conditions and to internal demand was hampered by such things as: clumsy licensing systems for investment, exports and imports, and domestic and foreign payments; lack of proper exchange rates and convertible currencies; centrally-set targets for production, and buying and selling; fixed prices; centrally regulated wages; centrally controlled credit and financing systems; central accounting; withdrawal of a large part of net incomes; and control over use of liquid assets. All of this overregulation combined with lack of interest to cause the failure of modernization and proper structural changes.

A further cause of low efficiency was the disorganization which itself stemmed from those doing the work having no interest in its result. The lack of information which accompanied bad organization led to gaps in production and consumption, goods and services of low quality, and weak market connections.

Yet another reason for low efficiency was the prevailing ideology of both intellectual and material egalitarianism.

Despite the later principle of 'to each according to his work', and the many ways in which the political and economic leadership made clear their intentions to effect distinctions among workers, the original communistic idea of egalitarianism endured in people's attitudes. There were several experiments in enforcing higher motivation – one such being the Hungarian reform – but they met with limited success. As a drag on overall achievement, even more significant than material levelling was intellectual egalitarianism, since the efficiency of production depends above all on the intellectual virtues of management, leadership, organization, innovation, research, and education.

The result of all this was the weak operation of the whole economy. However, agriculture in most socialist countries performed considerably worse even than the average. This was due to a number of causes:
- Agriculture was pushed into the background, because it was felt that it was industry that would drive growth.
- Capital was withdrawn from agriculture for industry. In socialist countries there were ideological as well as practical reasons for this. Neither the peasantry nor the workers of production cooperatives were

considered sufficiently reliable allies of 'socialism- and communism-building worker classes' and so it was not considered desirable to strengthen them economically. More important than ideological reasons, however, was that the central leadership considered that only fully state-owned enterprises could be kept well enough under control, and producer cooperatives, however state-directed, were not such. They therefore tried to transform the cooperatives into state farms in the Soviet Union, and in other socialist countries, and to absorb them into the nationalized sector of the state economy.

- The withdrawals were high, and mainly took the form of compulsory deliveries and low prices. Compulsory deliveries were imposed to meet export requirements and city food supplies, which had suffered from low agricultural productivity and production, but were usually unsuccessful in their aim of improving supply. The state wanted to support industry by keeping food prices low, which allowed them to keep down wages and labour costs. By low costs of procurement they also wanted to boost earnings from exported goods. They also had in mind the winning over of the urban working class through low food prices. At the same time, lack of interest in agricultural production led to ever more serious food and export shortages, which in turn hindered industrial development.

Eventually the governments were forced into developing socialist agriculture owing to the steady shortages and to substitute equipment for the flow of labour into industry. The development was, however, half-hearted and patchy and was carried out in an extensive manner similar to industry. Mechanization was mainly restricted to grain and the main arable crops, even in the relatively developed East European countries, and was not accompanied by sufficient expenditure on the items required to raise yields – such as fertilizer, pesticides, and high-yielding seed. Low production made mechanization expensive. Cultivation of many crops for industrial purposes, and for fruit and vegetables, was hardly mechanized at all, and livestock farming insufficiently. In those livestock farms which were mechanized, investments and relatively high fodder costs were not recuperated owing to low productivity.

The inadequately mechanized agriculture, because of the low productivity resulting from lack of motivation, was constantly struggling with labour shortages, especially in the more industrialized – mainly European – socialist countries. The declining workforce was not equal to the labour intensive task of producing fruit and vegetables, potatoes, industrial crops, livestock etc., and so the production of goods fell or did not rise according to demand.

Characteristically, the household farms of producers' cooperatives and small part-time farmers on officially-limited small areas of land, produced a significant proportion of the fruit and vegetables, potatoes, animals and dairy products, as shown on table 2.6.

Table 2.6
Percentage of total production by individual producers in the CMEA countries (1980)

Product	Bulgaria	Hungary	Romania	Soviet Union	Czecho-slovakia	GDR (1988)
Grain	12.5	11.1	13.9	1.4	3.6	..
Potatoes	53.4	69.6	58.4	64.1	19.7	..
Vegetables	27.6	47.9	41.7	32.7	39.3	..
Fruit	38.9	52.9	49.5	42.1	59.6	68.4
Beef	25.5	25.7	44.7	18.9	4.1	..
Pork	39.2	56.2	32.7	40.3	10.0	17.8
Lamb & goat	47.5	12.4	46.3	40.0	30.2	..
Poultry	45.4	36.7	47.0	37.6	6.4	37.2
Milk	25.9	31.1	56.6	29.6	5.0	..
Eggs	55.5	62.0	60.0	32.1	40.6	47.3
Wool	28.5	17.4	42.8	20.6	47.6	29.5

Sources: *CMEA Yearbook 1981,*
information from the Agricultural Economic Research Institute, Budapest,
A Világ Mezőgazdasága, Budapest, vol. XXII, no 23, p. 8

In completely collectivized socialist agriculture, small plots for private use (typically half a hectare or less), were granted after collectivization to the members of the collective and their families and they could keep a limited, and later in some countries an unlimited number of livestock. In addition to this, many people – agricultural and non-agricultural workers alike – had gardens or household plots, from which they obtained agricultural produce. In some countries, such as Hungary, some agricultural land was allowed to be held privately.

The part-time small-farmers worked at first to supply themselves, but later some of them turned to selling their produce. Although they were badly equipped and their labour productivity was low, as a result of intensive cultivation and the relatively high prices they could get because of the quality of their goods, their 10-15 per cent of the land produced 20-30 per cent of the gross agricultural product, and a very large proportion of labour-intensive agricultural products. In Hungary, for example, the small farmers spent twice as much time on their 15 per cent of the land to produce 30 per cent of the production than workers on the collective farms spent to produce the other 70 per cent. (Időgazdálkodás or Time Management, 1989).

The efforts of individuals could not entirely substitute for the weak performance of large farms on the 85 to 90 per cent of land they cultivated. Although socialist countries aspired to self sufficiency, scarcities appeared in more and more of them and the import requirement grew continually.

Table 2.7 shows how production growth fell over the years in European socialist countries, culminating in an absolute fall after 1990.

Table 2.7
Average annual growth rate of gross agricultural output at constant prices

	Bulgaria	CSFR	GDR	Hungary	Poland	Romania	USSR	Yugo-slavia
1971-75	2.9	2.2	4.1	4.6	3.7	6.5	0.8	3.2
1976-80	0.9	1.9	1.4	2.4	-1.7	3.8	1.5	2.4
1981-85	-0.6	1.8	2.3	0.7	2.1	3.7	2.1	0.7
1986-90	0.0	0.5	..	-0.7	0.8	-3.5	1.1	0.0
1989	0.4	1.8	1.6	-1.3	1.5	-5.4	1.3	5.0
1990	-6.0[a]	-3.7	-	-6.5	-1.4	-3.0	-2.3	-7.0
1991	-6.4	-8.8	-	-3.0	-2.0	1.2	-7.0	..
1992	-12.9	-12.0	-	-22.7	-11.9	-9.2	-8.0[b]	..

[a] estimated
[b] Russian Republic

Sources: *Comecon Data,* 1990, 1991
World Economic Survey, 1992
Osteuropas Landwirtshaft, 1992, 1993

The Soviet Union and other European socialist countries were forced into rising grain imports to ensure supplies of food and animal fodder. The Soviet Union's annual exports of 5 million tonnes of grain in 1969/71 turned into a net import of 38 million tonnes by 1983/85.

Recognizing the need for production incentives in Soviet agriculture, Gorbacsov's *perestroika* programme of transformation included a proposal to set up a system of heritable of tenancies, and even envisaged the privatization of land. The plans in large part, however, did not come to fruition.

Reforms in socialist countries

Divergence from the more or less accustomed agricultural performance of socialist countries was manifested in those countries where economic reforms were carried out. In Europe these were typified by Hungary, and in Asia, by China and Vietnam. In Hungary in the second half of the 1950s, national reform measures also affected agriculture. In 1957 compulsory deliveries came to an end and producer prices were raised. Central plan targets only remained valid for state farms in agriculture. However these measures were followed in 1960-61 by enforced almost total collectivization. Production cooperatives accounted for 75 per cent of cultivated land, and state farms 15 per cent.

Most new cooperatives, however, in contrast to other socialist countries, received significant state support. Between 1965 and 75 arable farming was completely mechanized, and modernization of technology significantly raised yields, approaching the standard of the most advanced European countries. Data from The International Statistical Handbook 1991 of the Central Statistical Office, Budapest, shows that the three-year average yields per hectare from 1986 to 89 was, in tonnes:

	Wheat	Maize
Hungary	4.84	6.02
Austria	4.76	8.07
France	5.10	6.81
FRG	6.33	7.14

Central control and regulation of the producing cooperatives was also more liberal then in other socialist countries, allowing system to develop which generated a high degree of motivation. Some rudimentary democracy also took hold, both for election of the leaders, and in the area of involvement by the cooperative members in the running of the farm.

The general economic reforms of 1968 brought further freedom of action to the farms. Their diminished obligations allowed them to take charge of their mode of production and trade, and the disposition of their incomes. Even state farms were no longer tied to a central plan. It thus became possible to extend into high-earning industrial, trading and service activities at first in a limited way, but freely from the end of the 70s, and sell the products from these. (Many industrial prices were also largely liberalized in the reforms.)

In the early and middle 70s, a counterattack by forces opposed to reform led to the dead weight of state regulation being restrengthened. Subsidies also fell because of signs of the deteriorating economic situation and the state deficit.

Another liberalizing wave at the end of the 70s brought significant changes. These brought a strengthening of the subsidiary businesses, which compensated in some measure for the reduction in support (accounting for 30 per cent of agricultural production on average, but 80 or 90 per cent in the case of naturally less well endowed farms), and the encouragement of individual farming.

The overwhelming majority of large farms wanted to free themselves from labour intensive production (Burger, 1988/a and b). Their mechanization had been thwarted in the 1970s through lack of capital, and due to emigration from agriculture and the low productivity of the remaining manual labour on large farms there was a lack of manpower. *Wage increases were* also made difficult by progressive tax on earnings. This, and the many problems associated with managing labour-intensive production, caused the leaders of the farms to hand over a large part of the livestock to household plots and contract out the cultivation of grapes and fruit to individuals and families, only retaining the mechanical work and sale of the goods, to rent out part of the land and the equipment, and to decentralize the larges into well financially-motivated small units, among others small and specialist cooperatives.

In the mid-1980s individual producers took over the farming of 80 per cent of vegetables and potatoes, 65 per cent of fruit, 50 per cent of wine and poultry and more than 50 per cent of pork.

In the latter part of the 1980s many production cooperatives turned into a mix of production, procurement, sales, services and processing cooperatives. Many of them took on a form which only really corresponded to the concept of 'production cooperative' in the area of completely mechanized arable crops and beef and sheep farming requiring large fodder areas.

The favourable policy towards agriculture meant that there was no food shortage in Hungary from the early 1960s, and it was able to export 1/3 of its agricultural produce.

Some Asian socialist countries have moved towards private operation of agriculture.

In Chinese agriculture, the commune system remained rigidly in place between 1958 and 1978, based on the principle of total equality and eliminating wages and finance, and resulting over the two decades in a significant decline in many areas of production. From being a net exporter of grain, China became a net importer. Forty per cent of supply to the city population was imported. Real income in the villages in 1977-78 was at the same level as in 1957-58.

In 1978 a decision of the Communist Party Central Committee brought in an experimental contractual system known as the 'system of household responsibility'. Communes rented out land to households and prescribed delivery quotas, agricultural taxes and a sum for the collective reserve funds via contracts. Producer prices were raised. Households were free to use the surplus as they wished. Such was the success of the system that by 1983, 95 per cent of village households had contracts. Production doubled between 1978 and 1984, and household incomes rose 2½ times. Compulsory delivery was brought to an end for most categories of produce in 1984-85, so that only producers of grain and cotton still had to hand over a certain percentage, those households specialising in fruit, vegetables and animal-rearing becoming completely free. Long-term, 15-year leases were the norm, with lifetime or even heritable leases in some provinces.

Despite all this the communist leadership stood by the ideological principle of superiority of collective farming, and regarded the whole exercise as a transitional one to get over certain difficulties.

Similar developments took place in *Vietnam and Cambodia*. Family contracts were brought in Vietnam since 1979. Selling prices grew and private trade was permitted. 70 per cent of trade in produce became private, part of this being foreign. Compulsory deliveries and the central distribution of machinery ended in the mid 1980s. Price support for agriculture stopped at the same time, and there was a further liberalization of the food and agricultural produce market. Rationing was abolished.

Striking results were achieved here too, with a considerable rise in agricultural production. From the major rice imports of the 1970s, Vietnam started exporting rice.

Transformation of agriculture in the Central-East European former socialist countries and the CIS

The stagnation characterizing most socialist countries turned to serious decline in the 1990s. As table 2.7 demonstrates, agriculture did not escape the overall decay.

Termed a 'transformation recession' by the economist Kornai (Kornai, 1993), it had many causes, only a few of which are known yet, and knowledge of their relative importance is still incomplete. Economics has still to elaborate a comprehensive theory. Below I attempt to outline a few causes of agricultural decline, noting that some of them concern the whole economy.

The first cause is undoubtedly bound up with the past. Decline started before the political changes, due to factors already mentioned.

Other causes appeared in the wake of the democratic changes in the *Central-East European countries* which took place in the 1990s and are largely responsible for the seriousness and duration of the recession.

Uncertainty of ownership is an important factor throughout the entire economy, including agriculture. Uncertainties caused by the long parliamentary and governmental disputes over privatization are felt most strongly by the managers of agricultural organisations and often by the workers too, provoking doubts over their future and the worth of their efforts, and the uncertain outlook for production.

The privatization laws which have been brought in have not made the situation any better. They have in many cases been contradictory, and instead of real privatization, only half-solutions or the pretence of privatization has been offered, (division of state enterprises and formal establishment as share or other kinds of companies, or worker or citizen ownership). Even this has been carried out with delays caused partly by bureaucratic inertia, and partly by the behaviour of powerful groups standing to lose from privatization or from a particular law.

The Central-East European countries have only managed to privatize 10-15 per cent of their state holdings. They have still not succeeded in diminishing uncertainty and apathy in the other 80-85 per cent, where the rigours of restructuring, bankruptcy, financial rescue and layoffs are no less common.

The uncertainty of ownership in agriculture has progressively worsened.

East European countries (Bulgaria, Czechoslovakia, which in 1993 divided into the Czech and Slovak Republics, the Eastern part of Germany, Hungary and Romania) passed laws in 1991 and 92 covering land privatization, cooperative property titling and the requirement for agricultural producer cooperatives either to be transformed into private farms, or if they prefer to continue to work cooperatively, to register themselves as new cooperatives or other types of companies. Privatization of state farms has also begun.

The laws that land privatization take the form of restitution to former owners. The situation may be contrasted with that of industry where, with local variations, there was very little reprivatization, or return of property to former owners, and more sale or free distribution of property, or manager or workers' buy-outs. The deciding factor in land ownership, however, was the desire to give back property to its former owners or their descendants (e.g. in Hungary cooperative members who had not previously owned land may only receive 1-2 hectares).

The aim of the land reprivatization laws was to establish individual farmers on the Western model, however it resulted in separating land ownership and farming. Because of the earlier large drift of population away from the land and the ageing of those remaining, many owners or their descendants no longer work in agriculture or have retired. In Hungary, for example, the ongoing compensation scheme could lead to a situation where half, or even two-thirds, of the agricultural land is owned by such people. Similarly, the working members of a cooperative could end up with only 40 per cent of non-land cooperative property after the rest has been distributed, in the form of shares, among retirees and people outside the business (Horváth, 1993).

Despite the intended aims of privatization, most countries' cooperatives (except those of Romania and Albania where cooperatives have been divided in favour of widespread private farming) have been reformed as new cooperatives or other companies. Private farms have not become common, because cooperative members lack the relevant experience, and most of the farms that would be available to them would be very small, ill-equipped and unviable; even if they did opt to become private farmers they would not, due to the economic situation of the country, get the required support or cheap credit. The reduction of demand for agricultural produce does nothing to make the outlook any better, and so even with all its uncertainties, common farming seems more secure than the alternative of going private. Only 10-20 per cent of new landowners have opted to work privately, except in eastern Germany, and even there the figure is not more than 25 per cent (Wagner, 1993). It seems that even in Romania, production associations are being revived because farms with less than 2 hectares to lack equipment, and their owners have inadequate farming skills or knowledge of the markets. By summer 1992, large companies were operating on 47.7 per cent of the land (Vincze, 1993).

In the re-established production cooperatives and companies a strange situation is taking shape, where a large part of the land does not belong to the members. In Hungary the law actually denies ownership of land or property by the cooperative, and so they have to rent land. Many of the landowners are likely to be external. Some of the other property is also owned by outsiders, because the Hungarian law provides a property entitlement for all those who were at any time members of producer cooperatives, or their descendants.

The contradictory nature of the privatization laws is compounded by delays in their application both to the land, and to the state farms, which in different countries can account for between 15 and 30 per cent of the land. Slowness is an aspect of the process which is shared by privatization in other sectors.

The unresolved issue of possession has had a bad effect on cultivation, with many areas lying uncultivated, and the use of seeds, fertilizer and pesticides, as well as investment, falling to a minimum.

A further reason is to be found in the general economic difficulties.

Price liberalization in the former socialist countries has led to greater rises on the input than the output side. Agricultural subsidies have considerably reduced. Cooperatives are now denied the income they once received from food processing and other industrial and service activities since they split off or closed down. In the recession following the changes, food consumption fell due to rising prices and unemployment. (Hungarian statistics record a 30 per cent drop between 1988 and 1991, a further 13 per cent in the following year, and 20 per cent up to June 1993 relative to the same period of the previous year). Exports have also fallen as a result of the collapse of the Council of Mutual Economic Aid trade system. Demand has fallen to such an extent that even the former net food importers find themselves with surpluses despite the fall in production.

Indebtedness, and the need to accept credit at rates which their income cannot repay, is forcing many state farms and cooperatives into bankruptcy. It is not only uncertainty surrounding future of large farms, but also simple lack of money which reduces their expenditure. They have already shed large numbers of workers (in Hungary nearly half), swelling the numbers of unemployed.

Private farms are doing even worse. Many of them aim to produce only for subsistence, rather than for the market.

Production has been further depressed by the collapse or deterioration of the state ordering, purchasing and distribution systems, without the emergence of a viable replacement. In the past, small farmers produced for the cooperatives a significant proportion of the animals, fruit, vegetables, grapes, potatoes and other crops requiring a lot of labour through a system of contracts, and the cooperatives then handled all the commercial aspects. This has completely stopped, and the contracting role of the food industry has also shrunk as a consequence of privatization, restructuring, a decrease in demand and bankruptcies.

In the CIS countries, the factors determining the fall in production are in some ways similar, with terms of trade deteriorating, i.e. input prices growing faster than output prices due to price liberalization, and subsidies being reduced. Loosening of the obligation to sell to the state has led to a severe fall in the amount of food sold through state enterprises. There have been serious losses not only in trade but in harvesting too.

Privatization is progressing slowly. In Russia in 1992 every *kolkhoz* (producers' cooperative) and *sovhoz* (state farm) was required to declare whether to retain its former organizational structure or to convert itself into some other form of association. By the end of that year about two-thirds had become share or some other kind of company, a third opting to retain their former structure. Although the number of full-time private farms in Russia is growing, they still account for only 10 per cent of the land, although if part-time and household farms are included this figure rises to 25 per cent.

The question of land ownership still remains to be settled. Land could not be bought or sold until, in October 1993, the President issued a decree allowing privatization of land. This however is only likely to come into effect under the new constitution, since under the current one land is declared to be state property. Privatization is also inhibited by local and central bureaucracy. (Osteuropas Landwirtschaft 1992, 1993).

The Ukrainian Parliament made a provision in 1992 for 10 per cent of that country's agricultural land to be privatized. The law requires farmers to work the land for three years to attain the right to buy the land, and to wait another three years before it passes into their possession. They cannot employ outside labour. Vineyards and orchards cannot become private property (Szabó, 1992).

It seems, therefore, that the former socialist countries' road to the transformation of their agriculture will be a long and bumpy one.

The faltering and slowing of growth across the world

The principles of growth were laid down at a time when mixed economies were taking shape in developed countries. Free competition no longer met the demands of economies predominantly made up of large monopolistic corporations. Large swings in prosperity were threatening the giant corporations with failure, which could have brought down the whole economic system. It was just such a domino-like series of company failures which led to the greatest ever crisis, that of 1929-30.

After this crisis, the New Deal was established in line with Keynesian principles, and after the Second World War, similar policies came to dominate economic policy in European countries.

Mixed economies replaced pure capitalism. The state played a part in the economy and its management. State sectors, large and small, took their place mostly in infrastructural and service areas. State enterprises were to some extent able to balance the cyclical swings of capitalism through the effects of their operations and investments. The state could keep them running at full capacity even through a recession while state investments stimulated the rest of the economy, and during a boom the state could withhold investment to prevent the economy from overheating, thus avoiding the oversupply and fall in demand which could lead to depression and crisis. Anticyclical effects were also the aim of economic policies which stimulated or held back private investments.

The Keynesian theory is built on the cyclical development of capitalist economies. There are upwardly and downwardly curving cycles. The upward, boom period is one when the industrial outlook is good. Expectations of growing profits stimulate investment activity, employment and demand rise, investment demand brings with it a demand for credit, interest rates and wages rise and demand for consumer goods increases prices. Demand for investment goods further stimulates growth in employment and the production of consumer goods through the multiplier effect, while growing demand for consumer goods further raises investment demand and the production of investment goods. This self-generating process accelerates after a while, and the rising prices of goods and of shares and rising interest rates cause demand to appear greater than it really is. A large proportion of goods become unsaleable, that is savings exceed investments, and so part of the investment goods also remain unsold. The overheated economy starts to decline. Reduced investment activity means less demand for credit, employment and consumer demand fall, and these in turn affect the demand for capital goods. Because there is less demand, prices, rents, interest rates and share prices all go down. The depression reaches its low point when producers, even at the much reduced level of production, are forced to replace worn-out capital equipment. This revitalises investment activity, the economy begins to pull itself out of crisis, and the whole process starts over again.

To save the economy from falling into increasingly frequent and ruinous crises, Keynes suggested that states introduce anticyclical measures. These would dampen the acceleration of a boom in order to avoid overheating and stimulate demand during a recession by promoting the growth of investment and employment. State intervention would primarily be aimed at influencing investment activity; this would in turn allow the desired level of employment to be achieved. Measures taken to hold back investments in a time of boom included raising interest rates, bank reserve ratios and taxes, issuing government bonds, decreasing budget expenditure and imposing other financial restrictions. During a recession, investment was elevated through reducing interest rates, bank reserve ratios and taxes, increasing the money supply and budgetary spending, buying government bonds, and state investment in infrastructure and welfare.

The mixed economy and state intervention worked particularly well in the post-war period. The effects of post-war reconstruction, the technical revolution, and such developments as the mechanization of households and agriculture, and the redefinition of the car as a consumer article, all served, at that time at least, to give new momentum to capitalist economies. In the 1960s growth rates of 5-6 per cent became common (in Japan 12-13 per cent) compared to the earlier 1-2-3 per cent broken often by stagnations and recessions. Large scale infrastructural investments and the state's taking on of social and cultural responsibilities – the so-called 'welfare state' – also helped in stabilising employment and income and had a damping effect on fluctuations in demand.

At the end of the sixties, unbroken growth looked set to continue indefinitely, when certain warning signs began to appear. There were the first indications of structural crisis in the developed countries. The leading post-war industrial sectors – such as the motor and machinery industries, and those of transport, household appliances, and traditional audio and television systems had saturated the market. As their products became harder to sell, their profits fell and they were forced to lay off some workers. Signs of crisis spread to the supply industries of coal iron and steel and their dependants. Growth slowed down, periodic recessions deepened and unemployment grew. Pollution related to industrial growth was a matter of increasing concern. Prognoses were made warning that at current rates of growth, the world's reserves of energy and raw materials would run out. Population growth accelerated in the developing countries and there were increasing food shortages and poverty.

In 1968, in recognition of these warning signs, a group of leading scientists and experts from many fields came together with the purpose of assessing the future of mankind. Known as the Club of Rome, it commissioned various research groups to make prognoses for the future. The principal question which was to be addressed was whether there would be enough resources for economic growth in coming generations. Would there be enough raw materials and energy for rising production, and would pollution resulting from their use endanger mankind? Ultimately, could agriculture feed the rapidly multiplying number of mouths?

The world food crisis of 1972-4 and the oil shocks of 1973 and 1979 appeared to confirm the validity of these questions.

Before 1972, many developing countries, mainly in Asia and Africa, had suffered from bad harvests in consecutive droughts which had exhausted their food reserves. In 1972 there was even a bad harvest in the USA, the world's greatest grain-growing nation. For the first time in many years, the USA ended the year with zero stocks of grain. The USSR suddenly increased its grain imports, taking in significant quantities from the start of the 1970s. China also started importing and the amount of grain bought by oil-exporting countries jumped to a new level. The results of all this were food shortages, especially in developing regions, and large rises in world market prices.

After the food crisis came the 1973 oil crisis, when oil producing countries combined to multiply their prices.

The oil price rise was followed by a rise in price of other raw materials, and when they worked through to finished products, large scale inflation resulted. The price shocks reduced demand and consequently production stagnated and then fell back, starting off 'stagflation': double digit inflation (Britain and Italy) combined with stagnation and recession. This was a new phenomenon, since hitherto booms had been accompanied by mild inflation and recessions by falling price levels.

For some time, state economic policy could not find an adequate response to the new situation. Prolonged stagnation was followed by a further doubling of the oil price in 1979, bringing in its wake another wave of inflation and a particularly deep recession.

Countries' economic policies changed. Governments needed to stop inflation and reduce debts and deficits in their budgets and balance of payments. This led them to discontinue Keynesian demand incentives and bring in the supply-side policies put forward by the 'new monetarist' school. The leading proponent of the monetarist approach, Milton Friedman (Friedman, 1969), advocated reassertion of the strengths of the free market in place of the regulated economy of the past. Monetarists took the view – and still do – that the state should only seek to influence the economy in providing incentives for supply through regulating the money supply.

Cuts in public spending, privatization of state companies, reducing subsidies, deregulation, whittling down welfare benefits and other restrictive measures for squeezing the money supply, at the same time as reducing taxes, achieved their desired affect of reducing inflation and the economy went into a new upswing. This upturn was mainly due to the structural changes (the electronic revolution) which took place during the recession. Economic growth started up again in 1984, but was lower than it used to be and was more often prone to downturns.

Even those governments most forcefully professing monetarist principles – the British and American – did not entirely renounce Keynesian anti-cyclical regulatory measures; neither did they do away altogether with the mixed economy in favour the free market. They also felt themselves unable to dispense with the welfare state with its social security protections for fear of risking a large-scale backlash to the benefit of their oppositions. Many subsidies were also left in place, especially to agriculture, whose ending would have set off political unrest in the farming community and other sections of the population.

The developing countries suffered even more severely from the recession as a consequence of their weak position. Most of them, mostly the less industrialized, were unable to bring in structural changes like those in South-East Asia, and have still not recovered from the consequent decline. Higher world prices made imports more expensive, and slackening world market demand reduced their ability to export, so that serious balance of payments deficits followed. High import prices and government debt set off rapid inflation in most of them. The green revolution also came to a temporary halt because fertilizer and other means of production became more and more expensive and there was no money to support major investments such as irrigation. Shortages of food and other goods became common in many countries.

In order to stop their situation deteriorating further, these countries borrowed significantly in order to reduce their balance of payments deficits. Banks in the developed countries generously lent out at low rates of interest the petrodollars being deposited with them. However in the early 1980s, in the course of counter-inflation measures, real rates of interest rose. Developing countries which could hardly survive even with the help of all this credit, suffered mounting difficulties in keeping up repayments. During the trough of the recession between 1982 and 84, many developing countries, among them socialist Poland, announced a moratorium on debt services. The 'debt crisis' had arrived.

International organizations, primarily the International Monetary Fund (IMF), but others as well, such as the 'Club of Paris' representing the main bankers of the developed countries, tried to find a way out of the crisis. Some leading capitalist countries, such as the US, also came up with plans to deal with the crisis, mostly for Latin America and the Philippines. These were the Baker and Brady plans of 1985 and 89 respectively, named after the US treasury secretaries of the time. The plans were aimed at strengthening the countries' capability to keep up repayments and outlined ways of moderating the burden of debt. These measures were: interest rate cuts, extending repayment period, making it possible for the affected countries to buy back some of their debts at reduced rates, selling debt bonds on foreign capital markets in exchange for shares in domestic companies etc. The new debt conditions were negotiated individually be each nation and their creditors, with the organizations who devised the plan mediating and often providing guarantees. The guarantee conditions were usually acceptance of prescribed reconstruction measures. These were also the terms for offering new credit.

The IMF has played a central role in renegotiating debt conditions and providing new credit. Although the IMF's own lending capacity is relatively small, its loans are mostly long-term and at low interest rates. Besides this, the IMF's offer of a loan to a particular country is often taken as a guarantee by commercial banks for their own lending.

When the IMF offers countries mediation in the negotiations of revised debt conditions and it gives new loans, it usually ties them to implementing a set of measures for reducing their budget deficits based on monetarist and free market principles:
- import liberalization
- currency devaluation
- introduction of full or partial currency convertibility
- freeing fixed prices
- stopping inflation through restrictive measures and tightening the money supply
- reduction of budget deficits by reduction of public spending and drastic reduction of subsidies and welfare payments.
- privatization of state enterprises, which are in most cases loss-making and subsidized.

The effect of these measures has proved to be double edged. Import and price liberalization have largely eliminated shortages, but the consequent price rises have greatly reduced the purchasing power of the population. This has affected the poorest sections of society most severely. In many countries, implementation of the measures was followed by hunger protests and riots (in Sudan, Morocco, Jordan, Dominica and Venezuela). Many countries responded to these by wholly or partly, or temporarily, abandoning the austerity measures.

Devaluation was intended to stimulate exports, but this effect has to be set against internal price rises due to more expensive imports. In the event, exports have shown little positive response because of the countries' economic weakness and low level of development, and the lack of readiness of export industries. Exports of raw materials and agricultural produce face a range of limitations set by developed countries: quotas, customs duties, levies and other import barriers. At the same time import liberalization renders their weak industry and agriculture defenceless against competition from foreign goods.

Those who came up with the plan and promote its implementation argue that the rise in food prices, although putting a burden on urban populations, encourages agricultural production and will benefit the whole population in the long run. But owing to import liberalization there is an opportunity to import food and the import competition weakens domestic food production (as in Egypt and Mexico). Tax increases brought in to help balance the budget are a further discouragement to domestic production.

Reduction of subsidies, including those of food and agricultural produce, put a further strain on the ordinary consumers and on agricultural producers. Paring down social security is hard on those who were badly off even on the previous level of benefits. Replacement of normative subsidies and benefits by needs-targeted benefits – the offering of free or cheap goods and services to the most poor – not only fails to substitute for benefits given as a matter of civil rights, but serves to humiliate the recipients.

The unambiguously favourable aspects of the measures are: reduction of the debt burden, the restraint of inflation (where it is successful), deregulation and privatization, which cause a significant decrease in state expenditure and raise motivation to produce.

The IMF hopes that time will vindicate all of its recommendations. We will have to wait and see.

World models of growth

World events have confirmed the relevance of the question posed by the Club of Rome in the 1960s: is mankind being threatened by dangers arising from economic growth?

Several projections of economic development and the resources required for it were commissioned by the Club of Rome and other organizations such as the UN.

The first of these were cast as mathematical models, and later as verbal models as well. In contrast with former growth models, natural resources, including agriculture, assumed a central position. Two models drew the most attention: those of D.L. Meadows (Meadows et al, 1972) and M. Mesarovic and E. Pestel (Mesarovic and Pestel, 1974). Both were computer models of dynamic system growth.

Meadows and his research group at MIT published the final report of their model under the title 'The Limits to Growth'. According to this, five basic factors were built into the model: industrial growth, reduction of non-renewable resources owing to industrial growth, environmental pollution, growth of population and food production. The group analysed interdependence and mutual effects of these factors in the process of economic growth. There was also a range of accompanying sub-factors.

The model looked at growth trends between 1900 and 1970 and extrapolated them to 2100. There were twelve variants.

The first variant assumed continuation of the hitherto exponential growth into the future. Other variants took into account varying resources, increased reserves due to discoveries, wider use of nuclear power, recycling of materials, birth control, higher levels of environmental protection, and increasing agricultural production.

The first variant of the model charts the effects of exponential growth as reserves of raw materials diminish: industry cannot grow any further. Therefore, and also because of the rising environmental pollution; agricultural production falls; the death rate rises from the effects of pollution and lack of food. The system can only be maintained until 2020 and then collapses.

In the next eight variants, the collapse of the system is pushed to the middle and end of the next century, but is still eventually unavoidable.

The 10th version is the 'No. 1 stabilization model'. This assumes a halt in population growth in 1975 and in industrial growth in 1990, so that industrial production stabilizes at three times the 1970 level. The following measures were implemented in the model: a reduction of pollution; recycling of materials; the extension of the lifetime of investment and other capital including land by better maintenance; control of erosion and land improvements; and the turning over much of industrial production to food production and to services. Because of the greater amount of investment directed towards agriculture, there would be enough food.

The eleventh variant, the 'No. 2 stabilization model', considered delayed stabilization of population and growth. Population would stabilize at a higher and industrial production at a lower level.

The final, twelfth, variant showed that the later that the necessary measures are brought in, the less hope there is for mankind. If the measures of the

64

previous two variants were delayed until after 2000, equilibrium would break down in the middle or end of the next century.

This model of world growth, with its somewhat pessimistic results, was widely criticised. The criticisms mainly concerned its globalization, all assumptions and measures being applied uniformly across the world, and its neglect of the possible effects of scientific progress. As far as the first criticism is concerned, it is clear that the starting points – and therefore the conclusions – regarding economic and population growth should be different for, say, India and the United States. The average effects can be calculated mathematically but not verified economically. Regarding the other point, critics noted that mankind had never yet come across such intractable problems that innovation, science, new inventions and discoveries couldn't find a way round. There was no reason to believe that the future would be different in that respect.

Avoiding the trap of globalization was one of the main aims of the Mesarovic-Pestel model, whose final report was entitled 'Mankind at the Turning Point'. Their model simulated the world as ten geographical regions of varying levels of development and examined the mutual effects of regional changes. The regions were: 1. North America, 2. Western Europe, 3. Japan, 4. Australia, South Africa and Israel, 5. Eastern Europe, 6. Latin America, 7. North Africa and the Middle East, 8. Tropical Africa, 9. South Asia, 10. China, North Korea, Mongolia and the then North Vietnam.

They described the regions' development in terms of hierarchical levels:

(a) environmental level (climate, land, water, air, raw materials, living organisms, plants and animals.
(b) technological and technical level (from agriculture to space research)
(c) demographic-economic level (based on economic and population statistics)
(d) social level (individual values, along with their biological and physical effects and conditions.

The different levels were interconnected in the model. The individual and social levels constitute a system for setting aims.

The period in question was 1975-2025. About 100,000 interrelations were calculated, compared with the few hundred of the earlier model.

The final report identified as most important among a range of world crises threatening mankind those of population explosion, environmental damage, scarcity of food and raw materials, and energy. The authors considered stopping economic growth to be the least desirable way of dealing with the crises.

They stress that growth has to be organic rather than exponential as it had been up to that time. As the world develops, the deciding factors must be the working of functional relationships, as in organic systems, rather than the quantity of growth. The comparison is made between exponential growth and the runaway growth of cancerous cells in a sick person, in contrast with the normal, organic growth in a healthy system. In changing over to the period of organic development mankind has reached a turning point in his history.

The various crises (population explosion, environmental pollution, scarcity of food etc.) are local and regional in character but in contrast to crises of the middle ages – plagues and wars – which remained local, these set in motion a chain of events that could threaten a general catastrophe. The authors felt that study of the features of the various regions at different levels of development was an important step which could help to avoid crises or temper their effects.

For a realistic analysis, the world has to be viewed as a system of mutually influencing regions. The culture, traditions and level of political and economic development of each region is different. Much more likely than a general collapse would be for individual regions to experience crises of diverse causes, perhaps not too far in the future, but whose influence, due to links between regions, would be felt everywhere. Regional crises could only be avoided or, if necessary, overcome with the cooperation of the whole world.

To avoid world-threatening crises, every region requires good economic and social conditions at all times, and economic growth, but of an organic nature, rather than the undifferentiated 'wild' growth which accelerates the oncoming of crises.

Holding back growth, far from offering a solution to the great problems of mankind, could itself lead the way to collapse.

The success of these two well-known models was in forcing people, particularly intellectuals and politicians, to recognize the dangers the world is threatened with. From different approaches and levels of intensity, both models reach the conclusion that mankind will have to look after what it has, especially the natural environment, more cautiously in the future. Attempting to continue the rapid industrial growth enjoyed hitherto can only lead to our very existence being threatened. Environmental protection and the status of agriculture must be given higher priorities, and exploitation of nature must give way to cooperation with it. More must be done for future generations instead of pursuing immediate returns. This calls for people from all over the world to work together for common aims.

The theories stated in, or inferred from, these models therefore tend to speak against the idea of rapid growth rather than for it. They say that human well-being is not completely identical to material wealth. It is useless for one region to be materially well off if the air and water are poisoned, or its resources are running out, or if the greater part of humanity is threatened with starvation.

Without doubt the warnings have had some effect – consider for example environmental protection measures in many countries or the aid or trade preferences offered to developing countries by developed ones – but the desired aim is far from being fulfilled.

Many subsequent models were devised to show that the first ones painted too black and white a picture, and that the dangers could be avoided with international collaboration, sensible policies and helping each other (Korán, 1980).

One of the better known of these models was the input-output growth model developed by Leontief and his research group (Leontief, 1976) for the UN.

In 1973 the UN commissioned Leontief to examine the possibility of fulfilment of the UN's international development strategy for the world, considering the restricted supply of resources, whereby the annual growth target was 6 per cent, the per capita growth rate 2.5 per cent and the population growth 2.5 per cent for the developing countries.

The study set out to determine how the pursuit of the targeted economic growth would be influenced by the available natural resources, industrial pollution, environmental protection costs, and whether the resources of the different regions were sufficient to meet the aims of regional development.

The Leontief input-output model divided the world into 15 economic-geographical regions, and examined 45 sectors and their subsectors. Its time period was 1970-2000. The main sectors were: agriculture, raw material and energy extraction, manufacturing industry, engineering industry, services and infrastructure.

The modellers analysed the possibilities for food supply and agricultural production, the state of mineral and energy resources, the costs of reducing pollution, the future of investment and industrialization, world trade changes and balance of payments problems, as well as the possibilities for a new world economic order.

The question of adequacy of resources received a broadly positive answer. Thus in their opinion agriculture could satisfy the demand for food if cultivated land was extended by 30 per cent and yields improved by a factor of three throughout the world.

The Earth's mineral reserves were considered to be sufficient to satisfy demand. According to their calculations, environmental protection expenditure would not exceed 0.5-1.6 per cent of GNP and 5-8 per cent of total capital stock. These expenditures would not put insurmountable obstacles in the way of accelerated growth.

They asserted that to close the gap between rich and poor countries, growth in the developing countries must be faster, and the rate of investment much greater, than those aimed at by the UN's international development strategy. The rate of investment in the developing countries has to be greater than that in the developed ones. For growth of 4-6 per cent the 20 per cent investment rate prescribed by the UN development strategy would be enough in developing countries. For 7-8 per cent growth, 30 per cent would be needed, however, and for 9-10 per cent sustained growth, 35-40 per cent. A precondition of faster growth is fast industrialization.

It was necessary to change world trade for the benefit of developing countries, and that they get their balance of payment deficits under control. For this they outlined the alternatives of a new international economic order. They stressed that establishment of such a new order was essential for a sustained closing of the gap between developing and developed countries. Such an order called for a fundamental change in economic relations between the two sets of countries. The main points of their suggested changes were:

- Prices of primary goods (raw materials and agricultural products) have to be raised more quickly than those of industrial goods.
- Developing countries have to reduce their dependence on imports.
- A greater proportion of their exports must be processed goods.
- Developed countries should give more aid of the relevant kind, and more selectively.
- Developed countries should provide capital goods to the developing countries on a larger scale.

To bring all this about, the developed countries have to increase their imports from the developing, liberalize their trade and offer preferential terms to developing regions. They should increase aid as a proportion of their GNP.

The report calls for fundamental social, political and institutional changes in the developing countries, such as land reform, more just and equal distribution of goods, better welfare benefits and so on.

The new international economic order was the subject of the Club of Rome's third report entitled RIO (Reshaping the International Order). The report was prepared by a 21-member research group led by the Nobel prize-winning Dutch economist Jan Tinbergen (Tinbergen, 1977) in response to the declaration of the 6th extraordinary meeting of the UN General Assembly in 1974 which called for, in the interests of the development of poorer countries, a new international economic order and an action plan to implement it.

The RIO model looks at the period 1975-2000, and has a verbal basis, in contrast with the previous mathematical models. It has three parts. The first part sets out the case for a new international economic order and enumerates the questions to be investigated. The second part outlines the possible variants of development, the possibilities for breaking down the current inequalities, and strategies for doing the work. The third part details and systematizes the recommended measures.

The main measures for forming a new world order are:

- The setting up of a reserve fund for Third World development by the IMF.

- A major transfer of resources from rich to poor.
- Self-sufficiency to be achieved in each region through collaborative efforts. Political, social and economic reforms such as land reform are preconditions for raising food production. Developed countries must hand over production technology to developing ones.
- A dynamic, progressive industrial strategy which supports comparative advantages. Regional specializations should be adapted in overpopulated countries to implement dual technological systems (factory and hand crafts). Developed countries should reduce their import restrictions on manufactured and semi-finished goods from the third world.
- No special measures are required regarding the overall supply of energy and raw materials.
- A wide-ranging inspection of multinational companies.
- Internationalization of measures to protect the human environment.
- As a fundamental precondition of the new world order's implementation, disarmament and the prevention of wars.

Within these main headings there are many other important considerations, such as the ending of poverty and unemployment, and the guaranteeing basic human rights to food and shelter.

The RIO report is clearly best regarded – in the same way as those of the other models – as a way of drawing the attention of the world's countries to the problems facing them, and its recommendations should be seen as the agenda for international negotiations, rather than a plan of action for rapid implementation.

In one respect the reports reached a positive achievement in demonstrating that the resources required for growth are not infinite: they have to be used more sparingly than in the past, and efforts must be made, and measures taken, to secure the supply of food to the rapidly rising population of the world.

Part II
AGRICULTURAL TRADE

3 Some principles of trade

The evolution of trade

Ancient cities and states – Babylon, Phoenicia, Carthage, Egypt and Greece – carried on trade at high levels of sophistication. Rome imported oil and wine from Hispania (today's southern Spain) and traded it on to southern Italy, Tunisia and Egypt in exchange for grain. From its North African colonies – Africa, Numidia and Mauritania – it brought in minerals. The sailors of ancient Phoenicia were well-known for their trade in wood, copper, iron, gold and ivory. Besides the sea routes, trade was taken from Carthage through the Sahara to the interior of Africa.

In the Middle Ages, the Chinese, Arabs and Levantines, and people from the Italian city-states were known traders. At the beginning of the modern age trade spread from the Mediterranean and the continent across the Atlantic, mainly by the Portuguese, Spanish, English, French and Dutch.

Trade underwent occasional rises and falls in intensity throughout history, suffering decline along with the eclipse of the trading states, but became a stable, integrated part of countries' economies only with industrialization.

Whereas agriculture accounted for the overwhelming majority of the national product, complemented by some artisan industry and in some places mining, only a very small amount of agricultural production made its way into circulation as trade. The majority of food was produced by those who consumed it, with little being required by the markets in whatever small towns there were. International trade in agricultural produce was virtually negligible; in past centuries only the richest and most powerful Europeans could afford 'colonial goods' from far away places, mainly consisting of spices, sugar, coffee and tea.

The industrial revolution saw the beginning of a division of labour between various economic sectors, starting in England and then spreading to other European countries and those overseas countries that had been settled by Europeans. Industrial goods were not produced for consumption by those who produced them, but in exchange for other goods. They had to be exchanged partly for raw materials, including those of agricultural origin, such as wool, flax, hemp, cotton, vegetable oil and rubber, and partly for food for the growing industrial cities. Agriculture started to buy more industrial goods, equipment and consumer goods, for which it had to hand over more of its produce to the market. In this way it gradually shed its subsistence character and itself became a commodity producer of goods. This process of exchange stabilized and became an integral part of the economies of industrialized countries.

Trade altered the structure of agricultural production. Whereas hitherto it was climate and soil which more or less dictated what and how much farmers produced, now the market started to make its effect through the type and quantity of goods that it demanded, and the distances over which they had to be transported. Specialization emerged. Subsistence farming is always necessarily diverse, since one farm has to supply the family with all of its food, and in pre-industrial times it was also the source of raw materials for manufactured goods which were needed and made at home. Subsistence farms usually only sell whatever they cannot consume themselves, if they sell anything at all. As trade becomes a steady and integrated part of the economy encourages the development of production purely for sale, and specialization of production according to the needs of the market. The nature of this specialization is determined, among other factors, by how far the producers are from the market.

Thünen's theory of location and rent

The principle of the geographical location of agricultural production and the effect of location on rent was put forward by the German economist von Thünen, who was also a practising farmer in the Mecklenburg region (von Thünen, 1827; also Morgan and Munton, 1971)

In his theoretical model, Thünen determined firstly the rents, dependent on the distances over which farm produce has to be transported to the market, and secondly the distribution of farms specializing in different types of produce in response to production costs which vary according to distance from the market.

His model contains the following assumptions:

1. Agricultural production takes place within an isolated country with only internal trade.
2. There is only one city market in the country.
3. The quality of the farmland producing goods for market is everywhere uniform. This is a crucial condition in the model, since it allowed Thünen to get round Ricardo's principle of differential rents, which stem from the different production costs depending on the quality of the land, thus enabling higher or lower income. The assumption of uniform land quality implies uniform production costs of the same produce, so that it concentrates attention of the effect of transport costs on differentiating income.
4. The ability to transport to market is uniform. Roads extend radially from the city. The mode of transport, which was universal at the time, is the horse and cart.
5. The market is supplied by farmers who have a direct interest in the net income.

Considering that each product is sold at a more or less uniform price, and the cost of production of the same produce does not vary from place to place, the transport cost is the only factor that can differentiate the margin obtained from selling the goods. The further the farm is from market, the higher the transport cost, and so the lower the net income. And as the distance to market, and hence the transport cost, increases, so the spending on production has to be reduced in order to maintain profit. Production therefore has a geographical limit where marginal cost equals marginal price and beyond which it is not worth producing for the market even at low production costs, because the profit would be negative owing to higher transport costs than income. The rent of location may be expressed as a formula:

$$L_r = Q(p-c) - Qdf$$

where

L_r = rent of location

Q = quantity of product

p = price of product

c = production cost

d = distance of transport

f = unit freight cost per unit of product (e.g. tonne/km)

Thünen drew various production zones around the city, based on farming and selling practices current in Germany at the time. These zones are called Thünen rings and are shown in figure 3.1.

The first zone, near the city, produces the perishable milk, dairy products and vegetables which cannot be transported over long distances, and are relatively expensive to produce. Yields, and with them production costs, rise with the use of horse manure which is available in large quantities from the horse-drawn transport of the city can supply. The transport costs are therefore least in this zone, but production costs are relatively high.

The second zone is occupied by forests. In Germany of that time wood was the main source of energy and it was advisable to produce it near to the city since it was bulky and the costs of transporting it were high because of the wide areas of land required to produce it.

The third zone from the city provides grain and potatoes, grown intensively in crop rotation. With increasing distance from the city, grain production becomes more extensive, and more and more grazing and fallowing is brought into crop rotation.

Finally, as distances get longer and production costs have to decrease, we arrive at the margin beyond which it is not worth carrying grain to market, because the transport cost absorbs the entire .

In Thünen's model, the horse-and-cart transport limit was also the limit of production for the market. At that time, Thünen calculated this to be 239 km. Beyond this, only extensive animal grazing and subsistence production was worthwhile.

Thünen's model contains many simplifications. He does not allow outlets other than the single market, such as foreign trade. A solitary market with radial access roads, uniform land quality and circular zones of production were constructs which did not correspond to reality. Thünen attempted to alleviate the closed nature of his model by employing other factors, such as river transport (since cities are normally set beside rivers and wood, for example, is normally transported this way), and admitting other, small-town markets. These new factors did not, however, change the substance of the model or the consequences drawn from it.

Many see Thünen's rent of location theory as outdated. Whether by rail, air or sea, the developments in transport and in cooling technology since the principle was formulated have transformed the movement of food. Even perishable goods can nowadays be carried over enormous distances, with the costs per kilometre tending to diminish distance increases. In a related development, the significance of agriculture in foreign trade has grown enormously since Thünen's day. The prevalence of food processing is another factor, making irrelevant the distance between the farm and the point of ultimate consumption.

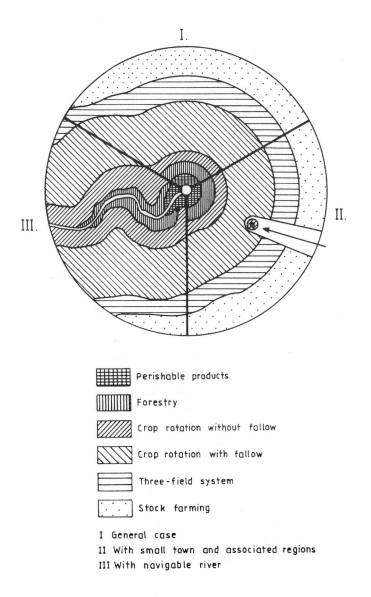

Perishable products

Forestry

Crop rotation without fallow

Crop rotation with fallow

Three-field system

Stock farming

I General case
II With small town and associated regions
III With navigable river

Figure 3.1   **Thünen's concentric agricultural zones around one or more cities**

However, outwith its original, narrow set of circumstances, the model contains much that is still relevant. Nearness to markets and freight distances still influences production and trade of goods. Processing industry may be considered as a market in the same way as the point of sale to consumers. Even nowadays, processing industries are usually located close to production areas – or production areas grow up around the factories precisely in the interests of keeping down transport costs. Vegetable-growing and dairy cattle areas are usually found near cities. It is true that the importance of California, Southern Europe, North Africa and others as suppliers of fruit and vegetables to distant cities is almost the same as the local supply belts of these cities, however transport costs are still an important factor. It is just that the higher transport costs are compensated by the lower production costs of the more advantageous ic sites.

Evidence for the continuing validity of the theory in its wider sense may be found in the phenomenon, following the rise in transport costs arising from the 1970s' oil price explosion, of the revival of the supply belts around cities in the north-east of the USA. At the same time, many Central and Northern European horticultural companies responded in an opposite way in order to cut their energy costs, by moving to South European and North African countries, because the resulting decrease in energy expenditure more than compensated for the negative effect on profits of higher transport costs. Since then, relative costs and prices have more or less evened out, even on a higher level. The oil price has gone down, and energy conservation technology has improved. The fact that the Netherlands remains, as before, Western Europe's largest supplier of expensively-produced and distantly-transported greenhouse tomatoes, needs no principle to explain it: Dutch production simply receives a large amount of subsidy. Protectionism therefore tends to invalidate the principle of rent of location, but it has the same effect on any other free-market principle.

Schultz (Schultz, 1953) extended the principle of advantages of location in agriculture to F. Perroux's (Perroux, 1950) idea of growth centres. This holds that in areas surrounding rapidly developing urban industrial centres, where the markets for both capital and consumption goods are more dynamic, agriculture also grows faster than elsewhere. Even in Hungary's agriculture there could be seen, in the 1980s signs of the beneficial effects of proximity to urban and industrial centres, although most produce was bought at uniform prices, irrespective of transport costs. (Szűcs, 1990). The benefits were a result of free selling prices of some products (for vegetables, fruit, poultry, eggs and others) and opportunities for faster general development.

Although Thünen based his location rent theory on domestic trade, it has proved its validity for foreign trade too. Commodities like cereals, which are bulky and have low production costs and can be stored for long periods, are transported most economically by sea. It is no coincidence that it was countries with large ports that became the great grain exporters: USA, Canada, Australia, Argentina and France. The same can be said for other high-volume, non-perishable produce, such as coffee, whose leading exporting countries are Brazil and Columbia. Further, within the exporting countries themselves, these crops are often produced either near the ports (e.g. coffee in the region around Santos in Brazil) or near water routes leading to the ports (e.g. the Mississippi valley and surrounding areas in the USA).

The tendency for produce which is relatively expensive to produce, or is perishable, (e.g. fruits and vegetables) to be transported over shorter distances also applies to external trade (Enyedi, 1971): apart from its sensitivity to being carried over long distances, the high cost of rail and air transport squeezes profit margins.

The development of foreign trade

With the widening of industrial production, domestic markets proved too narrow, and more and more products were sent abroad. Internally too, demand widened for items not produced domestically, or at least not in sufficient quantities: for certain industrial goods, mineral and agricultural raw materials, and food. Thus countries had to import increasing quantities. With exporting and importing becoming customary, there evolved a division of labour between countries. This process drew distant countries, with traditional economies, into the exchange activity along with the industrialized and industrializing countries. And those already comparatively highly industrialized felt the need for more raw materials from further away. The growing engineering industry needed jute, sisal, palm oil and the motor industry used large quantities of rubber. Food production in many industrializing countries, such as Britain and Germany, did not keep up with demand thus necessitating imports. Their suppliers were overseas countries who received industrial goods in return.

From the start, the exchange between developed and underdeveloped regions was unequal. Large trading companies were founded at the beginning of the 17th century in the then developed countries for pursuing trade with the countries of Asia, Africa and America. The best known of these were the East India companies established in England in 1600 and Holland in 1602. These companies had a monopoly of trade between the Cape of Good Hope and Cape Horn, i.e. all the way form Africa to America. Their trade monopolies went along with political power delegated to them by their home states.

Frequently fighting each other, the companies represented the states of England and the Netherlands on the territories where there writ ran, building forts, conducting wars and founding colonies over which they assumed the rights of administration and legal jurisdiction. In addition to straightforward plunder, the companies employed various schemes to coerce the subjugated areas into handing over their goods, including imposing levies, and setting unequal contracts many of which were later broken. They enforced the production of various export goods (coffee, tea, latex, cotton, tobacco and drugs), and imposed compulsory deliveries.

As colonization became more systematic in the 19th century, and the demand for food and raw materials grew considerably, several trade organizations were developed with authoritative powers overseeing production, procurement, processing and export of many kinds of products (Coffee board, Tea board etc.). A large part of their function was to meet s from the parent country for export goods by overseeing the work of small producers in areas where there were no white plantation owners, or to supplement plantation production. Thus started export production of rubber in Malaysia, cocoa in Ghana, Nigeria and Ivory Coast, tea in China, India and Ceylon, sugar cane in Jamaica, jute in Bengal, and palm oil in West and Central Africa.

In 1925 the English built a system of irrigation canals in Sudan between the Blue and the White Nile on the Gezira Plain for cotton growing, with which the now independent state of Sudan irrigates 1 million hectares. This is the largest irrigation system in the world under single control. The Gezira System incorporates 6 state companies renting out to tenants in 17-hectare pots. Cotton is grown in rotation on a quarter of the territory, with materials, machinery and seeds being provided by the companies and irrigation water by the state, and the producers being obliged to supply the cotton. A substantial part of the cotton price is deducted as rent. The companies process the cotton and pass it to the Cotton Public Corporation for export.

The French wanted to build a similar large-scale irrigation system in Mali based on the River Niger. However the scheme only reached 85,000 hectares. The area is the property of the Office du Niger, nowadays also a state enterprise, and the land is similarly rented out in parcels to producers. Originally cotton was the intended crop here too, but nowadays a large proportion is given over to rice production. Half of the countries' cotton and one third of its rice is produced by the Office du Niger.

The authoritarian trade and other organizations and companies involved in production certainly played a positive role. They untied producers from the constraints of traditional cultivation and taught them the principles of modern production; in turn the producers started to demand industrial goods and strove to produce more in order to increase their income.

At the same time, physical and other punishment, imprisonment, high taxation, pressed labour (in mines and public works) and other means of coercion, unequal contracts and compulsory sales at low prices kept trade inequitable. It is a striking fact that compelling production for export did not affect the traditional ways of producing food. In Africa, for example, where traditionally it is the women who grew the crops and support the family, the colonizers contracted the men to produce export crops, giving them land, more modern implements and skills. This had a doubly negative effect on families: 1. They dropped out of money earning. 2. Those supporting the family did not learn modern means of cultivation (Boserup, 1990).

After gaining independence, the new states took over the existing organizations which supervised production of export crops. But producers fared little better under the new régime than under the colonial one, with unfavourable contract conditions, compulsory deliveries, low purchase prices and high taxes largely being maintained or stepped up. In Egypt, for example, it was only in the 1980s that compulsory deliveries of cotton and grain were discontinued.

Despite the slow development of agriculture in most developing countries, most of them began to bring it into the trade system. About 20-40 per cent of developing countries' basic foods are bought and sold. Land given over to cash crops constituted more than 30 per cent of the cultivated total in the 1980s. The highest proportions were in Papua New Guinea (95 per cent), some South-East Asian countries (Malaysia 78 per cent), and a few developing countries in the Caribbean (Costa Rica 67 per cent, Cuba 66 per cent, Trinidad and Tobago 72 per cent, Dominica and Jamaica 43 per cent.). In Brazil, the percentage was 38, in Ecuador 39 and it was also significant in some African countries (Liberia 71, Egypt 47, Ivory Coast 43, Uganda 39, Tanzania 34). (Braun and Kennedy, 1986).

The applicability of Ricardo's principle of comparative costs

Ricardo's Principle of Comparative Costs (Ricardo, 1817) states that in free international competition:
1. Countries export what they can produce at higher productivity, i.e. lower costs, and import what they would only be able to produce at lower productivity, i.e. higher costs.
2. In this manner, countries can get better exchange prices abroad than at home.

This may be illustrated by an example: Assume that amongst the trade between two countries, A and B, there are two products: wheat and combine harvesters. A is less developed than B, and so produces things at lower productivity than B, hence its domestic prices are higher. They trade with each other on world market prices and within their countries on domestic prices. Expressing the prices of both countries' goods in dollars, suppose that

World price $

	World price $
1 combine	$ 50,000
1 tonne wheat	$ 120

Country A

	Domestic price $	Exchange of combine for tonnes of wheat within the country	abroad
1 combine	65,000	542	417
1 tonne wheat	120		

(Since

$$65,000 \div 120 = 542 \text{ and } 50,000 \div 120 = 417,$$

the machine price is 130 per cent of·and the wheat price the same as, the world price.)

Country B

	Domestic price $	Exchange of combine for tonnes of wheat within the country	abroad
1 combine	40,000	365	417
1 tonne wheat	110		

(Since

$$40,000 \div 110 = 365 \text{ and } 50,000 \div 120 = 417,$$

the machine price is 80 per cent of and the wheat price the same as the world price)

It can be seen that the price ratio in each country are reversed: in A 130/100, in B 80/92. It is thus worth exchanging goods. A can get more machines for its wheat abroad than at home, whereas B more wheat for its machines.

Ricardo's principles are valid in free-trade circumstances. In reality free competition in trade was not unlimited in the past, nor is it now. In Ricardo's time the industrially developed, politically strong Britain was set against weaker, servile partners, mostly its colonies, which it compelled to supply raw materials in exchange for industrial products. Free trade and the lowering of barriers was in the interests of Britain's strong industry, since its goods thereby had easier access to world markets, and was itself able to withstand international competition. In 1846, it even removed agricultural import duties by repealing the Corn Laws, the longest-surviving restriction on imports. Its agriculture largely being in the hands of big capitalist-run estates, which did not demand much protection, the country could profit more from completely free trade than from protectionist policies. The most developed European countries followed England in removing import duties, but with the exceptions of Denmark and the Netherlands they all reapplied the agricultural duties at the end of the 19th century when American wheat began to flow onto the European market. The economic crisis of the 1930s also hit agriculture very badly. In its wake countries intensified their intervention in agriculture, which included protectionism. A system of subsidies was established in America which essentially still remains. Some countries introduced quantitative limits, import quotas, and France and Germany started purchasing produce at centrally fixed prices.

The cold war which followed the Second World War strengthened countries' resolve to become self-sufficient, leading to wide-ranging systems of subsidy appearing nearly everywhere. 1958 saw the foundation of the EEC's system for common protection and support of its internal market. The Community became self-sufficient in food at the beginning of the 1970s and by the end of the 1980s became an agricultural exporter second only to the USA (see figure 3.2); indeed in beef, poultry, sugar, dairy products, wine, olive oil, wheat and barley, it took first place. At the same time, it was the world's largest food importer.

Despite the large-scale increases in production over the last few decades, support has hardly reduced, and the influential farmers' organizations still demand their continuation. Behind the farmers' organizations is the agricultural workforce, which constituted 20-25 per cent of total employment in the post-war period and were therefore a powerful political force at the time when protectionist economic policy was being formulated. Although nowadays farmers are only a small proportion of the population, they are still a force to be reckoned with, since they might hold the balance of power in elections. Governments are therefore reluctant to risk opposing them.

A large proportion of agricultural producers really do depend on support. Most small holdings cannot provide a livelihood comparable to that of workers in most other industries. In the middle of the 1980s, for example, 62 per cent of the USA's farms provided an annual income of less than $20,000. Only 28 per cent reached the $40,000 mark, which the US Department of Agriculture

83

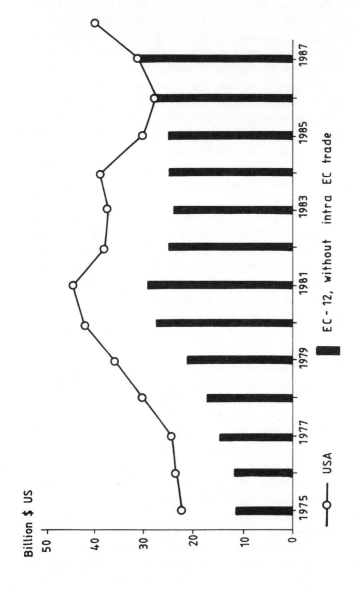

Figure 3.2   Change in the value of exports from the USA and the EC between 1975 and 1989

Source: *United Nations Trade Data, 1990*

84

considered as the threshold of viability at that time. However, those 62 per cent earning less than $20,000 only accounted for 5.2 per cent of the total agricultural income. Farms bringing in more than $100,000, making up 12 per cent of the total, produced 66 per cent of income.

The situation is similar in most other developed countries. The income of most farmers' households deriving from agriculture is less than incomes of households of those employed in other industries. More than 50 per cent of farmers' income comes from outside farming. In Japan this proportion is even higher, more than 70 per cent. In these countries, too, the greater part of production comes from the small number of large farms.

All farms enjoy support, including those who could not survive without subsidies and the large ones. The same universality applies to market protection against external competitors. Subsidies based on the needs of unproductive small farmers causes prices to be much higher than would be warranted by the productivity of the large farms which provide most of the production. The incentive to produce is thus much higher than it needs to be, and production rises to the extent that there is a large surplus for export. The production passed on to the world market depresses world market prices, which become much lower than the internal prices in most developed countries. Countries are therefore subsidising exports and further encouraging production.

In most developing and other low-income countries, among them the former socialist countries, the discriminatory agricultural policies already described cause a diametrically opposite tendency to prevail. Governments keep producer prices low and in many cases exact export taxes in the hope of increasing their income and export earnings. This naturally works its way back, acting as a counter-incentive and depressing production.

In contrast to the previous example, then, the domestic prices of products getting into domestic and international trade are actually given by

	combine harvester	Wheat
Country A	$65,000	$80 / tonne
Country B	$40,000	$80 / tonne

Country A withdraws the income from wheat, forcing its price to 50 per cent of that of the world market, B on the other hand supports it and raises it 50 per cent above the world price. Country B thus encourages the production and export of wheat with internal price supports, even though it would be better favouring the trade in its more productive machinery over trade in wheat. Country A, although its intended prices make it more favourable to export wheat, discourages its production by the same means and reduces the quantity available for exports.

So it is in fact comparative disadvantage, rather than advantage, which determines world trade for less developed countries (Dunn, 1988). The causes of this are:

1. There is no proper international division of labour. Developing countries do not specialize in what they can produce efficiently, but instead sell their natural resources.

2. Their production is not sufficiently diversified for them to select efficient products for export and change them according to the changing world market prices.

3. Their internal markets are so restricted that they cannot choose freely between selling internally or externally.

4. Because of the policies of agricultural subsidies and levies practised by the developed countries, there is no free competition on the world market.

5. Agricultural price regulation in both developed and developing countries mean that prices do not reflect the domestic productivity ratios, and so do not appropriately orient to production and export. Price support brings in its wake agricultural overproduction and world price depression, thereby putting at a disadvantage those exporters whose countries do not support them.

4 Agricultural world trade

Agricultural protectionism

Table 4.1 shows the developed countries' support for agriculture in terms of the percentage of the total value of production and table 4.2 shows support in percentage of unit value of individual products in some developing countries.

The average support, known as Producer Subsidy Equivalent (PSE), that developed countries gave to their agriculture in 1991, is indicated on table 4.1, and amounted to 45 per cent of its total value, with the EC countries giving 49 per cent, the USA 30, Canada 45, and Japan 66 per cent. Support by European countries outside the EC was even greater than the EC's. The lowest levels of support were in New Zealand (4 per cent) and Australia (15). Levels of support fluctuate, occasionally falling and more frequently rising, with the exception of New Zealand, where subsidies have fallen drastically in the last few years, as shown in figure 4.1. New Zealand and Australia are the least subsidized of the OECD countries. At the other extreme are the developing countries of India, Pakistan, Nigeria and Argentina, where, as can be seen on table 4.2, governments impose taxes and otherwise extract income from most production, the balance between support and withdrawals being negative. Brazilian wheat, and other products in Mexico and South Korea, however, receive significant subsidies.

In Hungary, the average support (PSE) is less than in developed countries, and there are even some products with negative support (Borszéki and Mészáros, 1991). The average support per unit value of production was 5 per cent in 1982-86 and the net PSE 18 per cent in 1986, 27 in 87 and 8 in 1988. Hungarian producers of wheat and maize received 42 per cent of the EC price for their goods, the corresponding figures for beef and pork being 51 and 94 per cent respectively (Mészáros and Spitálszky, 1991).

87

Table 4.1

Net percentage PSE[a] of all agricultural products

Country	1979-86 average	1987	1988	1989	1990 (estimate)	1991 (provisional)
Australia	12	11	10	10	15	15
Austria	33	48	48	41	50	52
Canada	32	49	42	36	45	45
EC[b]	37	49	46	41	49	49
Finland	58	71	72	69	72	71
Japan	65	76	74	70	66	66
New Zealand	25	14	7	5	5	4
Norway	71	74	75	73	76	77
Sweden	44	57	52	52	61	59
Switzerland	68	79	78	73	80	80
USA	28	40	34	28	29	30
OECD	37	49	45	40	45	45

a The percentage net Producer Subsidy Equivalent (PSE) expresses the market price support, direct payments and other support after deduction of the feed input in percentage of production at the farm gate.

b EC-10 1979-85, EC-12 1986-91. 1990 and 1991 include former GDR.

Source: Agricultural Policies, Markets and Trade, OECD, 1992

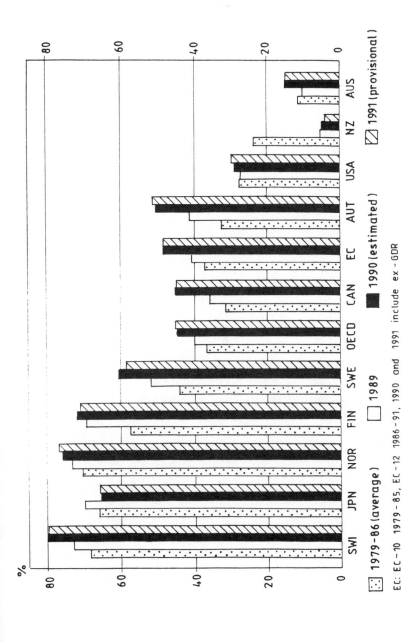

Figure 4.1   Changes in percentage PSE

Source: *Agricultural Policies, Markets and Trade, 1992*

89

Table 4.2
Average PSE[a] per unit value for some developing countries' agriculture
(percent)

Country/ Product	1982	1983	1984	1985	1986	Average 1982-86
India						
wheat	-30.9	-23.1	-40.1	-47.9	-31.7	-35.3
rice	-39.6	-18.2	-12.0	-17.0	-4.9	-16.9
soybeans	-13.3	-11.7	-19.5	-4.4	-12.8	-11.4
rapeseed	16.8	20.3	11.6	-15.7	-13.0	3.0
peanuts	8.4	30.5	26.7	19.0	1.8	17.3
cotton (med staple)	6.1	-34.9	-17.5	-13.9	-9.9	-14.0
cotton (long staple)	-21.0	-37.9	-45.3	-19.1	3.8	-23.9
7 commodity PSE	-27.4	-14.8	-15.6	-21.9	-11.2	-17.8
Pakistan						
cotton	-28.1	-11.6	-25.6	3.7	-36.1	-19.8
Nigeria						
wheat	-12.5	-35.8	-44.6	-14.4	24.9	-18.7
corn (white)	2.0	2.9	2.9	2.8	3.4	2.8
rice (polished)	-47.8	-56.1	-53.3	-35.5	-22.9	-42.6
sugar	-139.6	-169.5	-294.5	-244.1	-124.6	-189.4
cotton	-158.5	-118.6	-242.9	-140.4	-91.0	-135.8
cocoa	-158.6	-209.8	-438.8	-370.4	-286.6	-296.6
6 commodity PSE	-34.3	-37.3	-65.0	-40.1	-26.9	-40.8
Thailand						
rice	-0.3	0.4	1.1	1.8	4.3	1.3
Indonesia						
rice	22.8	1.4	9.7	17.8	19.7	14.4
Argentina						
wheat	-14.6	-29.2	-41.2	-0.5	16.6	4.8
corn	-27.4	-19.7	-25.0	-8.8	11.8	0.3
sorghum	-34.6	-38.5	-67.3	-30.4	-16.1	-27.4
soybeans	-20.4	-18.0	-45.3	-15.1	-11.9	-14.7
4 commodity PSE	-21.7	-25.2	-40.0	-9.1	1.7	-5.4

Table 4.2 contd.

Country/ Product	1982	1983	1984	1985	1986	Average 1982-86
Brazil						
wheat	77.2	55.2	63.2	63.5	52.3	63.4
soybeans	2.4	13.0	-13.1	3.4	27.6	0.1
beef	11.7	4.4	-14.5	-134.0	-	-33.1
poultry	12.6	17.9	5.1	5.3	-	6.2
corn	16.7	5.2	-23.5	11.6	58.5	4.0
5 commodity PSE	19.5	18.8	-3.6	12.0	-	9.2
Mexico						
wheat	5.0	7.5	17.6	25.2	-	18.8 [b]
corn	73.8	59.0	50.9	50.0	-	53.1 [b]
soybeans	41.9	34.5	41.3	50.8	-	45.0 [b]
sorghum	46.1	25.0	32.7	42.5	-	36.5 [b]
cotton	42.0	43.3	-0.1	-4.7	-	14.3 [b]
5 commodity PSE	50.3	44.1	37.2	41.8	-	41.3 [b]
South Korea						
wheat	64.4	58.7	53.7	51.4	60.8	59.9
corn	55.1	53.7	53.6	61.6	70.9	59.4
rice	66.7	71.3	71.7	72.4	76.6	72.1
barley	63.8	66.1	61.7	64.5	74.8	65.6
soybeans	76.4	76.0	70.3	74.4	78.1	74.9
beef	76.9	77.6	75.0	59.8	50.2	66.4
pork	31.6	16.7	-14.0	1.8	-31.4	-1.2
chicken	37.4	36.8	37.8	46.8	46.6	41.5
eggs	8.8	16.7	16.2	12.4	4.2	11.8
milk	48.6	52.9	64.0	28.8	44.2	46.4
10 commodity PSE	60.4	62.1	59.9	58.2	57.5	59.5

[a]   Unit PSE: the subsidies shown on the table are expressed as a percentage of the total value of the product divided by its quantity

[b]   1982-85 average

Source: US Department of Agriculture, Estimates of Producer and Consumer Subsidy Equivalents: Government Intervention in Agriculture 1982-86, April 1988. Quoted in Aziz, 1990.

Table 4.3

Nominal protection coefficients[a] 1980-82

Country, region	Wheat		Coarse grains		Rice		Beef, lamb		Pork, poultry	
	producer	consumer	producer	consumer	producer	consumer	producer	consumer	producer	consumer
Australia	1.04	1.08	1.00	1.00	1.15	1.75	1.00	1.00	1.00	1.00
Canada	1.15	1.12	1.00	1.00	1.00	1.00	1.00	1.00	1.10	1.10
EC[b]	1.25	1.30	1.40	1.40	1.40	1.40	1.90	1.90	1.25	1.25
Other Europe[c]	1.70	1.70	1.45	1.45	1.00	1.00	2.10	2.10	1.35	1.35
Japan	3.80	1.25	4.30	1.30	3.30	2.90	4.00	4.00	1.50	1.50
New Zealand	1.00	1.00	1.00	1.00	1.00	1.00	1.00	1.00	1.00	1.00
United States	1.15	1.00	1.00	1.00	1.30	1.00	1.00	1.00	1.00	1.00
Average	1.19	1.20	1.11	1.16	2.49	2.42	1.47	1.51	1.17	1.17

Table 4.3 contd.

Country, region	Dairy products		Sugar		Average		Average for 1991	
	producer	consumer	producer	consumer	producer	consumer	producer	consumer
Australia	1.30	1.40	1.00	1.40	1.04	1.09	1.16	1.09
Canada	1.95	1.95	1.30	1.30	1.17	1.16	1.69	1.45
EC[b]	1.75	1.80	1.50	1.70	1.54	1.56	1.94	1.76
Other Europe[c]	2.40	2.40	1.80	1.80	1.84	1.81	-	-
Japan	2.90	2.90	3.00	2.60	2.44	2.08	2.67	1.96
New Zealand	1.00	1.00	1.00	1.00	1.00	1.00	1.04	1.04
United States	2.00	1.40	1.40	1.40	1.16	1.17	1.39	1.24
Average	1.93	1.49	1.49	1.68	1.40	1.43	1.78[d]	1.62[d]

[a] Domestic price/import price at border. Averages are weighted by the values of production and consumption

[b] Except Greece, Portugal, Spain in 1980-82. In 1991 it includes ex-GDR.

[c] Austria, Finland, Norway, Sweden, Switzerland

[d] OECD average

Source: World Development Report, 1986, and Agricultural Policies, Markets and Trade, 1992.

Table 4.3, which shows the ratios of domestic prices to border prices, indicates the high levels of support in the European countries and the lower levels in Australia, Canada and the United States. Only in New Zealand are the international prices equal or near to the world market price. It should be borne in mind that price support in the EC has dropped since the end of the 1980s.

The development of agricultural imports and exports

The large scale expansion of agriculture, encouraged by the support systems, turned the developed countries into the greatest agricultural exporters, reversing the previous situation with regard to their former colonies. This trend can be seen in table 4.4: whereas in 1970, developed countries accounted for only 55 per cent of agricultural exports, by 1989 this had become 71 per cent, taking an ever-growing share of the world market. Developing countries only held on to their leading position in the export of a few tropical fruits and some raw materials. Cotton was one important raw material in which they lost their primary trading position. Whereas in 1970 developing countries' cotton exports outstripped those from the developed by a factor of 3.5, by 1989 their share was less than half of the total world exports. Developed countries' share of cereal export was 85 per cent, and of meat and animal products, 89 per cent. It is worth noting, though, that the export position of developing countries in some product areas was better at the end of the 1980s than in the preceding period, notably in oilseeds, cereals, meat and animal products. Two Asian countries, India and Vietnam, and several Latin American countries, changed from being net importers to net exporters of cereals.

Between 1970 and 1989, developed countries' agricultural external trade grew 12-fold, compared with developing countries' scant 6-fold. Figure 4.2 shows the changing composition of the OECD countries' exports and imports by percentage share in world trade. It can be seen that although their share of cereals fell in the 1980s, it still constituted the largest component making up exports. The second highest item was meat, with an increasing share, followed by dairy products, fruits and vegetables and feed. In imports, the proportion occupied by meat between 1981-83 and 1988 was the largest, and showed an increase throughout the period, followed by fruits and vegetables and oilseeds, which both fell, and feed, which rose. About 50 per cent of OECD trade, and 60 per cent of EC trade is internal.

Countries with the highest percentage share of exports in various product categories are shown on table 4.5. Developed and rapidly developing countries have a marked superiority in most product areas.

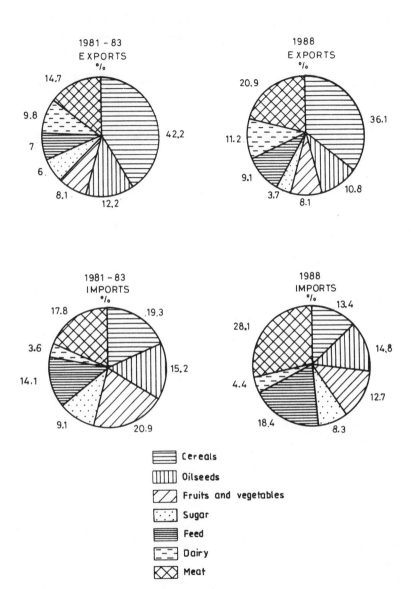

Figure 4.2   **The composition of OECD trade in unprocessed agricultural goods in value terms as a percentage share of the world's unprocessed agricultural exports and imports**

Source: *OECD Agricultural Data Base,* December 1990

Table 4.4
Percentage share of developed and developing countries in agricultural world exports in value terms

	1970 Developing	1970 Developed	1980 Developing	1980 Developed	1989 Developing	1989 Developed
	countries		countries		countries	
Sugar and beverages	93	7	85	15	78	22
Sugar	81	19	66	34	62	38
Coffee	100	0	100	0	93	7
Cocoa	100	0	100	0	92[a]	8[a]
Tea	99	1	100	0	100[b]	0[b]
Oil seeds, fats and products	37	63	34	66	45	55
Oil seeds, fats and vegetable oils	39	61	31	69	40	60
Oil seed cake and meal	34	66	45	55	63	37
Cereals	18	82	13	87	15	85
Rice	44	56	60	40	63	37
Wheat	6	94	5	95	7	93
Coarse grains	25	75	8	92	8	92
Meat, milk and milk products	17	83	12	88	11	89
Bovine meat	30	70	13	87	15[c]	85[c]
Sheep meat	7	93	11	89	29[d]	71[d]
Pig meat	2	98	4	96	11[e]	89[e]
Poultry meat	1	99	16	84	21[f]	79[f]
Canned and other meat	27	73	20	80	13[g]	87[g]
Butter	1	99	1	99	3	97
Cheese	..	..	1	99	1	99
Powder & other milk products	..	..	2	98	3	97

Table 4.4 contd.

	1970		1980		1989	
	Develop-ing	Develop-ed	Develop-ing	Develop-ed	Develop-ing	Develop-ed
	countries		countries		countries	
Raw materials	74	16	55	45	50	50
Cotton lint	78	22	43	57	46	54
Jute	100	0	96	4	100	0
Hard fibres	100	0	99	1	100	0
Natural rubber	100	0	98	2	98	2
Hides and skins	24	76	14	86	10	90
Other commodities	23	77	23	77	20	80
Citrus fruit	..	..	30	70	27	73
Wine	18	82	3	97	1[h]	99[h]
Tobacco	34	66	43	57	47	53
Total agricultural products[i]	45	55	31	69	29	71
Total agricultural products in million US Dollars[i]	15,167	18,342	67,442	153,760	85,700	214,200

[a] Including cocoa products
[b] Net exporting countries
[c] Beef and bovines
[d] Sheep meat and ovines
[e] Pig meat and swine
[f] Poultry meat and poultry
[g] Other meat
[h] Wine, vermouths, etc.
[i] Do not include trade in fisheries and forestry products

Source: FAO Commodity Review and Outlook 1970-71, 1980-81 and 1990-91

Table 4.5
Exports of agricultural products of major exporting countries and their percentage share in the world's exports
(1989-1991 average)

Wheat and Meslin		
Country	100 MT	%
USA	317,381	31
Canada	174,964	17
France	165,064	16
Australia	111,998	11
Argentina	52,347	5
UK	39,208	4

Maize		
Country	100 MT	%
USA	510,813	71
France	65,648	9
China	48,968	7
Argentina	29,136	4
South Africa	17,693	2
Thailand	12,160	2

Rice		
Country	10 MT	%
Thailand	488,719	36
USA	259,267	19
Vietnam	134,800	10
Pakistan	93,426	7
Italy	57,884	4
China	53,546	4

Fresh and Frozen Meat		
Country	10 MT	%
Netherlands	150,228	13
USA	134,898	11
France	107,029	9
Germany (FR+NL)*	98,254	8
Australia	89,838	8
New Zealand	71,622	6

Tomatoes (Fresh)		
Country	MT	%
Netherlands	611,982	25
Mexico	425,192	18
Spain	368,250	15
Jordan	192,002	8
Bel-Lux	164,427	7
USA	129,120	5

Lemons and Limes		
Country	MT	%
Spain	374,520	37
USA	134,980	13
Turkey	117,247	11
Mexico	70,942	7
Italy	62,175	6
Argentina	51,433	5

Apples		
Country	MT	%
France	666,215	18
USA	368,344	10
Chile	345,507	9
Hungary	326,530	9
Italy	296,503	8
Argentina	252,625	7

Wine + Vermouth + Similar		
Country	MT	%
Italy	1,381,045	30
France	1,267,907	28
Spain	552,978	12
Germany (FR)*	276,730	6
Hungary	172,712	4
Portugal	160,923	4

Table 4.5 contd

Sugar (raw equivalent)		
Country	MT	%
Cuba	691,948	23
Thailand	280,349	9
France	278,969	9
Australia	275,661	9
Germany		
(FR+NL)*	146,747	5
Brazil	140,489	5

Coffee Green Roast		
Country	MT	%
Brazil	988,166	20
Colombia	726,740	15
Indonesia	386,658	8
Mexico	234,177	5
Cote d'Ivoire	195,521	4
Guatemala	191,007	4

Tea		
Country	MT	%
India	200,529	17
Sri Lanka	210,609	17
China	200,972	17
Kenya	169,960	14
Indonesia	111,954	9
Argentina	41,819	3

Cocoa Beans		
Country	MT	%
Cote d'Ivoire	694,807	37
Ghana	249,357	13
Malaysia	160,005	9
Brazil	107,289	6
Nigeria	119,333	6
Indonesia	99,709	5

Bananas		
Country	MT	%
Ecuador	2,231,304	24
Costa Rica	1,420,158	15
Colombia	1,202,360	13
Philippines	880,449	9
Honduras	786,612	8
Panama	709,777	8

Cotton Lint		
Country	MT	%
USA	1,587,348	30
Former USSR	591,948	11
Pakistan	482,173	9
Australia	302,438	6
Paraguay	221,457	4
China	213,862	4

Wool Degreased		
Country	MT	%
New Zealand	144,944	38
Australia	88,829	23
UK	26,933	7
Argentina	16,568	4
Former USSR	15,192	4
France	12,109	3

Natural Rubber		
Country	MT	%
Malaysia	1,313,594	31
Indonesia	1,155,168	27
Thailand	1,148,378	27
Sri Lanka	83,312	2
Nigeria	78,226	2
Viet Nam	64,859	1

* 1991 unified Germany

Source: FAO Trade Yearbook, 1992

But there were some developing countries which increased their share of certain categories. Particularly interesting is the progress made by Saudi Arabia, one of the richest desert oil countries, which with 16 million tonnes has become the world's 7th-largest exporter of wheat in the 1989-91 average. China's exports of many products – maize, rice, tea and cotton – ascended the world rankings. In a similar way, the former rice importing country of Vietnam has taken a major role in rice exports. Argentina still shows up strongly in wheat, maize, tea, cotton and lemons; Brazil in sugar, coffee and cocoa; Thailand in rice (world's highest) and sugar; and Pakistan in rice and cotton. Mexico's tomato, lemon and coffee exports did well. Indonesia exports large quantities of coffee, tea and cocoa, and Ivory Coast coffee and cocoa. Cuba has kept its first place in the export of sugar, and Ecuador, Colombia and the Philippines have made progress in banana sales along with the Central American countries.

Developed countries' agricultural trade, although significant in the world market, makes up a minor proportion of their own total trade (see table 4.6). Its 1988 export share was 8 per cent in the EC, and 13 per cent in the USA. Within the EC, Denmark, Germany and Ireland stand out with 22-23 per cent (similar to Hungary's) and the Netherlands with about 20 per cent. Denmark led with meat and dairy products, Ireland with meat and Greece with fruits, vegetables and citrus. Holland is a big exporter of meat, vegetables, flowers and tulip bulbs. Among OECD countries it is Australia and New Zealand which stand out (figure 4.3). Both export large quantities of meat and wool, Australia cereals and New Zealand milk products.

Table 4.7 shows the level of self-sufficiency of the OECD countries in some significant commodities. Outside the EC, production of cereals outstrips consumption in Canada, the USA, Australia, New Zealand, Austria, Sweden and Turkey; within the EC this is true primarily for France, but also Denmark, the Federal Republic of Germany, Greece, Spain and Britain. Putting this alongside the fact that according to the 1992 FAO Trade Yearbook, in Central and South America, only St Vincent, Argentina, French Guyana, Guyana, Paraguay, Surinam and Uruguay, in Asia only Burma (Myanmar), India, Pakistan, Thailand, Turkey and Vietnam, and in Africa Uganda and Zimbabwe had positive cereal balances, we can get a good impression of the OECD's superiority in this area too.

Production outstripped consumption in sugar only in Australia, Belgium-Luxembourg, Denmark, Germany and France. In beef, this is true for Canada, Australia, New Zealand, Austria, Finland, and within the EC to the greatest extent for Ireland, followed by France, Denmark, Holland and Belgium-Luxembourg.

Table 4.8 shows the EC as a whole to be a net food importer, but within it France, Netherlands, Denmark and Ireland are major exporters, and Spain less

Table 4.6
Trade in agricultural products as a percentage of value of total traded products

Country	Export			Import		
	1981-83	1988	1991[a]	1981-83	1988	1991[a]
Canada	11.5	8.2	8.3	7.6	5.6	6.2
United States	19.0	13.2	9.1	7.3	5.1	5.5
Japan	0.6	0.4	0.6	12.9	14.6	14.5
Australia	37.7	35.1	..	4.4	4.8	..
New Zealand	66.4	59.1	..	6.5	7.9	..
EC-12[b]	9.2	8.0	..	12.9	10.7	..
Belgium-Luxembourg	7.8	3.8	9.0	11.3	9.4	8.9
Denmark	23.1	22.7	26.5	13.9	10.1	11.8
France	14.9	12.1	13.7	10.9	10.5	9.4
Germany[b]	4.0	3.3	5.0[c]	12.8	10.1	9.3[c]
Greece	29.4	22.1	28.0	8.7	12.4	12.7
Ireland	34.2	22.9	22.5	13.6	9.6	11.0
Italy	5.9	5.2[d]	6.5	11.7	12.3[d]	11.9
Netherlands	21.5	18.2	19.6	18.1	16.4	11.7
Portugal	12.5	8.6	7.2	26.9	24.3	11.1
Spain	13.3	14.6	13.6	15.4	14.2	10.7
United Kingdom	6.4	5.8	7.4	12.3	8.0	10.3
Austria	4.8	3.7	3.2	7.7	..	5.0
Finland	5.6	2.9	2.4	7.2	6.1	5.7
Iceland	2.9	2.2	..	11.1	8.5	..
Norway	1.8	2.0[d]	7.4	7.0	..	5.9
Sweden	2.9	2.1	1.9	6.9	6.6	6.7
Switzerland	3.8	3.1	..	9.5	7.3	..
Turkey	47.1	26.1	..	3.5	6.6	..

[a] Food, beverages and tobacco
[b] Without GDR
[c] Unified Germany
[d] 1987

Source: *Agricultural Policies, Markets and Trade, OECD, 1991 for 1991 data: International Economic Indicators. 1993*

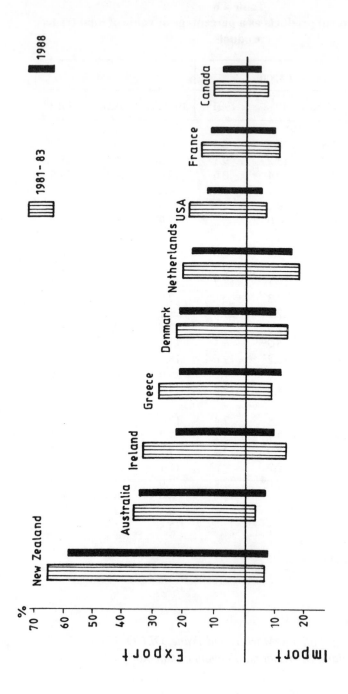

Figure 4.3   Agricultural product trade of some major exporters as a percentage share of total merchandise exports in value terms

Source: *OECD Foreign Trade Data Base and Agricultural Data Base, December 1990*

Table 4.7
Level of self-sufficiency in the OECD countries in per cent
(production/consumption)

Country	Cereals[b]			Sugar[c]			Beef (carcass weight)		
	1981 -83	1987	1988	1981 -83	1987	1988	1981 -83	1987	1988
Canada	213	186	147	12	13	4	104	100	105
United States	155	127	192	64	90	87	93	92	93
Japan	4	4	5	27	34	28	72	64	60
Australia	386	334	361	396	439	434	209	236	232
New Zealand	96	120	112	0	0	..	351	407	408
EC-12[a]	100	114	..	133	..	..	102	106	103
Belgium-Luxembourg	51	50	55	263	202	225	109	136	148
Denmark	108	120	136	208	189	261	412	295	253
France	177	220	223	225	..	..	115	125	121
Germany[a]	91	93	106	140	122	132	112	121	114
Greece	105	102	108	110	76	64	53	26	41
Ireland	87	96	..	145	180	..	507	692	754
Italy	81	80	77	99	112	97	60	55	54
Netherlands	29	27	..	174	176	..	113	133	118
Portugal	25	52	45	0	0	0	97	83	85
Spain	62	99	113	106	101	..	92	96	97
United Kingdom	108	104	107	55	59	57	84	83	75
Austria	112	123	126	133	106	91	117	142	139
Finland	103	78	95	59	36	68	113	119	108
Iceland	..	..	..	..	..	..	100	..	..
Norway	65	70	61	0	0	0	108	100	95
Sweden	119	118	119	98	88	86	113	105	97
Switzerland	39	46	55	42	39	45	89	93	86
Turkey	103	103	103	134	106	92	105	94	97

[a] Without GDR
[b] Cereal grains and cereal preparations
[c] Refined sugar

Source: Agricultural Policies, Markets and Trade, OECD, 1991

so. Among other comparable countries, USA, Canada, Turkey and Norway are net exporters.

1988 figures show the former CMEA countries' share in world agricultural trade to be 7 per cent, compared to 10 per cent in 1981-83. Their share of imports was a minimal 2-5 per cent, despite the Soviet Union's and Poland's occasional significant imports of cereals. Their foreign trade, as can be seen in table 4.9, continued to recede after 1990, a consequence of falling production and general recession. Hungary's exports grew by 7 per cent in 1992, but national statistics show a fall of 12 per cent in the first seven months of 1993. Agricultural exports suffered a similar fall.

Table 4.8
The EC countries' and some other developed countries' agricultural[a] balance of trade

Million ECU's in 1988

EC		Others	
EC 12	-9,742	Britain	-7,887
Belgium-		Turkey[b]	2,392
Luxembourg	-868	Norway	462
Denmark	3,507	Sweden	-1,727
FRG	-9,197	Switzerland	-1,994
Greece	-660	Austria	-806
Spain	575	Finland	-608
France	5,527	Soviet Union[b]	-8,525
Ireland	2,532	United States[c]	5,680
Italy	-8,019	Canada	3,240
Netherlands	5,556	Japan	-23,201
Portugal	-829		

[a] Food, drink and tobacco
[b] 1987 data
[c] SITC, Rev. 2

Source: EUROSTAT, Statistische Grundzahlen der Gemeinschaft, 1990, Luxembourg

Table 4.9
Annual percentage change of export and import volumes

	1987		1988		1989		1990		1991[a]	
	Export	Import	Export	Import	Export	Import	Export	Import	Export	Import
Bulgaria	1.8	-1.4	2.4	5.3	-2.3	-4.6	-24.2	-24.2	-30.0	-50.0
Czechoslovakia	3.4	4.3	3.2	2.9	-2.0	2.7	-4.2	9.7	-20.0	-35.0
East Germany	-0.1	9.0	0.2	4.7	0.5	2.4	..	-15.0	..	..
Hungary	3.9	3.2	5.0	-1.9	0.3	1.1	-4.3	-3.4	-10.7	-2.3
Poland	4.8	4.5	9.1	9.4	0.2	1.5	13.7	-17.9	-1.4	39.0
Romania	-4.3	-6.3	7.4	-5.8	-10.8	3.7	-46.0	4.0	-30.0	-5.0
Eastern Europe	1.4	3.4	3.6	3.3	-1.9	1.2	-7.9	-8.6	-16.1	-14.7
USSR	3.3	-1.6	4.8	4.0	..	9.3	13.1	-1.4	-25.0	-27.4

[a] Preliminary estimate

Source: World Economic Survey, 1992

As well as an overall decline, foreign trade underwent a major structural change, so that the previously dominant CMEA trade decreased sharply in favour of business with developed market economies. Overall figures show that of exports from the region's countries, 50 per cent were previously internal, and of imports 55 per cent in 1980 and 60 per cent in 1989. Internal CMEA trade of agricultural commodities was 46.5 per cent of the total in 1970 and 52 per cent in 1980 (World Economic Survey, 1991).

Three-quarters of Hungary's total exports were to the CMEA in the 1960s, two-thirds in the 1970s half in the 1980s, 23 per cent in 1989, falling to 18 per cent in 1990. However, it has experienced some growth since that time, and in 1992, its East European export share went back up to 22 per cent (Konjunkturajelentés – Conjunctural Report – 1993/1).

With the dissolution of the CMEA, the former CMEA countries changed over their trade to hard currency. The lack of this currency and the lessened ability of some countries, including those of the former Soviet Union, to import, turned the focus of trade to the West, as indicated in Table 4.10. The restructuring of trade was assisted by the EC's relieving discriminative quantitative restrictions and the so-called 'specific restrictions' against the Eastern European countries. The seven Central-Eastern European countries and the Baltic states received the Generalized System of Preferences (GSP) status, which gave them similar trade advantages to those accorded to developing countries. In 1992, the EC signed an association treaty with Hungary, Poland and the Czech and Slovak Republic which prescribed mutual reductions in customs duties and trade quotas, but with the reductions to be quicker on the EC side. Similar treaties are under negotiation with Bulgaria and Romania. The free-trade treaty signed by Hungary, Poland, the Czech Republic and Slovakia with EFTA is also being implemented asymmetrically, and one for Bulgaria and Romania is being prepared.

In granting easier access to the Eastern countries to Western markets, these agreements have resulted in a sudden increase in trade with the West. This has had the added effect that the value of exports has not fallen as much as the volume. This was a particular feature of the early stages, when low-priced Eastern trade was replaced with trade at higher, Western, prices. Thus in 1990 Bulgaria's exports with the West grew in volume by 11 per cent but in value by 25 per cent. The corresponding figures for Hungary were 12 and 27 per cent respectively, and for Czechoslovakia 5 and 19 per cent. But rises in imports and import prices from the West grew even more, so that the terms of trade and trade balances deteriorated (Economic Bulletin for Europe, 1993).

Although the total exports from the smaller former Eastern bloc countries were in large part reoriented from an eastern to a western direction, (those of Hungary, Poland, Czech Republic and Slovakia by nearly 70 per cent), this was less marked for food exports. The reason for this was that Western

Table 4.10
Geographical structure of exports in per cent 1989-1992

To	Bulgaria		Poland	Czechoslovakia		Romania		Hungary		USSR/Russia		
	1989	1992 QI-II	1989	1989	1992	1989	1992 QI-II	1989	1992 QI-II	1992 QI-II	1989	1992 QI-II
Eastern Europe	12.9	6.4	16.4	20.1	5.8	10.2	10.4	15.9	4.7	6.1	24.4	23.2
USSR/CIS	49.3	20.5	24.4	26.5	11.0	14.5	9.3	25.1	14.9	14.5	..	..
Developed market economies	19.6	34.4	43.2	37.6	73.7	47.7	64.9	43.1	47.8	67.9	41.8	55.6
Developing countries	15.8	26.5	9.0	9.7	7.7	23.2	11.3	9.5	23.0	7.3	25.8	12.7

Notes: 1989 figures are calculated at standardized rouble/dollar crossrates
The former GDR is included in the 'Eastern Europe' aggregates
The intra-trade of CIS is excluded from the exports.

Source: Economic Bulletin for Europe, 1993

107

countries eased protectionist policies towards agricultural goods far less than towards industrial ones. Neither did the free-trade agreements signed with the EC and EFTA greatly reduce import restrictions in the agricultural area. The Western market for agricultural products was in any case largely saturated and unable to absorb any more. Thus the former Soviet Union's imports from Hungary were approximately 50 per cent food in 1992, and accounted for 46 per cent of Hungary's food exports. (Konjunkurajelentés, 1993/1).

As important as the change in direction of the Eastern countries' exports is the change in their composition. More than 50 per cent of CMEA's internal trade consisted of investment goods, engineering goods, machines and equipment. This was replaced in trade with the West by raw materials, agricultural products, and industrial chemicals. Trade of investment goods between former CMEA countries also virtually evaporated and trade was limited largely to raw materials, consumer goods and food.

Engineering goods have suffered a serious drop in sales, chiefly because they are not sufficiently up to date or of high enough quality for developed market economies. Despite the relaxing of import restrictions by the Western countries, they import comparatively few of these kind of goods, and the Eastern countries are either importing less because of the deep recession, or, in the new hard-currency trading régime, can buy better quality from the West.

Western initiative, involving among others UN staff, suggested the setting up of a Central European Payments Union (CEPU) to facilitate trade among Eastern countries and ease their payment problems. However, the plan did not meet with sufficient enthusiasm in the East-European countries. Among the reasons for refusal was that such a payments union would not help the former socialist countries, mainly those of East and Central Europe, to break out of the eastern trading arena. The wish for the break was partly political, stemming from antipathy towards the Soviet Union as a former occupying power, and the mutual antagonisms among the smaller countries stemming from ethnic problems – in particular Hungary, Slovakia, Romania and Yugoslavia – and partly economic. Among the economic reasons, particularly significant is the economists' argument that if trade was once again regional, it would remain backward.

It is true that in the preceding 40 years the Eastern countries forged many trade links with each other, but the most important were with the Soviet Union, accounting for at least a quarter and up to a half of trading each country's activity, as against the 10-20 per cent with the other Eastern countries. The collapse of the Eastern trade situation thus had a serious effect on trade, and indeed on production, in all of them.

Some time after the collapse of CMEA trade there were some attempts to restore it, at least partially. In 1990, an EC initiative led to the Visegrad Summit, where Czechoslovakia, Hungary and Poland agreed to multinational economic cooperation. In 1992, the 'Visegrad Countries' signed a free trade agreement, by which they would gradually bring down customs and other trade barriers, leading to complete trade liberalization by 2000, in the same way as the associate agreement with the EC.

Trade with the former Soviet Union also revived. To get round currency difficulties, a 'quasi-barter' system evolved through bilateral agreements and a direct barter system. Estimates put the proportion of the former Soviet Union's trade constituted by bartering at 8-9 per cent (Economic Bulletin for Europe, 1992). Direct trade between Eastern-European companies and those in Russia, Ukraine, Belarus, Moldova and Kazakhstan also underwent an increase.

Much export-import activity was conducted through third parties located in Western countries. In 1992, 9 per cent Hungary's exports and 10 per cent of its imports were effected in this way, and 21 per cent of its agricultural exports. 37 per cent of total energy imports, 10 per cent of raw materials and 20 per cent of agricultural products arriving from Eastern Europe were handled by third parties (Konjunkturajelentés, 1993/1).

Foreign trade was less significant for the former Soviet Union than for the Central-Eastern European countries. Whereas about 50 per cent of the NMP (Net Material Product) of Czechoslovakia, Hungary and Poland was foreign trade, exports from the Soviet Union constituted only 6 per cent of its NMP, and imports 14 per cent. Inter-republican trade is still more significant, although it has fallen to nearly half its former level since 1991, mainly in 1992. This fall is due to lower production, shortages, measures which restrict exports and the collapse of the common currency system. The decline of inter-republican trade following becoming foreign trade has had its effect on decreasing NMP. The reduction varies according to each country's dependency on exports and imports, which is weakest in Russia, where external trade was 15-17 per cent of NMP in 1990, 25-40 per cent in Kazakhstan and Ukraine, and 50-60 per cent in Belarus, Moldova and the Baltics (Economic Bulletin for Europe 1992).

Taken together, the East-European countries were approximately self-sufficient in food, but the level of self-sufficiency had declined over the years, as table 4.11 shows. From time to time, the Soviet Union, Czechoslovakia, East Germany and Romania were obliged to import grain. The region's largest food exporter was Hungary, but the quantities of exports were far from sufficient to satisfy the region's import requirements.

With the exception of the Soviet Union, all of the countries in the region exported more animal products than they imported. Hungary, Bulgaria and Romania exported significant quantities of fresh and processed fruits and vegetables.

The European CMEA countries' exports of food, beverage and tobacco goods constituted 4.7 per cent of their total exports in 1986 and 10.9 per cent of their imports (Nemzetközi Statisztikai Évkönyv – International Statistical Yearbook – 1989, KSH).

Table 4.11
Self-sufficiency ratios* (per cent)

	1961/63	1969/71	1979/89	1983/85
All European socialist countries	99	99	93	95
Albania	94	100	102	104
Bulgaria	114	114	112	114
Czechoslovakia	84	87	90	98
GDR	83	88	91	91
Hungary	102	109	118	124
Poland	100	98	93	99
Romania	106	106	101	104
USSR	100	99	91	92

* 26 crops and 6 animal products
Source: World Agriculture: Toward 2000, 1988

In Hungary, the proportion of exports constituted by food was higher, at 19-20 per cent of total exports (Külkereskedelmi Statisztikai Évkönyv – Statistical Yearbook of Foreign Trade – 1988). About a half of these were fresh or processed meat, 24 per cent fresh and processed fruits and vegetables, and 16 per cent cereals. Food accounted for only 7 per cent of total imports, the greater part of that being protein feed, coffee, tea, cocoa, spices and tropical fruits.

Since the end of the 1980s, in accordance with tendencies already outlined, the proportion of agricultural exports in total exports has risen in Hungary. In 1991, this reached 25 per cent, but fell back to 24 per cent in 1992. Cereal exports increased (to CIS countries) and other previously strong export sectors decreased sharply – meat, poultry, milk products, canned goods and sweets. Imports of many products grew because of liberalization, especially those of processed foods. Table 4.12 shows the structure of Hungarian agricultural trade and how it has changed from 1991 to 1992. In the first six months of 1993, Hungarian exports were almost 40 per cent lower than the same period in the previous year.

Table 4.12
Percentage structure of Hungarian agricultural export-import in US dollars and changes between 1991 and 1992

	Exports		Imports	
	Ratio	1992/1991 (%)	Ratio	1992/1991 (%)
Livestock and animal products	32.3	74.0	13.3	230.7
Crops	36.2	135.2	28.0	72.0
Fats, oils & waxes	4.3	102.4	4.0	119.5
Processed foods & drinks	27.2	110.7	54.7	116.1
Raw agricultural products (all)	36.1	121.7	25.7	69.8
Processed foods (all)	63.9	91.9	74.3	121.4

Source: Konjunkturajelentés (Conjunctural report), 1993/1

The North-South dilemma and the GATT negotiations

The disadvantaged position of developing countries due to the unequal terms of trade has been on the agenda of international organizations since the 1960s and throughout this time has been the main cause of conflict between North and South. The Swedish economist Myrdal (Myrdal, 1957 and 1970) stated that the disadvantaged, poor countries were getting progressively poorer and the rich countries richer.

Similar principles are part of the neomarxist theory of the core and the periphery (Wallerstein, 1979 and 1984). This states that in the development of international division of labour, the world is divided into core and peripheral areas. Those enjoying favourable terms of international trade develop rapidly, while those on the periphery are left behind. Between core and periphery are the semiperipheral countries, which have started on the road to development and with luck can catch up with the core (e.g. Mexico, Brazil, Argentina, South-East Asian countries, but according to Wallerstein, Czechoslovakia and Hungary also belong to these), or those countries which became semiperipheral through a change in international terms of change (e.g. the oil-rich countries) or those which slip further from the core (e.g. the GDR). The unequal exchange allows the core to acquire a large part of the surplus created in the periphery, and to develop even more rapidly, the periphery therefore becoming even less able to develop (see figures 4.4 and 4.5).

A UN resolution of 1976 set the goal of resolving the North-South dilemma. This is also the partial aim of some international talks whose purpose is the lowering of protectionism and the liberalization of trade with the intention of, among other things, improving the lot of less-developed countries in international trade.

The Uruguay Round

The General Agreement of Tariffs and Trade (GATT), founded in 1948, strives to bring down obstacles and barriers to free trade and to liberalize a greater part of international trade.

It thus organizes series of negotiations involving the relevant countries. Before the Uruguay Round started in 1986, seven rounds had already been completed. The first round, in 1948, involved 23 countries. The negotiations led to 45,000 agreements to loosen trade restrictions to the value of 10 billion US dollars. In the last, Tokyo Round, 99 countries agreed US$ 300 billion-worth of tariff reductions (World Economic Survey, 1991).

Until 1986, the GATT negotiations did not put on their agenda general trade questions regarding agricultural commodities and raw materials, although some individual agricultural trade restrictions were discussed. Thus in the 1960s in the so-called Kennedy Round there was a clash of interests between the free agricultural trade aspirations of the US and the protectionism of the EC. Additionally, of 32 complaints made to GATT concerning unjustified trade restrictions, 17 have been agricultural complaints against the EC. However, agricultural commodities do not appear in the GATT's paragraphs against non-tariff trade barriers (paragraphs 11 and 16). The principal reason for this was the USA's previous insistence that internal measures could not be the subject of international limitations, and it is internal measures, rather than customs barriers, which make up the most important obstacles to free trade in agricultural products.

By the start of the Uruguay Round in 1986, it seemed that the time had come at last to deal with liberalization of agricultural trade. Budget expenditure on agriculture protectionism had risen to intolerable levels, in the USA from US$ 4 to 26 billion between 1981-86, and in the EC from US$ 13 to 22 billion in the same period (Moyer and Josling, 1990, and see figure 4.6). In 1989, 62 per cent of the EC's budget was spent on supporting agriculture (Europe in Figures, 1989/90). The burden this imposed on taxpayers and consumers provoked ever sharper protests from representative organizations.

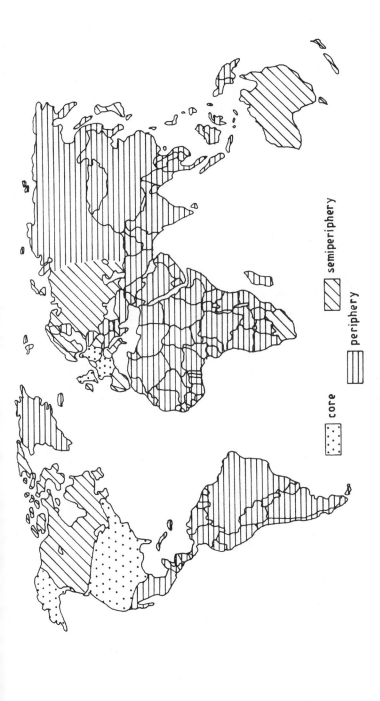

semiperiphery

periphery

core

Figure 4.4   **Wallerstein Regions c 1900**

Source: *Terlouw, 1985*

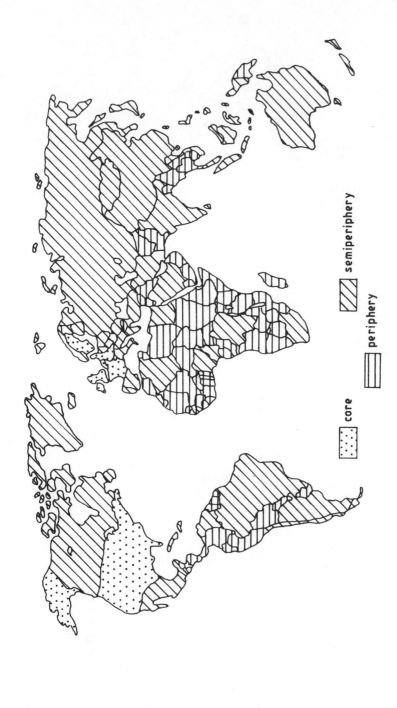

semiperiphery

periphery

core

Figure 4.5 **Wallerstein Regions of the world at present**
Source: *Terlouw,1985*

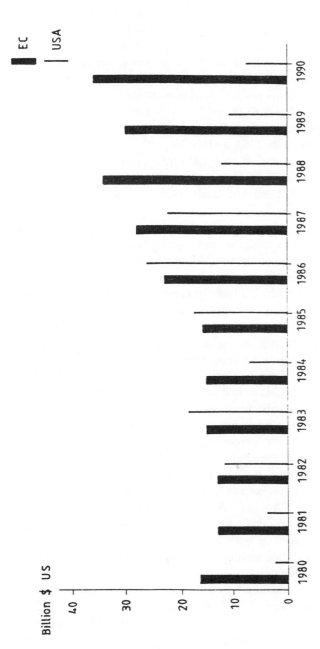

Figure 4.6   Budget expenditure for agricultural price and income support in the USA and the EC between 1980 and 1990

Source: USDA and EC Commissions

115

Protectionism caused enormous growth in developed countries' stocks of goods which could either not be sold or only sold at low prices. For the US, it became increasingly urgent for the strongly protectionist EC-Japan markets to open up to their products. The developing countries also demanded access to developed countries' markets and the reduction of their production to make world prices fairer. Studies based on model calculations showed that world market prices would rise significantly if protectionism decreased (Valdes and Zietz, 1980; Anderson and Tyers, 1986 and 1987; Parikh et al, 1988).

A notable feature of the Uruguay Round is the centring of the dispute around negotiations between the USA and the EC rather than the developing countries. The developing countries' interests were represented by the Cairns Group, whose members were: Argentina, Australia, Brazil, Canada, Chile, Colombia, Fiji, Hungary, Indonesia, Malaysia, New Zealand, the Philippines, Thailand and Uruguay.

In the Punta del Este Declaration, all negotiating parties expressed their agreement on the urgency of bringing down protectionist measures. There were considerable differences of opinion, however, on how this should be achieved. The USA and the Cairns group recommended that all agricultural support and import barriers which adversely affected agricultural production and trade should be done away with in the long term. Japan, Switzerland, Australia, the Scandinavian countries and the EC only accepted as aims the reduction of domestic subsidies and protectionist measures – and border measures including export subsidies (Alexandratos, 1990).

The negotiations should have reached a conclusion by December 1990. However, the parties were unable to find an agreement by that date. The EC's final offer was a reduction in subsidies of 30 per cent between 1986 and 1996 (and in fact of this, they had already reduced 15 per cent), not specifying the reduction in import barriers and export subsidies. The USA and the Cairns Group wanted a 75 per cent reduction in farm subsidies and 90 per cent in export subsidies in the same period. The Swedish compromise version recommended a 30 per cent cut equally in domestic subsidies, import barriers and export support (World Economic Survey, 1991). In the absence of an agreement, the talks were suspended.

The negotiations were taken up again in 1991. The GATT Director-General and Chairman of the Trade Negotiating Committee, Mr Dunkel, presented a transitional solution for agriculture.

The proposed draft provided that:

a) Non-tariff border measures should be converted into tariff equivalents. The base periods shall be the years 1986-88. Customs duties should be reduced by 36 per cent on a simple average basis in equal instalments between 1993 and 1999. Minimum access opportunities of imported goods for domestic consumption should be maintained and raised.

b) All domestic support measures should be reduced by 20 per cent in equal instalments from 1993 to 1999 with the exception of measures which have no or most minimal trade distortion effects (the so-called Green Box). The base periods shall be the years 1986 to 1988.

c) Export subsidies should be reduced by 36 per cent and subsidized export quantity by 24 per cent from 1993 to 1999. The base period shall be the years 1986 to 1990 (Agricultural Policies, Markets and Trade, 1992).

Although an agreement appeared close on the basis of this recommendation, the EC declined to accept it, mainly because of France's opposition to the provision on export subsidies.

In 1992 a bilateral agreement, the so-called 'Blair House Accord', was reached between the EC and the US, similar to the Dunkel Plan, after the US demanded the EC's liberalization of trade in oilseed and threatened a trade war if its demand was not complied with.

According to the Blair House accord,

a) import restrictions would be converted to import tariffs and reduced by 36 per cent over 6 years from their level in 1986-88. Every customs item would be reduced by a minimum of 6 per cent.

b) Import contingencies would gradually rise.

c) The aggregate measure of support would fall by 20 per cent over 6 years from the 1986-88 level. Reductions implemented by the EC since 1986 would be counted. Items in the Dunkel-plan's 'Green Box' would be exempted from reductions, as would direct support for land and livestock.

d) Export support would fall by 36 per cent in the 6 years from 1986 to 1988 and the subsidised quantity by 21 per cent.

Neither the recommendations of the Dunkel Plan, nor the terms of the EC-USA agreement tackled processed goods (Manegold, 1993).

At last on December 15 1993 the Uruguay Round negotiations concluded in an agreement. Participants agreed upon 40 separate agreements. Farm trade, textiles and services have been brought under GATT disciplines for the first time. The overall cut in tariffs is around 40 per cent.

All trade barriers in farming are to be converted into transparent tariffs, which will be cut in rich countries by an average of 36 per cent and in the case of tropical fruits by 40 per cent, and the quantity of subsidized export curbed by 21 per cent in six years. Agricultural subsidies, including export subsidies, should be reduced in these countries by 20 per cent in the same period.

In four months a tidied version of the agreement is to be formally signed in Marrakech, in Morocco.

The agreement will come in to force on January 1, 1995. (The Economist, December 18, 1993; Handelsblatt 16.12.1993 and Heti Világgazdaság, vol. XV, no. 52-53, 1993).

5 Regional trade agreements and market regulation systems

The EC and its agricultural market regulation system

The European Economic Community was formed in 1957 from 6 countries: France, the Federal Republic of Germany, Italy and the Benelux countries. It was brought into existence by the Treaty of Rome in 1958. In 1967, after merging with the European Coal and Steel Community and Euratom, it took on the title Economic Community. It expanded in 1973 with the admission of Denmark, Britain and Ireland, and then Greece joined in 1981, and Spain and Portugal in 1986.

The EEC, later EC, aimed to achieve a free flow of commodities, capital, labour and services within its borders, and also to harmonization of economic and monetary policies. On 1 January 1968, the customs union came into existence, with a single common customs border for countries outside the EC. The same principle had led, in the previous year, to the introduction of an identical system of Value Added Tax in all EC countries. The principles of the Common Agricultural Policy were laid down in 1962. Later harmonization measures encompassed energy, the environment, education, research, consumer protection and fishery policies. The European Regional Development Fund was set up in 1975, and the European Monetary System (EMS), a system of stabilizing exchange rates between members' currencies, in 1978. The EMS in turn introduced a device for common accounting, European Currency Unit (ECU), whose value was based on the basket of member countries' currencies weighted according to GDP and foreign trade. Since 1981, the accountancy currency of the common budget has been the ECU and it is one of the means of payment between the Central Banks of the member states. The ECU is gradually becoming a real means of payment, finding more and more application in the financial transactions of companies, banks and

118

private individuals. The agricultural version, the so-called 'Green ECU', was tied to the Deutchsmark in 1982 and was converted into national currencies by at special 'green rates' protecting member countries against exchange rate changes to be transmitted to their agriculture.

In 1986, the 12 member countries signed the Single European Act, which modified and supplemented the Treaties of Rome and Paris to provide for the complete elimination of political and economic borders between the 12 countries, that is the complete integration of newly joined countries and those who have been granted a few years' delay. The agreement provides for the complete abolition of physical frontiers, common passports for citizens, free choice of place of work and living, mutual recognition of educational qualifications, unimpeded circulation of goods, capital, labour and services, and total freedom of location for businesses. It unifies standards, the financial system, tax support and VAT keys. It abolishes all obstacles to transfer of capital. Citizens can hold money in any currency in any countries' banks, may purchase shares anywhere and take out insurance anywhere. It is intended to set up a common European bank and a common currency. Harmonization of social, health, education research, and al affairs is another aim, as is the further development of the Community's supranational institutions. Finally, the treaty provides for the creation of unified foreign and security policies.

The Single European Act incorporated 279 specific measures. The measures were introduced in several steps up to 1 January 1993.

On December 11, 1991, the 12 member countries agreed in Maastricht to work towards Economic and Monetary Union, called European Union (EU), by 1999, whereby the states would have common economic, foreign and defence policies, a central European bank and a common currency. After positive votes in referenda in some countries (in France, and at the second referendum in Denmark) and long parliamentary debates, the treaty was finally accepted by all member parliaments. However even after ratification, it was not clear how they were going to satisfy the strict monetary conditions required for the treaty to come into force. At the moment several member countries do not meet the strict monetary criteria for Maastricht and through currency difficulties some were even forced to suspend their membership of the EMS in 1993.

The EC has at its head several supranational organizations: The Council of Ministers, the Parliament, the Court, the Economic and Social Committee, and the apparatus for preparing decisions and carrying them out: the European Commission.

The Common Agricultural Policy (CAP) is one of the key questions of Community regulation. According to clause 39 of the Treaty of Rome, the common purpose of agricultural policy is: raising agricultural productivity through technical progress; ensuring an appropriate standard of living for the agricultural population; market stabilization; guaranteeing regular supply; and guaranteeing reasonable prices for consumers (Koester and Bale, 1990). Similarly, as with the policy of the Community as a whole it aimed to implement free movement of capital, products and labour inside the Community and the protection against outside competition. Its principal means were common market order, common guaranteed prices for agricultural products, common subsidization systems, common tariffs and levies, and common finance. Unification of the market was especially important, because price level differences in different countries strongly differentiated real wages and thus industrial competitiveness.

Of the 279 measures in the Single European Act, about 100 relate to agriculture. In order to remove obstacles on the road to free circulation of goods, first of all the member states must achieve unification, or mutual recognition, of various animal health, crop protection and food regulations and standards.

From the beginning, agriculture was the Community's weakest sector and therefore the one most requiring of support. It set out to protect and support the many small producers, many of whom had insufficient land to make an income close to that of an industrial worker. Free competition would obviously have led to mass bankruptcy and endangered the aspirations to food self-sufficiency, seen as all the more important because of the persisting cold war, and would have brought in its wake serious dissatisfaction among the still-numerous agricultural community.

Differing opinions on the question of market regulation were held by the food-importing and exporting member countries. The big producers, primarily France, insisted on a strong system of subsidization and protection of the internal market from outside. The large-scale importers (Germany, and later Britain) were reluctant to give up their cheap food from external sources and were concerned about the burden of more expensive food on the consumers and the costs to the state and consumers of farm support policies. (EC consumers currently pay more than the world market price by a factor of five for milk powder, four for butter, two and a half for sugar and cheese, two for beef, and one and a half for cereals.) Liberal, free-market principles were therefore much more strongly preferred by the importing countries, who took the view that farms had to be concentrated for agriculture to become competitive even without support from within and protection from outside, and at prices which would put a significant proportion of producers out of business. On the other hand, they could see that if they did not allow France, the Netherlands and Italy to protect their agricultural interests, and did not ensure a market for their protected products, then they would not be able to count on equal treatments of their own industrial exports (Tracy, 1982).

In 1968 the Agricultural Commission devised the Mansholt Plan, named after the head of the Commission of the time, aimed at restructuring farming on a more economic scale. The proposals for concentrating farms set off passionate debate and protest, and it was only in a much-diluted form that the Council of Ministers eventually accepted the Plan, in 1972.

Under the Plan, farms engaging in modernization became eligible for capital assistance and interest-free credit from the Common Agricultural Fund and national budgets. Farmers could retire early if they sold their land (either to the State or other farmers) or handed it to their adult descendants. In addition, training schemes were started for farmers to improve their skills or change to a new occupation. It is intended to freeze guaranteed prices and gradually reduce price support.

The results were unspectacular. From 12 hectares in 1960, the average size of Community farms only went up to 14 hectares by 1985, although this includes the entry of new countries. In 1987 the highest average was in Britain, at 51.5 hectares, followed by Denmark with 30.7, France with 28.6 and Ireland with 22.7.

In the event, support and protection policy was winning within the Community. The threads of regulation made up a complex mesh whose anchor points were the price supports. The principal elements of this system were:

1. Annually or seasonally declared target prices (the upper bound of market prices) and minimum intervention or guaranteed prices (the lower bound of market prices) for the most important products.
2. Intervention purchases by the state (recently, for some commodities, up to a maximum volume, even more recently from a maximum land area and after a certain time following harvest) at guaranteed prices.
3. Setting threshold prices (applied to, for example, cereals) derived from target prices, reference prices (fruit and vegetables) and lock prices (pork), which are related to market prices.
4. Variable levies providing revenues for the CAP budget, in order to stabilize internal prices, if the threshold, reference, or lock prices are higher than the import price and the budget supplying the difference if the world market price is higher than these internal ones.
5. Restitutions or refunds for exporters, which equalize the difference between the internal (reference) prices and the world market price.
6. Import quotas for certain products.
7. Import tariffs.

Apart from price support, the system provides assistance for structural improvement and product development. There are supports for investment, farm modernization, innovative restructuring, social benefits, al protection, regional development for backward areas, and schemes for early retirement.

The last of these applies to farmers giving up agricultural production, using their farm for non-agricultural purposes, or selling or renting it.

However, 80 per cent of the system is price support, affecting three-quarters of the produce. The higher levels of support go to cereals, milk and oilseeds (Borszéki, 1991). It all comes out of the common budget, whose source is import duties, import charges, VAT and certain percentages of other taxes, as well as from national budgets.

Some years ago, faced with overproduction, high budget expenditure, claims of international organizations (like GATT) and foreign trade partners, as well as criticisms of the system by its own producers, the EC was obliged to restrict its support or partly divide it in a different way. In 1988 the European Commission decided to limit farm expenditure to a certain fraction of growth of GDP, and to double spending on the regional, social and structural programmes.

A production quota system was introduced, first for milk and then for cereals, sugar, lamb and oilseeds. The payment of guaranteed prices was limited by production quotas or the application of the system of *maximum guaranteed quantities* (m.g.q.), such as in the case of cereals, oil seeds and sheep meat, according to which price support or direct payments decrease when production exceeds the maximum guaranteed quantity. For cereals, a *co-responsibility levy* was imposed for the m.g.q. which grows as the m.g.q. is overstepped.

Intervention prices were gradually reduced. Partly to balance this reduction, and partly to change the production-stimulating effect of the price support system, a direct support system was gradually introduced, and the intervention-related maximum guaranteed quantity was also phased out in favour of maximum guaranteed area.

In May 1992 the EC Council of Agriculture Ministers came to an agreement on reform of the support system. Price support was reduced, but new payments, having a neutral effect on production, were brought in for farmers taking part in a *set-aside* scheme. The new arrangement was primarily targeted at cereals, oilseeds and pulses.

First the system of a payment per tonne to oilseed crushers within the limits of a m.g.q. was replaced from 1992 onwards by a system of payments per hectare made directly to producers within the limits of maximum guaranteed areas (m.g.a.).

From 1993 an area-premium is to be paid for cereals in partial compensation for the lower intervention price. Small producers receive this unconditionally, larger ones only if they take part in set-aside. The Agricultural Commission had originally recommended that smaller farms should receive a higher premium than larger ones. This would reduce the current unfairness of 80 per cent of payments going to 20 per cent of producers (Blick durch die

Wirtschaft, 1991). This was not accepted by countries with big farms – the UK, Denmark and, in the interest of large eastern German farms, the newly-unified Germany – and so an equal-area premium was decided on by the EC Council of Ministers.

A similar premium, with a higher area value, is in place for oilseed and protein plants.

The set-aside programme applies to cereals, oilseeds and protein plants. Large farmers must leave at least 15 per cent of their land fallow to be eligible for area support. For smallholders it is voluntary. Set-aside is done in rotation. The same parcel of land can be re-cultivated after a minimum of five years. Non-food produce, such as industrial crops or medicinal herbs may be produced on the set-aside area. The programme also pays a premium on the set-aside area.

Their have also been changes regarding animal breeding. A dairy cow premium balances 1993 reductions in prices and quotas for milk.

Intervention prices for beef are tied to maximum livestock levels per hectare. Both were reduced from 1993. In compensation, farmers receive a higher premium for bulls and calving animals.

Similar premiums apply to livestock levels per hectare of sheep, ewes and nanny goats. The ewe premium rose in 1993 despite sheep meat's receiving, at 75 per cent PSE, the highest level of support in the EC (Manegold, 1993).

Agricultural market regulation in the USA

In contrast to the regulation and support of prices which prevails in the European countries and Japan, market regulation in the US and other large food exporters, such as Canada and Australia, mainly takes the form of income support.

Farm assistance in the United States goes back to the 1930s. During the Great Depression, agricultural prices fell severely, by 64 per cent between 1923 and 1933. In 1933, the government directed the Commodity Credit Corporation, the bank of the US Department of Agriculture to provide a nine-month interest-free loan for new yields of grain and tobacco. After the loan term had expired, the farmers either repaid the loan, or the government took their produce in lieu. This had the effect of supporting minimum prices by the amount of the total credit divided by the total product. This is called the loan rate. The prospective aim of the support was restoration of the high 1910-1914 prices (parity price) and these prices still appear as marked levels in the production prices index. (Their application is hotly debated, because yields have greatly increased since that time, so that earnings can stay the same or even grow at lower prices.) In later years, the CCC charged on their loans. If the market price rose above the loan rate, the producers sold their production and repaid the loan with interest, if not, they kept it on. The system was set in law by the Agricultural Adjustment Act of 1938 and the Agricultural Act of 1949. By 1938, loans were already tied to a requirement to leave a certain percentage of land fallow to prevent overproduction. The acreage set-aside requirement was only suspended during the Second World War and up to the end of the Korean War, and then in the export boom following the food crises of 1972-73. The scheme as a whole remained the dominant form of support until 1973.

The other, and nowadays basic, type, the *deficiency payment*, emerged in the 1970s. The 1973 Agriculture and Protection Act introduced the *target price*. Deficiency payment is paid to farmers as the difference between the annually set target price and the market price or loan rate, whatever is higher.

In the period since then the two basic types of support have interwoven, and the land diversion requirements and other production limiting measures have become conditions of both (Becker, 1989 and Food, Agriculture, Conservation and Trade Act, 1990).

Among commodities covered by loan-rate provisions in the 1991-95 farm program are wheat, rice, rye, corn, oats, barley, grain sorghum, soybeans, peanuts, upland and especially long-staple cotton, tobacco, honey and sugar. Those in the deficiency payment scheme are wheat, feed grains, cotton and rice. Other forms of support apply to wool, mohair, milk and honey.

The Payment In Kind (PIK) program was brought in for land reduction compensation from the surplus USDA stocks in 1983 (at that time 80 million acres were removed from production). Since that time, this form of support has been widely applied also to the implementation of other forms of support. Nowadays producers do not receive the products themselves but a PIK certificate with a face dollar value entitling bearers to any available CCC surpluses. This payment takes the form of bonds that can be bought and sold, or used for other purposes, such as repaying CCC loans.

Support can be given in a multitude of ways outwith the two basic schemes:
- Supporting commodity prices by intervention purchases (e.g. milk).
- Interest rate subsidies for loans provided for various purposes, as, for example, agricultural marketing and land purchases.
- Compensation for income loss from natural disasters.
- Paid acreage reduction outwith the terms of CCC loans and deficiency payments.
- Supports for 10 to 15 years for land withdrawals for conservation by planting conserving vegetation.
- Higher loan-rates are given to some producers under set quotas of production and growing area (e.g. peanuts).

- Nonrecourse loans and paid storage costs for farmers who enter the programme of farmer-owned reserve and place their grain in storage for up to three years.
- Dairy farms receive payments for withdrawing dairy cows from production if they do not replace them for five years.
- There are funds for various soil-conservation programmes, and for longer-term withdrawals and improvements of land in designated erosion areas. (In 1990, 34 million acres were under soil conservation schemes and it is planned to improve 40-45 million acres by 1995; apart from this, farmers receive help to rehabilitate waterways contaminated by pesticides and fertilizers, and to rectify other environmental damage on 10 million acres).
- The government gives assistance for crop insurance.

Market regulation is supplemented by import tariffs and quotas on the import of some products (milk and sugar) and by export subsidies.

The natural tendency of most of the American supports is to reduce overall production. The two basic forms, loan-rates and deficiency payments, are closely bound to varying obligations to withdraw land or, more rarely, to centrally-set quantitative production limits depending on the level of national production and the level of federal stocks.

The US Congress approves the support schemes and can alter their composition, scope, size and conditions from time to time. The responsibility for putting them into effect falls to the US Department of Agriculture's CCC bank.

In the amount that the US spends on its programs, it is not far behind the EC, as figure 4.7 shows, but the percentage of production that it represents is much lower (see table 4.1). It results in less distortion of the price system, as indicated by table 4.3, because the guaranteed prices (the loan rates) are close to market prices. Measures to reduce production have been in place for much longer than in the EC, starting as long ago as the 1930s. In recent times there have also been efforts to reduce the amount of support. Guaranteed minimum and target prices have been lowered, and the latter frozen for 5 years from 1990. These have not, however, led to easily visible results. Total subsidies continue to grow – according to estimates the deficiency payment for wheat went up by a factor of 4 in 1990-91, despite the lower target price – as do production and yields. Farmers try to avoid the effects of the land reduction program partly by taking their worst land out of production, and partly by increasing yields on what remains.

It is, however, beyond doubt that America's market regulation does not protect farmers to the same extent as the EC's. This is also demonstrated by the far higher level of concentration of American farms. The number of farmers has fallen from 6 to 2 million since the Second World War, and the average

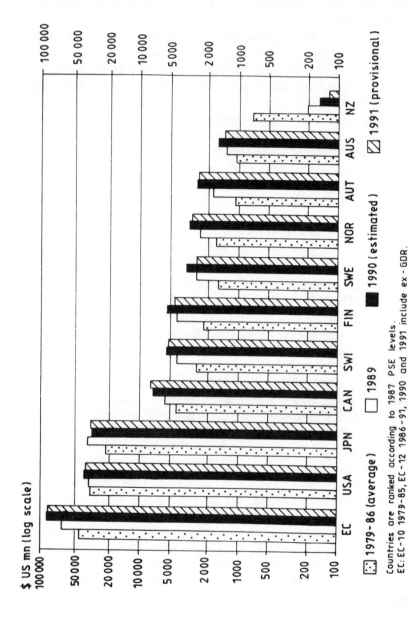

Figure 4.7 Net total PSE

Source: Agricultural Policies, Markets and Trade, 1992

farm size has grown from 65 to about 200 hectares. According the USDA, farms have become economically stronger: from 200,000 in 1985, the number of farms considered vulnerable fell to 100,000 in 1990 (The Farm Act, 1990).

International free trade agreements

There are many agreements in force to ease trade relations between countries. They range from customs concessions to customs unions and from free trade agreements to treaties aiming at partial or complete integration of all elements of economics.

Balassa (Balassa, 1961) identified four phases of international economic cooperation:

1. the free-trade area, in which customs duties are lowered or abolished.
2. the customs union, which involves a common customs border to third parties.
3. the common market, which allows free traffic of the factors of production (labour and capital) within the customs union.
4. economic union, which harmonizes the member countries' economic and financial policies and fiscal regulations.

What we encounter nowadays seldom falls into a pure form of any of these categories. Real groupings tend to carry elements of more than one phase, or are better described as being between phases or constituting a mixed phase. The evolution of mixed forms are strengthened by the tendency of the different treaty organizations to forge agreements between each other.

In Europe, the biggest association outside the EC is the European Free Trade Association (EFTA). Started in 1960, some of its former members (Britain, Denmark and Portugal) left on joining the EC. Its current members are Austria, Finland, Iceland, Norway, Switzerland and Sweden. Customs duties have been abolished for industrial goods. An agreement with the EC in 1972-73 introduced a free trade area for industrial goods. Cooperation became closer in 1984, and in 1991 they signed a treaty to form the European Economic Area, covering the lifting of some restrictions on the free flow not only of industrial goods but also of capital, services and labour, hence including some elements of integration similar in substance to article 238 of the Treaty of Rome. The agreement came into effect on 1 January 1993. The absence of provisions for free trade in unprocessed agricultural goods from among its articles is partly offset by treaties between individual countries in the EC and EFTA, and it was agreed that the EC and EFTA would sign special treaties to liberalize trade of food and other sensitive goods.

The European Community has signed agreements of association or cooperation with many countries: Greece in 1962, Turkey in 1963, Spain in 1970, Malta in 1970, Cyprus in 1972 and Yugoslavia in 1980. The purpose of the agreements was the creation of customs union or free-trade areas, and were usually implemented asymmetrically over a long period, with the EC bringing down their barriers more quickly than their economically weaker partners. Thus, for example, Greece and Spain undertook to adopt the EC import tariffs for trade with third countries by the end of the agreement period, while the EC gradually increased their import quotas. Regarding agricultural commodities, the EC did not go all the way to liberalization, stopping at the level of Most Favoured Nation (MFN) status for Greece and gradually reducing duties with respect to Turkey and Spain. The EC retained quotas for agricultural commodities from Malta and Cyprus. Turkey also received considerable financial assistance for the modernization, development and restructuring of its industry. Yugoslavia's goods, with the exception of certain products, like agricultural products, were allowed unlimited duty-free access to the EC market. Yugoslavia reciprocated with MFN treatment of EC countries.

Further EC agreements were for preferential trade and cooperation with the Maghreb countries (Algeria, Morocco and Tunisia) in 1969, and the Mashreg countries (Egypt, Jordan, Syria and Lebanon) in 1977, and with Israel in 1970 and 1975 (Dezséri, 1990 and Balázs, 1991). The agreements guaranteed duty free access of many commodities to the EC market and brought to an end quantitative restrictions. Tariffs on agricultural products were reduced. The two groups were obliged to extend Most Favoured Nation status to EC goods. Israel was to work towards complete removal of tariffs for EC goods.

The Lomé Convention links the EC to a number of African, Caribbean and Pacific (ACP) countries. First signed in 1975 by 46 countries, the number of signatories grew to 58 on its renewal in 1979 and to 66 in 1984. The current version, dating from 1989, includes 69 countries and covers the period 1990-2000. The Lomé Conventions offer unilateral concessions to developing countries. They liberalize EC access of industrial goods and many agricultural commodities. Most of their goods come into the EC free of customs duty or equivalent taxes. At the same time community exports to ACP markets enjoy MFN treatment. The EC investment aid to the Lomé countries provides financial support for development projects, grants, soft loans and interest rate subsidies, funds for stabilizing export earnings from agricultural and mining products, and to some extent liberalizing the flow of labour from these countries and frees undertakings (Europe: World Partner, 1991).

Hungary, Czechoslovakia and Poland negotiated an association agreement with the EC in December 1991, which came into force on March 1, 1992. (Because of the separation of the Czech and Slovak Republics, the two new countries negotiated separate agreements.)

Hungary had already secured unrestricted MFN status in a 1988 agreement which also provided for abolition of quotas by 1995. After setting up diplomatic ties in 1989, the EC joined with the OECD programme called Phare to assist Hungary and Poland, and later Czechoslovakia, with economic reforms, restructuring the economy, privatization, and development of education and research. In 1990 discriminative restrictions to which the former socialist countries had been subjected were removed, and non-discriminative ones reduced. Hungary, Czechoslovakia and Poland also received import preferences under the Community's Generalised System of Preferences.

The Hungarian agreement of association with the EC provides for free trade in industrial goods to and from the countries within 10 years. An immediate drop of 30 per cent in EC tariffs is to be followed by a further 30 per cent in equal steps over 5 years. The average EC duty of 10 per cent applying to textiles will disappear over 7 years. Textiles produced on commission are immediately freed from tariffs. The asymmetry allows Hungary to remove import tariffs on only 15 per cent of EC industrial goods over 3 years. The remainder will only be subject to gradual abolition of tariffs from 1995, one category over 3 years, another over 7. Both sides will also gradually phase out quantitative restrictions, but the agreement does not specify the dates.

The new associates obtained less favourable terms for agricultural commodities, even though these account for a quarter of exports to the EC for Hungary and Poland. Levies and tariffs for Hungary will diminish by 20 per cent in each of the three years from 1992 (60 per cent in total). Quotas will increase by 10 per cent per year over 5 years, so that Hungary will be allowed one and half times as much at the end. The measures overall affect 75 per cent of agricultural products (Meisel and Mohácsi, 1993). In exchange the annual relaxation of barriers for EC products will be 10 per cent for tariffs over three years and 5 per cent for quotas over five years.

The EC does not provide financial aid for the associated Central and East European countries apart from contributing to the Phare programme and the loans provided on preferential terms by the European Bank for Reconstruction and Development (EBRD). Neither does the agreement address free flow of labour, although it provides for the freeing of restrictions on resettlement in five years' time, whereby professionals, self-employed doctors, engineers, lawyers and so on will receive equal treatment if they set up practice in each others' countries (Heti Világgazdaság, 1991, vol. XIII, no. 48; Europe: World Partner, 1991).

It seems clear that in most of its agreements of association and cooperation, the EC is ready to free restrictions on those products with which it is itself competitive on the world market, however protects its less competitive sectors and industries, such as textiles, steel, and most especially agriculture. Thus the agreements give more rapid access at more favourable terms to industrial commodities than to the agricultural ones, which many countries at lower levels of development – and this includes Hungary – would most like to export.

Poland, Hungary and the Czech and Slovak Republic also made an agreement with EFTA for the establishment of a free trade area which is also asymmetric in character and came into force in 1992. The agreements provide for free trade in industrial and processed agricultural products but the terms of access for agricultural products are specified in a series of bilateral arrangements.

Free trade agreements entered into by the other great power, the USA, have mostly been with Latin American countries. It signed a free trade agreement with Canada in 1990 for gradually abolishing tariffs, import quotas, licences and other trade barriers, and ceasing the restriction on free flow of goods, services, investment and labour. A similar agreement was concluded with Mexico in 1993. In January 1994 the North American Free Trade Agreement (NAFTA) came into force, creating the world's largest free trade area in terms of volume of intraregional trade. NAFTA includes Canada, the USA and Mexico. According to the Agreement tariffs on 99 per cent of goods traded between the three countries will be abolished within a decade (Heti Világgazdaság, 1993, vol. XV, no. 47; Figyelő, December 9, 1993, The Economist, November 13, 1993).

Many countries have formed associations which do not involve the great powers of the EC and the USA, largely encouraged by the EC's example.

The Council of Mutual Economic Aid (CMEA or Comecon) brought together the Soviet Union and other European socialist countries. Founded in 1949, its aims were to facilitate trade, eliminate border tariffs and offer mutual economic aid for development. The latter was very narrow in scope and the CMEA remained largely a trade organization. Its founding members were the Soviet Union, Bulgaria, Czechoslovakia, Hungary, Poland and Romania. Albania joined in 1949 but withdrew later. The GDR joined in 1950, Mongolia in 1962, Cuba in 1972 and Vietnam in 1978. Yugoslavia was an associate member, and Finland had an agreement for cooperation from 1973, Mexico and Iraq from 1976. Laos, Angola and North Korea had observer status.

Unlike the EC, the CMEA did not have supranational institutions. Its highest organ was the Council. The Executive Committee operated with a system of 22 permanent committees.

Exchange of goods between the member countries was based on the coordination of their production plans as far as these affected or involved trade. State level agreements set quotas bilaterally. Shipments were valued in the transferable rouble at an arbitrary rate which did not properly reflect the real purchasing power of the currencies. Prices were themselves artificial, being based on world market prices five years previously. The lack of a real exchange rate, currency convertibility or correct prices deprived the system of

130

an accounting mechanism which could not have allowed multilateral trade, and the bilateral arrangements were restricted to the setting of quotas and so were effectively barter in character.

In an attempt to address trade difficulties and the inability of measuring its effectiveness, part of the 1971 'Complex Programme' set out to reform national price systems, establish real exchange rates and make the rouble convertible within the CMEA. However, these aims, which were stressed mainly by the Polish and Hungarian negotiators were given little weight even in the Programme itself, and were later effectively nullified in practice when the Soviet Union continued to regard as major aims coordination of planning, common long-term plans, specialization of production and cooperation in investment.

The CMEA broke up after the democratic reforms in Central and East Europe in January 1991 without making way for a successor organization. This was in keeping with the smaller members' determination to change over to market economies, even though in practice it was an aspiration they were far from achieving. This was coupled with the Soviet Union's view that it was no longer obliged to support them by providing oil and raw materials below world market prices in exchange for substandard industrial goods. CMEA undoubtedly extended the life of socialist economies. It allowed them to sell outdated, low quality products to each other, and especially to the Soviet Union, in exchange for the raw materials they needed. It thus propped up a rigid planned economic system which was insensitive to market influences and incapable of revival (Csaba, 1990). The closed economy and the unresponsiveness of state enterprises to competition rendered the socialist countries incapable of breaking out of their backwardness through either domestic or foreign competition.

International economic cooperation is pursued outside Europe and North America by a host of different customs unions and trade and economic associations. A good many of them exist only on paper, or do not really achieve their original goals. There are others which are quite promising or are already developing well. Space permits mention of only a few of them here.

The Association of South-East Asian Nations (ASEAN) exists to develop economic, social and cultural cooperation among Brunei, Philippines, Indonesia, Malaysia, Singapore and Thailand. In 1991 it worked out a treaty to bring about regional integration and a common market, the Asian Free Trade Area, over 15 years.

Argentina, Brazil, Paraguay and Uruguay signed a treaty in 1991 to start up the Common Market of the Southern Cone (MERCOSUR) in 1994.

On 1 January 1992 the Andean Pact, consisting of Bolivia, Colombia, Ecuador, Peru and Venezuela came into effect. A common market is to be established by the end of 1995.

In Central America there has been an attempt to revive the Central American Common Market which was originally set up in the 1960s but which disintegrated in 1969. Its members are Costa Rica, El Salvador, Guatemala, Honduras, Nicaragua and Panama.

The Caribbean Community (CARICOM) consists of 13 Caribbean countries. It is also attempting to create a customs union.

Notable organizations in Africa are the Preferential Trade Area (PTA), a trade organization involving eastern and southern African countries, and the Economic Commission of West African States (ECOWAS). Both of these are for developing economic cooperation and establishing customs unions, leading in the longer term to a common market. Other institutions of significance are the Economic Community of Central African States (CEEAC) and the Central African Customs Union (UDEAC).

In 1991 members of the Organization of African Unity signed a treaty establishing the African Economic Community. Its aim is to pass through the phase of a Free Trade Area and eventually evolve into a fully fledged Customs Union at the continental level (World Economic Survey, 1992, and Surányi, 1992).

Several other free trade associations exist throughout the world operating at various levels of effectiveness.

Part III
NATURAL ENDOWMENT AND FACTORS OF PRODUCTION

6 Agro-ecological conditions

The fundamental requirements for agricultural production are land and water, to which can be added suitable temperature and sunlight for crops. But natural conditions are not the whole story. There is no production without human effort. The farmer tames nature and reaps the fruit of his labour, helped by the materials, tools and machines which are at his disposal. And his interference with the ways of nature can in turn work its way through to the environment in ways that are as likely to be harmful as they are to be beneficial.

Here we look at the factors governing production and its environment. The basic factors of production are land, capital and labour. Within land is included ecological properties determining its productivity.

Arable land and its agro-ecological characteristics

Without land there is no cultivation of crops for food or animal feed. It is possible to grow crops or ornamental plants without soil in laboratory conditions or under glass, (e.g. aquaculture), but these are as yet of no significance in everyday practice.

Water is no less important than land. Water, taken up from the soil into the plant cells, carries with it the nutrients which along with the photosynthetic process, allow the plant to grow.

Agricultural production occurs optimally where good soil and sufficient and well distributed rainfall occur together. Such a happy conjunction is rare in nature.

The cultivator of the land has to improve it artificially by means mechanical and chemical, securing satisfactory yields by using natural and artificial fertilizer to raise the level of nutrients and supplementing inadequate rainfall with irrigation from other sources of water.

135

Whether land available for cultivation is sufficient can be determined through the number of people or animals it can support. Apart from the land area, this is dependent on the quality of the land and intensity of cultivation.

In some tropical and subtropical areas, especially in Africa, the population may be sparse, but the availability of land is offset by its soil's poor quality. Organic material decays quickly in the heat, so that little humus accumulates. Heavy rainfall causes much of the nutrients to leach away, leaving buildups of iron and aluminium oxides (red laterite and subtropical terra rossa soils are examples of where this has occurred). The thin cover is easily susceptible to erosion and is easily washed away by rain, especially if forests have been cut down without being replaced by protective plants. The poor, thin tillable soil limits the potential for intensive cultivation.

A different set of circumstances prevail in the temperate zones. Here the humus soil layers are thicker and less susceptible to erosion. Population is typically much denser, especially in the temperate regions of Europe, than in the tropics, and so the land per person is less. Intensive agriculture is thus both more necessary and more possible.

Inferior soils can still support high population densities if the conditions are right. In Egypt, the country's population of around 52 million has to be supported from 3 per cent of the land area, the rest of the country being desert. The answer lies in intensive cultivation coupled with careful soil protection and land reclamation from the desert and other poor, dry areas. Densely populated areas of south-east Asia also depend on intensive cultivation. Enhanced irrigation and wet rice cultivation conserves the soil as well as maintaining a relatively high level of production.

Conversely, the best cultivated soil can still lose its fertility. Restoring fertility by fallowing was common in the past; it is used nowadays only in sparsely populated areas of Africa, Latin America and highland areas of Asia, the more intensive forms of cultivation making use of natural and artificial fertilizers. Chemical fertilizers dominate modern cultivation mostly because the natural manure is not available in sufficient quantities for the required yields. Statistics revealing the use of fertilizer are good indicators of the level of advancement of agriculture, although by themselves, without considering local conditions, they can be misleading. In some large, sparsely populated countries, such as the USA, Australia and Argentina, where land is relatively cheap, it is more worthwhile to produce extensively, thereby obtaining the same quantity from larger areas at lower yields and therefore with less fertilizer cost compared with smaller areas at higher yields. Figure 7.5 in chapter 7 shows that the least-cost combination of land and fertilizer, where income is highest, is reached with more land and less fertilizer in the case where land is relatively plentiful.

136

The adequacy of rainfall is a function partly of the quantity of rain, partly of its distribution and partly of the temperatures influencing evaporation. The 50 mm of rain falling in the desert area around Cairo and the 50 – 100 mm in the dry central Asian steppe clearly need to be supplemented. It is not so clear why irrigation is necessary in the monsoon region of Hindustan, where annual rainfall is above 1000 mm. But with the soil rapidly drying out in the heat following deluge between June and September, no crops could survive without irrigation. The situation is similar in winter rainfall areas of the Mediterranean. Irrigation is thus essential for many crops in areas other than dry, steppe regions, in monsoon and mediterranean regions.

Rainfall is far less of a problem in temperate zone countries with oceanic climates (western Europe, New Zealand). The yearly total may be less than in many countries in warmer zones, but it tends to be spread out much more evenly and there is less evaporation.

The regions requiring least rainfall are continental areas with short summers and low annual average temperatures (Scandinavia, western Siberia, Canada and Alaska). There, the cool climate and very low evaporation allows land to become marshy even where annual rainfall is below 200-300 mm.

Land area

The ice-free land area of the world has a total area of 13.1 billion hectares. Of this, 4 billion hectares are forest, 3.4 pasture, 1.5 agricultural cultivation and 4.2 others (rocky desert, tundra, swamp, other unproductive land, and built-up areas). This is shown in figure 6.1 (FAO Production Yearbook, 1992).

Several surveys and forecasts have indicated that the land area currently cultivated could be doubled from the 11 per cent of today to a quarter of the world's land area, in the best case. If most of the world's cultivable land could be brought into use by 2000 – as FAO predictions claim is necessary – then the current world average of 0.3 hectares per head of population could increase to 0.5-0.6 hectares.

In 'Agriculture: Toward 2000 (1981)', the cost of bringing under cultivation one hectare of non-irrigated land was put at US\$ 424 in 1975. This includes \$50 for clearing rainforest and supplying production infrastructure (social infrastructural costs – housing, schools etc. – are not included in this figure).

Start-up costs for new land are therefore high. In addition, much of the land in question is in endangered rainforest areas with thin soils, or in areas where the soil is poor, the rainfall low or the growing season short.

FAO and the United Nations Educational, Scientific and Cultural Organization (UNESCO) started a world soil map project in the 1960s (Land Resources Future Populations Project) which enabled the food-production

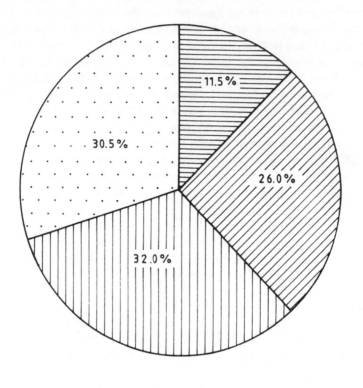

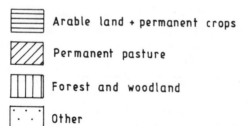

Arable land + permanent crops

Permanent pasture

Forest and woodland

Other

Figure 6.1 **Distribution of the world's land area**
Source: *FAO Production Yearbook,1992*

capability of various soils to be assessed. The regional soil maps were published between 1971 and 81 (Márton and Újhelyi, 1986), and by combining data for soil and climate, determined the agro-ecological zones which allowed available cultivable land in developing countries to be identified, in particular land suitable for growing basic foods.

Figure 6.2 presents the study's findings for potentially cultivable land in developing countries, showing that 12 per cent suffers from lack of rainfall, 36 per cent has low-quality soil or short growing seasons, 17 per cent is floodland and 2 per cent desert.

According to the publication Food 2000 (1987), different regions have widely varying proportions of cultivable land which are as yet unused. Table 6.1 and figure 6.3 show that in Africa, Australia and New Zealand, only 21-22 per cent is already under cultivation, in Central America the figure is about 50 per cent and in Europe and Asia there are hardly any reserves.

Table 6.1
Cultivated land area and reserves (million hectares)

Continent, region	Total land area	Cultivated land area	Cultivable area	%-age of cultivable land already in use
Africa	3,010	158	734	22
Asia (without the USSR)	2,740	519	627	83
Australia & New Zealand	820	32	153	21
Europe	480	154	174	88
North America	2,110	239	465	51
Latin America	1,750	77	681	11
USSR	2,240	227	356	64
World total	13,150	1,406	3,190*	44

* Nowadays largely meadow and pasture
Source: Food 2000, 1987

Distribution of land use throughout the world is the subject of table 6.2. It shows that Oceania and Africa has the lowest proportion of arable land and permanent crops, and the highest proportion of permanent pasture. The highest arable proportion is found in Europe, followed by the Far East, and the most forest and woodland is in South America, Central America and Europe.

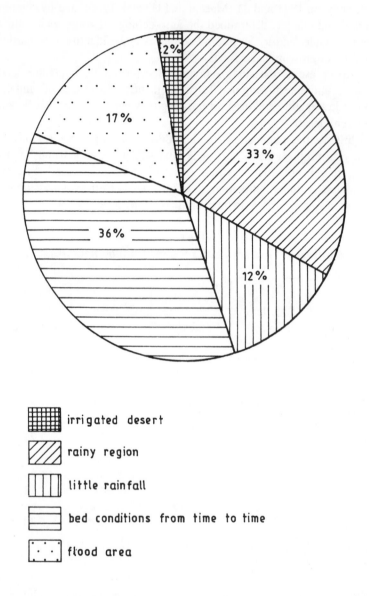

Legend:

- irrigated desert
- rainy region
- little rainfall
- bed conditions from time to time
- flood area

Figure 6.2   Quality of cultivable land in the developing countries

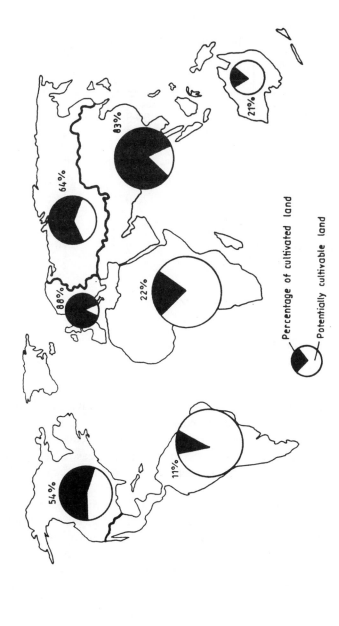

Figure 6.3 Cultivated land as a percentage of potentially cultivable land area according to continent or region

141

Table 6.2
Land use in 1990 in percent of land area

	Arable land and permanent crops	Permanent pasture	Forest and woodland	Other land
World	11.0	26.0	30.8	32.2
Africa	6.1	30.4	23.1	40.4
North and Central America	12.8	17.1	33.5	36.6
South America	6.5	28.2	47.3	18.0
Asia	17.0	28.4	20.0	34.6
Near East	7.1	26.9	7.9	58.0
Far East	19.6	28.6	23.6	28.2
Europe	29.4	17.6	33.2	19.8
Oceania	5.9	51.1	18.6	24.4

Source: *FAO Production Yearbook,* 1992

Agro-ecological potential of the world's regions

Africa

47 per cent of the continent's land area is too dry to be cultivated without irrigation. Only on 19 per cent is the soil completely productive, and 36 per cent of the soil is desert or semidesert. However, 600 million hectares rainfed area is available for cultivation, mostly in the rainy tropical areas. 22 per cent of the cultivable land, and only 15 per cent of the irrigation capacity is currently used.

The distribution of fertile land across the continent is uneven. A significant proportion of suitable land in North Africa, the Middle East, the Sahel and East Africa is already in use. In North Africa, cultivable land with sufficient rainfall is mainly confined to the coastal strip, the rest being desert, semi-desert, dry plains and mountainous areas. The greatest untapped land potential lies in the Central African countries. A large part of southern Africa is sparsely populated, but much of it is low-rainfall, dry savannah (Probáld and Szegedi, 1983).

In assessing potential for food production, the zones which are critical because of infertile soil or high population density are: the coastal and hilly areas of the Maghreb, parts of the Sahel between 12° and 20°N, the most densely populated parts of Kenya and the densely populated arc of East Africa from south-east Uganda through Ruanda and Burundi to Malawi. In the southern part of the continent, the critical zones are spread out between the Angolan coast through Botswana and Lesotho to the southern part of Mozambique.

South-west Asia

33 per cent of south-west Asian soils are desert or semi-desert, another 27 per cent having thin topsoil. Because of the highland regions, the growing season is short over 17 per cent of the area. More than 80 per cent of cultivable land is already utilised, despite the low population density of 25-30 per square kilometre.

The whole area is extremely dry, with only a few rainy areas. One of these is the Mediterranean coastal area with an annual rainfall of more than 500 mm, others the steadily wet southern edges of the Black and Caspian Seas. The 250-500 mm falling on the Syrian-Arab plain's northern borders is enough for growing grain. On the Mesopotamian plain, most of the Arabian Peninsula and the interior of the Iranian Basin, rainfall hardly reaches 250 mm. The mountainous south-west strip of the Arab Peninsula is affected by summer monsoon rains, and rainfed agriculture is therefore possible. Turkey is the only country in the region where the majority of the land does not need irrigation.

South-east Asia

The region is densely populated, and by 1975 already 92 per cent of the fertile land reserves were under cultivation. Soil and climate are best in the densely populated areas, and there farming is highly intensive. The greater part of the region is subject to the monsoon, and in the dry season cultivation can only be carried on with irrigation (Benedek, Karceva, Probáld and Szegedi, 1988). Most of the islands and the Malaysian peninsula experience daily rain.

Soils in the area are of the laterite, chernozem-like dry tropical and subtropical, grey-brown and podzolic mountainous, and along the rivers fertile alluvial types. The greatest population densities are mostly along the irrigated riverside areas (Benedek, Karceva, Probáld and Szegedi, 1988).

North America

Not counting Alaska and Hawaii, 63 per cent of the USA's land area serves some agricultural purpose. Arable cultivation is most widespread on the best soils south from the Great Lakes to the Mississippi valley and some distance west from there. This constitutes about one-fifth of the USA's land area. In contrast, eight mountainous states and Alaska, account for almost half of the country's area, but only one-tenth of the arable land. The dry Mid-West states are primarily suited to extensive grazing. 17 million hectares in the Mid-West and West are irrigated. There are major efforts going on to halt erosion, and many irrigation and improvement projects are supported by the government.

The country's southern reaches mainly consist of dry, desert areas. In California, irrigated fruit, vegetable and grape production is widespread .

Canada's land suitable for agriculture makes up only about 13-14 per cent of its total, and only a small proportion of this is utilized (arable 4.4 per cent, meadow and pasture 2.4 per cent) because of the unfavourable climate and soil characteristics. The sparse population, on the other hand, means that there is ample land. Arable cultivation is centred around the southern areas. The wet continental climate provides a sufficient 500-100 mm of rain, and on the Atlantic coast there is a substantial 1000-1500 mm. Drought is a problem in the south west of the prairie provinces and in the leeward side of the Rocky mountains. Here annual rainfall is a bare 500 mm.

Of good quality are the chestnut-brown and chernozem soils of the prairie and the brown forest soils of the Ontario peninsula and the St Lawrence plain. Four-fifths of the cultivated land is on the prairie provinces of Manitoba, Saskatchewan and Alberta. 600,000 hectares of the drier areas of the prairie are irrigated, half of these being in Alberta (Mészáros et al., 1987).

Central America

About 64 per cent of the region's land area is suited to rainfed cultivation. 44 per cent of the soils are fully fertile. Much of Central America is in the tropical rain belt, but on the leeward side of the mountains there is rain only in summer. Irrigation is often required there. There are many high mountains and small islands, which reduces the productive area. Approximately half of the cultivable land was being utilized in 1975.

The northern part of Mexico is desert and semi-desert, and it is here that most of the irrigation takes place. Most of the country belongs to the oceanic climatic zone, with upland and rainy high plains prevailing (Mészáros et al, 1987).

South America

The region is comparatively sparsely populated and there are ample reserves of land. Only 15 per cent of the potential was being exploited in 1975. (In Brazil, for example, the large estate owners work a mere sixth of their holdings.) The critical regions are principally along the Andes, in the cool and cold climatic zones, in the drought-prone areas in the interior of Brazil and along the Caribbean coast. The Andean areas suffer from by soil degradation and desertification.

Australia and New Zealand

Australia is the driest continent. In contrast to the world average of 660 mm, its average annual rainfall is 420 mm. There is only sufficient precipitation for crops in the perimeter areas of the north, east and south-west of the country. 70 per cent of the continent is desert, semi-desert and dry plain. Part of the dry area can be used for extensive animal breeding. The population is extremely sparse, at 2 per square kilometre. Most of the population is concentrated on the fertile coastal strip. Despite the exceptionally poor soil and rainfall conditions there are large reserves of cultivable land.

New Zealand's natural endowments are much more favourable. Its climate is mild oceanic. Annual rainfall is 600-1500 mm, although the leeward sides of South Island are much drier. Most of North Island is volcanic plateau, and much of South Island is occupied by the high contours of the Southern Alps. The sparse population (12 per square kilometre) is confined to the fertile coastal plain and smaller basin areas (Benedek, Karceva, Probáld and Szegedi, 1988).

Europe

This is the most densely populated continent, and not surprisingly almost all the cultivable land is already in use.

A significant part of western Europe is an area of oceanic climate with uniformly-distributed rainfall. This has given rise to a lot of very good pastureland.

The best loess soils are found in the warm temperate zone, made up of the Paris basin, Belgium, central Germany, Polish Silesia, the Hungarian and Romanian Plains, and the Ukrainian and Russian black-soil belt, but the rainfall in these regions is not more than 500-600 mm, and droughts are frequent.

The cool temperate zone extends northwards from this area. The summer in the northern region is short, with long days, and even with the small amount of rain, there are swamps. The area is sparsely populated.

The area of the Mediterranean climate with its rainy winters and dry summers is the home of wheat and subtropical crops (Probáld, Sárfalvi, and Szegedi, 1984 and Krajkó, 1987).

Irrigation

Irrigation is the ancient method of securing and increasing yields. The oldest irrigation schemes were in Egypt, Mesopotamia and Turkestan, in those areas where due to the lack of rain during the growing season, there was no other way to grow crops. Irrigation got under way in Egypt and Mesopotamia in the 4th millennium BC. By the end of the 4th millennium it was common along the River Nile. Along the Rivers Tigris and Euphrates dams, channels and slopes are found in the 2nd century BC (Grigg, 1974). Between the 5th and 2nd centuries BC, irrigated cultivation took shape in Turkestan, in the dry steppe to the east of the Caspian Sea, and also along the rivers which rise in the Hindu Kush and in Kopet Dag .

Wet-rice production originates in Thailand from about 3500 BC and it was established in areas of central China in the 3rd millennium BC, and in Gujarat in India around 1800 BC. It became dominant in China along the Huangho and its tributaries in the 1st century AD, spreading to the Yangtse in the 8th century and southwards from there. During the first millennium AD it also became widespread in South China and the Ganges and Brahmaputra deltas. By the 1400s, wet rice production was practised in China, Japan, northern Vietnam, Korea and other south-east Asian countries. In most places, the growers did not rely purely on monsoon and natural river flooding, but built embankments, water-lifting devices and canals.

In ancient irrigating societies, it was usually the state who took responsibility for maintaining the irrigation system. The 'Asian mode of production' was based on irrigated cultivation in Asian societies, which from ancient times prevailed in several countries up to the 19th century, with some vestiges surviving to the 20th century. In the Asian mode of production, the owner of the land was the state (usually the emperor of the country). The state directed the building of and maintained the irrigation works, and the farmers paid taxes in return. The tax-collectors were high ranking appointees of the emperor, who used their widespread network of officials not only to impose the taxes, but also to control the maintenance of the irrigation system, by organizing public works. Colonial interference by the Turks, and later the Europeans, broke up the ancient systems of administration and in many cases led to the decay of the irrigation systems. For example, in Mesopotamia the irrigation network collapsed at the time of the Ottoman conquest. And in India, the British organized the administration along European lines, so that when they conferred the right to rule on the maharajahs they did not oblige them to maintain the irrigation works.

In this century, after the 1950s, the green revolution gave new impetus to the establishment of irrigation schemes. The state built many large dams and reservoirs in India and China. Egypt built the new Aswan Dam, with Soviet assistance, between 1960 and 1971. This replaced the seasonal flooding of the Nile on 1 million hectares with continuous irrigation, and gave rise to the reclamation of 400,000 hectares of new fertile land. Earlier, the giant Gezira irrigation works were established in Sudan under colonial direction, as were the works on the Niger in Mali. Along with the favourable effects of the large dams, the darker aspects began to make their appearance. In many cases inadequate drainage led land becoming swampy and salinated. Soil erosion also increased. In Egypt, the fertilizing function of the silt left behind by flooding came to an end, with the silt building up in Lake Nasser instead. This had the added effect of the multiplying the amount fertilizer needed for farming.

More recently, there has been a preference for building small reservoirs rather than large dams. As well as being cheaper to build, they depend on local water sources and monsoon rains, have lower running costs, and are less damaging to the environment.

In the Middle East, where river water is scarce, every source of water is exploited for irrigation: streams, wells and cisterns. In Iran, Afghanistan and Oman, underground networks of channels collect the water and protect it from evaporation. In Israel, the River Jordan irrigation scheme and water from other rivers, streams, wells and treated sewage have increased the area of productive land by a factor of two and a half, and the irrigated land by a factor of five. Part of the Negev desert has also been made productive.

In recent years, artesian wells have been drilled on the Arabian Peninsula and in other oil-rich countries, such as Algeria and Libya, in the vicinity of the oil wells, and the water used for irrigation. With such artificial oases, these countries hope to raise their level of self-sufficiency in food. Saudi Arabia now exports grain, even though the cost of producing it by irrigation is several times the imported price.

The former Soviet Union set up enormous irrigation systems in the central Asian steppes and desert areas using the waters of the Amu-darja and Szir-darja. Three-quarters of the Soviet Union's cotton came from the Uzbek Republic. About half of the cotton was produced in the Fergana basin, irrigated by the Fergana Canal.

The USA also provides state support for irrigation works, as it does also for soil conservation projects. Most irrigation works were, as worldwide, built between 1950 and 1970. Californian agriculture is almost completely irrigated. It is also significant along the Mississippi and its tributaries.

Irrigation could also be put to good use in the dry continent of Australasia, but because of the small rivers, it has only so far found practical application on 2 per cent of the land.

A large proportion of the growth in irrigated land area has taken place between 1950 and 1980. In 1900, there were about 40 million hectares under irrigation in the world and in 1950 there were 94 million, but between 1950 and 1980 the area increased by a factor of three. The growth was especially fast in the 1950s and 60s (The State of the World in 1987, 1987). This was when the large-scale works on the Indus, the Ganges, the Brahmaputra, the Yangtse, the Huangho and other large rivers were established, but the agricultural boom and the rising demand for food encouraged a significant rise in irrigation in other parts of the world, such as North America and Europe – including the Soviet Union, as shown on table 6.3.

Table 6.3
Percentage rise in irrigated areas between 1950 and 1985 by world region

Region	Area irrigated (M ha)				
	Absolute	Amount of increase			
	1985	1950-60	1960-70	1970-80	1980-85
Asia[a]	184	52	32	28	8
North America	34	42	71	14	-11[b]
Europe[c]	29	50	67	33	9
Africa	13	25	80	27	13
South America	9	67	20	28	17
Oceania	2	0	100	0	0
World	271	49	41	26	8

[a] Including the Asian part of the Soviet Union
[b] 1980-84 values, for the USA only
    (USDA, Farm and Ranch Irrigation Survey, 1984)
[c] Including the European part of the Soviet Union

Source: *The State of the World in 1987,* 1987

In the 50s and 60s, the average annual rise in land covered by irrigation was 4 per cent, slowing down from the 1970s, probably because of the recession following the oil-price rises and the fall in agricultural prices in the 1980s. The annual rise during the 1980s fell to below 1 per cent. In the USA the irrigated land area has actually reduced.

The regions' irrigated land area, and its rise between 1975 and 1990, is shown on table 6.4. The greatest irrigated area is to be found in Asia, making up two thirds of the world's total and one third of its own arable land, and is concentrated in east and south-east Asia. The least is found in Oceania.

148

Table 6.4
Irrigated areas in 1990 and their growth

Regions	Irrigated area			
	million hectares	%-age of world's irrigated area	%-age of arable and permanent cropland	Growth 1990-1975 (%)
World	237.4		16.4	125.5
Africa	11.3	4.8	6.2	118.8
North & Cent. America	26.6	11.2	9.7	116.6
South America	8.8	3.7	7.7	138.8
Asia	150.3	63.3	33.0	123.4
Near East	20.4	8.6	23.9	113.0
Far East	131.6	55.4	34.3	125.2
Europe	17.1	7.2	12.2	134.2
Oceania	2.2	0.9	4.3	134.6
Former USSR	21.2	8.9	9.2	146.5

Source: *FAO Production Yearbook,* 1992.

The world's irrigated area expanded by around 26 per cent between 1975 and 1990, to the greatest extent in the former USSR, South America, Oceania and Europe. The least growth was in the Middle East and North and Central America.

According to the projections in World Agriculture: Toward 2000 (1988), two thirds of the increase in cultivated area up to 2000 will take place by irrigation, bringing the irrigated fraction of the world's farmland to 20 per cent from the 14 per cent of 1982-84. 85 per cent of this rise will take place in Asia, concentrated in India. But works for bringing water to crops are needed in many other places: in the Middle East and North Africa there is no more rainfed land which can be brought under cultivation. In Sub-Saharan Africa and in Latin America, however, the main source of new farmland will be from rainfed areas.

The average cost of building irrigation works, not including running costs, was $2,380 in 1975, ranging between $300 to $7,000 according to sophistication (Agriculture: Toward 2000, 1981). It is not, therefore, a cheap solution, and returns depend on yields and the types of crops which can be grown. Considering that world prices are depressed, and that yields –

especially in developing countries – are not high, costs in most cases cannot be borne without state assistance.

Fertilization

Overcoming the natural shortcomings of soils and maintaining their properties is mainly achieved by application of fertilizer. Fertilizer also raises the efficiency of rain and irrigation water.

Natural fertilizers have, since the middle of the 19th century, gradually given way to the chemical variety. Although natural fertilizer has many advantageous properties – it increases humus, is less damaging to the environment, and is cheaper where animals are reared – it is little used. The reasons for this are as diverse. In the developed countries, there is not usually enough for the required yields which give farmers high incomes. It is convenient to use only where animals are reared or in the area nearby, transport over long distances being problematic. Where the animals are kept on ranches or moving grazing, it is difficult to collect. And in low-income countries where fuel is scarce, it is too important as a source of energy.

Table 6.5 shows that more developed countries use more fertilizer, although the amounts they use do not vary according to world development rankings.

There is also a wide scatter within groups of similar average income. In the low-income group, the amounts of fertilizer used are Ethiopia: 7 kilograms per hectare; India 69; and China 262. In the lower middle income group Egypt stands out with 404 kg/ha, this being the only way to maintain the fertility of the desertifying soils along the Nile since the flooding was stopped.

The springboard for the especially large jumps in use of fertilizer in Asia and the Middle East has been the green revolution. In countries where the green revolution has been successful, most governments have provided assistance for fertilizer use, just as they have for irrigation and seeds.

Among the upper middle income countries, South Korea and Hungary stand out in the 1989-90 figures with 425 kg/ha and 246 kg/ha respectively. (Hungary's use of fertilizer has suffered a severe drop since 1990, with the consequent effect on yields). Some export crop-producing countries also use a lot of fertilizer (Costa Rica 203 kg/ha, Mauritius 330, Malaysia 157, Venezuela 151 and Greece 172).

The high-users among the OECD countries are Ireland (723 kg/ha), New Zealand (656 kg/ha) Holland (642 kg/ha) and Belgium (502 kg/ha), with the large, sparsely populated countries using very little: Canada applies 47, the USA 99 kg/ha, and Australia 23 kg/ha on their arable land.

Of the oil-producing countries, Saudi Arabia stands out with 401 kg/ha as a high user of fertilizer, in its attempt to achieve self-sufficiency in grain on its arid land.

150

Table 6.5
Fertilizer use

Country groups	GNP per capita US$ 1990[a]	Fertilizer use on arable land, kg of plant nutrient per hectare 1989-90
Low-income countries	350	94.6
China and India	360	138.3
Other low-income countries	320	39.4
Lower-middle income countries	1,530	60.1
Upper middle-income countries	3,410	82.4
High income countries	19,590	121.8
OECD members	20,170	120.6
Other[b]	..	401.9
Low and middle income countries	840	83.3
Sub-Saharan Africa	340	8.9
East Asia and Pacific	600	190.3
South Asia	330	68.9
Europe	2400	142.4
Middle East and N. Africa	1790	64.6
Latin America and Caribbean	2180	46.8

[a] Weighted average
[b] Classified as developing

Source: *World Development Report, 1992.*

Fertilizer use displays a closer relationship to the intensity of agriculture than to national product, as shown in table 6.6 and figure 6.4. Although both intensity and fertilizer use is determined by the level of development of the country, values can vary widely within the determined limits depending on a number of factors: the amount of land per capita of population, or per agricultural worker; how productive the land is; how much of agricultural production is for subsistence and how much for export; how developed the methods of cultivation are; and what is included in the average, i.e. which crops have a lot of fertilizer applied to them and which ones little.

Table 6.6 and figure 6.4 compare grain yields and average fertilizer use in some countries. Yields are clearly related to average fertilizer totals, but there are exceptions. In South Africa, for instance, most of the fertilizer is used on

Table 6.6
Yields and fertilizer use

Continent / country	Cereal Yields tonnes/hectare (1990)	Fertilizer use: kg of plant nutrient per hectare of arable land (1989-90)
Africa		
Mozambique	0.5	0.8
Algeria	0.6	28.3
Malawi	1.0	22.7
Ethiopia	1.3	7.0
Zimbabwe	1.6	60.4
South Africa	1.8	57.5
Egypt	5.7	404.3
America		
Argentina	2.2	4.6
Canada	2.6	47.2
USA	4.8	98.5
Asia		
Pakistan	1.8	89.0
India	1.9	68.7
Bangladesh	2.5	99.3
Israel	2.8	242.5
China	4.3	261.9
Saudi Arabia	4.7	400.8
Japan	5.8	417.9
Australia	1.7	22.6
Europe		
Hungary	4.5	246.3
Austria	5.6	200.8
West Germany	5.8	370.5
East Germany	4.7	..
Denmark	6.1	250.3
UK	6.2	350.2
Ireland	6.4	722.5
Netherlands	7.0	642.4

Sources: *World Development Report,* 1992
FAO Production Yearbook, 1992

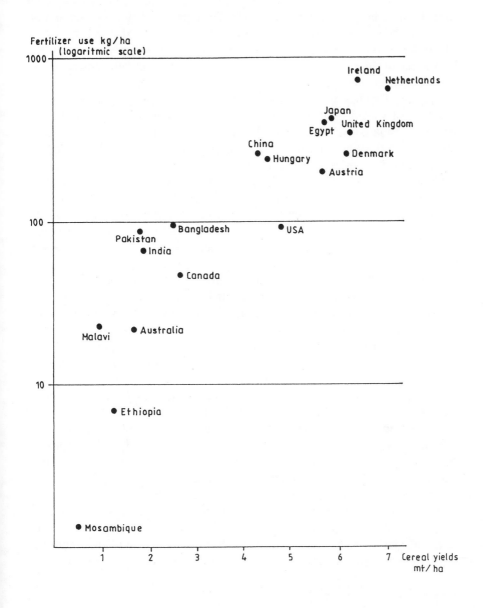

Figure 6.4   Fertilizer use and yields in 1990

153

white farms, where yields are higher, the national average being low because of the prevalence of traditional cultivation. A similar situation exists in Zimbabwe, where the average yield of wheat – grown mainly on white-run farms – is 5.8 tonnes per hectare, the national average grain yield being kept down by the low-yield types of cereals grown by black farmers.

The low fertilizer use and low cereal yields in the large grain-exporting countries of Canada, Australia and Argentina is striking. This is due to the same economic considerations which we have encountered before: the large amount of land per head means that it is cheaper to produce with low yields on a large area than on a small area with a lot of fertilizer. In the high corn-producing United States, wheat is produced in the drier western areas in preference to the higher-income producing maize. On the better-soil endowed Central Plain (Ohio, Iowa, Indiana, Illinois) maize is preferred, whose yields are raised by higher doses of fertilizer than are applied for wheat. The average American wheat yield was 2.7 tonnes per hectare in 1990, that of maize 7.4 tonnes per hectare.

In the Middle East and Asia, the scarcity of land compels maximum intensity of cultivation in most countries. It is China which has achieved the highest rate of growth of intensification. In the two decades from 1970, fertilizer use went from 41 to 262 kg/ha and the wheat yields rose by more than 2 tonnes. These results are due to the success of the green revolution and socio-economic changes whereby communes have been turned over to family farms.

The relatively high use of fertilizer in Israel is not accompanied by high yields probably because of the bad desert-like soil.

In Pakistan, Bangladesh and India, the green revolution is well established in some areas along the great rivers, but the relatively low overall figures show that fertilizer application and the consequent yields are sufficiently low in the rest of the country to bring down the nation's average.

Japan and the developed European states are textbook examples of the relation between large quantities of fertilizer and high yields. It is worth noting that many developed countries, like the UK, the Netherlands, Ireland and Japan have reduced fertilizer quantities in recent years, probably due to efforts to rein in overproduction and to higher levels of environmental protection.

Agricultural mechanization

A wide range of tools and machinery are used in agricultural production, ranging from simple implements like the digging stick, the axe, the hoe, the sickle the scythe, and the sugarcane knife through the animal-drawn plough and harrow up to powered machinery like tractors, harvesters, tractor-drawn machines and the various machines used in animal breeding. Irrigation works and machinery also belong here.

International statistics for means of production are poor. Apart from data for fertilizer and pesticide use, and some for irrigation, statistics are only available for certain machines, such as tractors, combine harvesters and milking machines. We can get an approximate impression of the level to which a country is equipped with modern agricultural machinery through the figures for machines per unit cultivated area, given in table 6.7. The picture is approximate because the data only includes the numbers of machines and not their power, even though there is a not immaterial difference between a 25 and a 200 horsepower tractor. There are similar differences between harvesters.

Table 6.7
Number of tractors and harvester-threshers per 1000 hectare arable land and permanent crop land in 1990

Region	Tractors	Harvester-threshers
Developed regions:		
North America	23.4	3.5
Europe	75.1	5.9
Oceania	8.3	1.2
former Soviet Union	11.4	2.9
Other developed	128.0	72.1
Developing regions:		
Africa	1.9	0.1
Latin America	9.3	1.0
Middle East	12.3	0.3
Far East	6.5	0.3
Other developing	6.4	0.4

Source: FAO Production Yearbook, 1992

The number of tractors and harvester-threshers per unit cultivated area is a simple function of level of development. The smallest number is in the developing countries of Africa and the Far East, followed by Latin America and the Middle East, the highest being in developed countries outside Europe, North America and Oceania (Japan, for example, has 461.3 tractors per thousand hectares and 278.5 harvesters), followed by Europe, North America and Oceania. The smaller number in North America compared with Japan and

Europe is connected with the smaller farm size in the latter areas: smaller farms are, like the large American ones, completely mechanized, but the machines are smaller.

The former Soviet Union had hardly half the level of tractor coverage of the US in 1990. Among the former socialist countries, the numbers per thousand hectares were: for Hungary 9.3 tractors and 1.9 harvester-threshers; East Germany 35 and 6.5; Czechoslovakia 27 and 4; and Bulgaria 12.8 and 1.9. It should be pointed out that the large farms in these countries tended to use high power machines. Since 1989 the level of equipment in many European former socialist countries has declined due to falling replacement and investment.

Tractors are relatively plentiful in the planned, i.e. socialist economies of the Far East compared with the regional average, with the greatest weight being carried by China's figure of 8.6 per 1000 hectares.

Environmental damage

The environmental conditions required for agriculture are in many respects endangered by human activities. Industry and transport are sources of emissions which among other things cause acid rain and destruction of trees. Factories giving out soot and CO_2 not only pollute the air and the water, but also contribute to reduced sunlight, the greenhouse effect, warming of rivers, seas and the climate. Agriculture itself can damage the environment. Transport and draught machines, for example, emit pollutants just as their counterparts in other industries.

The harmful environmental effects caused by, and felt by, agriculture include some that are unique to it. Of these, the most important are the following (Brown, 1987, and Our Common Future, 1987):

1. *Soil erosion and loss of cultivable soils* by inappropriate soil management and utilization. The soil nutrients and water-holding capacity falls, the soil thins and all these reduce the soils' productivity. The eroded topsoil makes its way into rivers and waterways, silts up ports and navigation channels, reduces water containment capacity, and increases both the danger and severity of floods.

According to the FAO studies, the developing countries of Asia, Africa and Latin America will see a fall in their non-irrigated cultivated area of about 550 million hectares in the coming years, if appropriate soil protection measures are not taken. Of India's cultivated land, for example, about 30 per cent is affected by soil erosion. In the former Soviet Union the arable land was increased by nearly a fifth by clearing the virgin land of Kazakhstan. But with the erosion of the soil, production is in continuous decline and most of the land is already barely considered cultivable.

156

The situation is similar in China, where Mao Zedung's slogan 'Grow more grain!' led to its being attempted on the ecologically unsuited western steppe country. Since then, the grain growing area has contracted by about 10 per cent, from 98 million hectares in 1976 to 88 million in 1986.

The high agricultural prices in 1972-74 encouraged USA farmers to grow cereals in the western Great Plain's dry and fragile grazing land, which is exposed to severe soil erosion. In the late 1970s almost as much arable land was lost as in the 1930s. Wind and water erosion affected one third of American arable land, most seriously the agricultural areas of the Mid-West. There, droughts periodically endanger production.

2. *Badly planned and built irrigation systems* lead to formation of swamps, alkilinization and salination. According to FAO and UNESCO estimates, half the world's irrigated areas are affected by these problems and cultivation will have to stop on 10 million irrigated hectares.

3. *Excess fertilizer and pesticide* seriously pollute the environment. The residues of protractedly used chemicals build up in soils and waterways, harmful agents also getting into the air and into food.

Overuse of nitrate fertilizer causes nitration of drinking water. In Hungary, a large proportion of water in rural wells and aquifers contains enough nitrate to cause death if regularly consumed by a child of less than 12 months . Pesticides upset the biological balance. Many species of birds have been lost and insects which kill pests have also largely been destroyed. The number of insecticide-resistant species of pests, however, is rising all over the world, at the same time as their natural predators are being killed off. The number of different types of pests has also multiplied. Fish stocks have been destroyed by water pollution.

It should be noted, however, that careful use of fertilizer and chemicals in appropriate quantities is not harmful and raises agricultural production. It is therefore still desirable to raise the amounts used in many developing countries from their current low levels.

4. *Destruction of forests*. The tropical rainforests once covered 1.5-1.6 billion hectares. Their current area is only 900 million hectares. Annually 10 million hectares are cleared. By the end of the century, little will remain of the rainforests of the Congo basin and the Amazon. In the latter, the forest area is mainly turned to grazing, and the weak soil rapidly deteriorates.

Forests are cleared for new cultivation, grazing, to extract wood and fuel, and to build roads and cities. The process takes place worldwide, but on the greatest scale in the developing countries and in tropical forests. Weak tropical soil used for arable or grazing purposes quickly erodes and deteriorates. Along with the forest itself, the recycling effect on precipitation is lost. Rainforests hold the rain and cause more rain after re-evaporation. Greater areas than those cleared are thus dried out. Reduced rainfall is experienced in areas well beyond the rainforests. If the rain forest is in the area of a watershed, then its destruction allows water to flow away freely and raises the danger of flooding. This is the cause of the increasing number of floods, like those experienced in India and Pakistan in recent decades.

The rainforests are being cleared at different rates in different parts of the world. There have been, and still are, forecasts predicting the disappearance of a major proportion of the rainforest by the turn of the century. The FAO (Agriculture: Toward 2000, 1981) is more optimistic. It puts the likely proportion of cleared forest, based on rates of loss of the 1970s, at 12 per cent between 1980 and 2000.

Compared to the debate about the rainforests, less talked about is the fate of temperate zone forests. It is true that cutting down the rainforests is much more spectacular and causes greater harm, but the clearing of the temperate forests is also a danger to the environment. It leaves the area defenceless to pollution, reduces precipitation and contributes to climatic change. The rapid clearing of the Buda forests in Hungary, for example, which was partly due to the zoning of the land for housing and partly to wasteful forest management, threatens to take away the last air filtering and oxygen-producing green belt from around Budapest, which is already choking from exhaust fumes and other pollutants.

5. _Extinction of species and races._ Wild species and races are a vitally important resource for a host of different aims. They are used in improving domesticated plant and animal strains in order to rectify defects and degeneration, increase yields and strengthen resistance. Half of today's drugs originated from wild organisms. Industry also profits from them: rubber, vegetable oils and fats, resins, pigments, tannin, insecticide and many other raw materials are obtained from wild plants. Derivatives of wild oilseeds are involved in the production of detergents, hardeners and foods. There are grounds for saying that the 'green revolution' is giving way to the 'genetic revolution' which will look to wild species and types as sources of genetic material. But the number of species and races is rapidly decreasing. With production concentrated on a few highly improved strains, the genetic variety of species and races of many cultivated plants and domesticated animals has been lost. Today's genetic pool of rice and maize, for example, is a fraction of what it was a few decades ago.

Estimates put the natural rate of extinction over the last 2000 years to be 900,000 species per million years, or less than one per year. The current rate, set by man, is hundreds or even thousands of times higher.

A significant contribution to this rate of extinction is the destruction of tropical and temperate forest. At least half of rainforest species are unique to their locality.

The shrinking pool of species and races endangers further work on cross-breeding. Existing varieties might degenerate if there is no possibility of crossbreeding them. It also reduces their chances of adapting to environmental and climatic changes.

Mexican botanists working on maize improvement recently discovered a perennial type and a protein-rich type. The first could save on ploughing and planting, the other could lead to a type of corn which may allow more protein to be available in Africa, where for the people of many countries, maize is the staple food. This could be the start of the maize green revolution. Without wild species, such improvements would be impossible.

The FAO, UNESCO and other international organizations, with assistance from governments and scientific institutes, aim to set up biosphere reserve systems, gene banks and other projects to preserve the gene pool. Considering the scale and urgency of the task, however, their results so far have been minimal.

6. The advance of deserts is particularly threatening. About 29 per cent of the world's land area is undergoing desertification, with 6 per cent outright desert. In the mid-1980's, 850 million people lived in very dry areas, and 230 million of those in seriously desertified areas. Desert area is growing continuously by 6 million hectares per year. The danger exists in the largest scale in North America, Asia and Africa. Among developing countries, the advance of desert is felt most strongly in the natural geographical region of Sudan's Sahel belt, where 80 per cent of all people affected by desertification live.

Desertification is a joint result of climatic change and human intervention. Clearing forests, inappropriate arable and pastoral use, and overgrazing all speed up the encroachment of the desert. In Sudan's Sahel region, for example, the traditional pasture and cultivation can support 15 persons per square kilometre. The actual number trying to survive there is 20 per square kilometre. Nowadays the forests are completely cleared for firewood and to provide arable land, whereas the old practice of leaving part of it protected the soil. Fallowing time is shorter and shorter and permanent cultivation is more and more common without sufficient fertilization. Thus the soil cannot regenerate sufficiently. More and more soil is losing its natural fertility, forcing the population to move further and further south (The Sahel Facing the Future, 1988).

7 Social and economic conditions of production

Agricultural population and workforce

In 7000-6000 BC, there were probably about 5-20 million people on Earth. By the time of Christ the number had grown to 160-250 million, and by 1600 barely 500 million, during which time wars and plagues routinely took their toll. The 14th century plague killed 25 million people in Europe alone, one third of its population. But between 1700 and 1850, the world's population went up from 600 to 1,200 million, so that the doubling time, having been 500-600 years at the time of Christ, was now only 150 years. It doubled again by 1950 to 2,500 million (Baade, 1964). In 1980, the world's population was 4.4 billion, in 1991 5.4 billion. A 3 per cent annual rate of increase implies doubling in 24 years, a 2 per cent rate 36 years.

With such a scale of population growth, the urgent question arises as to whether food production can rise at the same rate, or more simply, will there be enough food for all the new people?

Theories of population growth

T.R. Malthus (Malthus, 1933) answered the question with a definite 'no'. In 1798 he stated his famous thesis that the number of people and animals grows geometrically, but the food supply only arithmetically. Balance between the two was maintained by the death rate. If the population grows faster than the available food, then famine occurs and the death rate rises, whereas if the food supply improves, the death rate falls, and so population growth accelerates again. Periodic wars and epidemics also contribute to the death rate.

Malthus's theoretical conclusions fitted the facts of his time and before. The birth rate at that time was more than 4 per cent, about equal to the death rate. At the time of Christ there were about 6 million babies born in the world

160

annually, of which 3 million survived. Agriculture developed very slowly over the centuries. In Ireland there was widespread famine even in 1845. Malthus did not notice, however, that large-scale changes were taking place even in his own time. These were leading on one hand to the unprecedented increase in food supply, and on the other to lower birth and death rates in the industrialized countries.

In industrially backward regions the changes only occurred partially. The rise in food supply remained slow. The birth rate did not fall or hardly fell. In the middle of this century, however, developments in health care and the prevention of epidemics significantly reduced mortality. The result was a squeezing of the per capita food supply, culminating in the food crisis of 1972-74.

Its effect promoted neo-Malthusian theories claiming that it was also true for our own time that food supply could not keep step with population growth. They pointed to the decimation of people by starvation and of animals, as on the overgrazed Sahel, by lack of pasture.

According to the 'demographic transition model' (Stevens and Jabara, 1988), rapid population growth is only a transitional stage. Population growth in the developing countries will fall to the level now current in developed countries by the next century. This will happen through rising per capita income, urbanization, spread of family planning and the acceptance that, when the death rate is lower, less children are needed to be born for the desired number to survive. (The latter factor is important for labour-intensive family farms, where labour is provided by farm members. Hence the failure of China's centrally-planned population reduction measures, despite their carrying the threat of punitive taxes.)

The demographic transition model appears to be borne out by the data in table 7.1.

Table 7.1 shows that in the last few years, the population growth in developing countries, outwith black Africa, has reduced. Of course the averages conceal considerable variations, with population in Arab countries, for example, actually rising faster.

Malthusian and neomalthusian theories are widely repudiated, among others by Marxist thinkers. Their main argument is that there is no reason why the rates of growth achieved by agriculture in the 19th and 20th centuries should not continue in the future. The developed countries' agriculture could already provide enough food, they say, to supply the whole world. In backward countries, the limits to production are not natural, just social and economic. Before backwardness is overcome and faster economic development gets under way, considerable benefits could result from institutional reforms (from the Marxist viewpoint, revolutionary changes) bringing with them more equitable distribution. Thus everyone could have bread, even if not much of it.

Population growth could also be expected to slow down through the rise in wealth and standard of living.

Table 7.1
Average annual growth of population*
(per cent)

Country groups	1965-80	1980-90	1989-2000 (projection)
Low and middle countries	2.3	2.0	1.9
Sub-Saharan Africa	2.7	3.1	3.0
East Asia and Pacific	2.2	1.6	1.4
South Asia	2.4	2.2	1.8
Europe	1.1	0.1	0.8
Middle East and North Africa	2.8	3.1	2.9
Latin America and Caribbean	2.5	2.1	1.8
Other	1.0	0.9	0.7
High income countries	0.9	0.6	0.5
OECD members	0.8	0.6	0.5
Other	2.5	1.8	1.4

* Weighted average

Source: World development report, 1992.

One anti-Malthusian theory is represented by the Danish researcher Ester Boserup's agricultural development theory (Boserup, 1965, 1981, 1990). Her view is that it was population growth itself which forced agriculture to become intensive, raise yields and thus provide food to the rising number of people. In Northern Europe, according to her view, rising population set off the change from hunting and gathering to pasture and long cultivation. It forced fallowing to become shorter and shorter, and firstly change from long fallow to bush-fallow, then to short-fallow and the three-field rotation system, and finally to permanent crop rotation.

In Scandinavia, shifting agriculture by slashing and burning the forest was still the norm in the 19th century, and in the rest of Europe, annual harvest only became standard in the 18th century. Pasturing took hold when the fallow was too short for the forest to regrow, and the area became grassland. With land increasingly turned over to the three-field system and later permanent crop rotation, grazing was confined to fallow land, or the latter was alternated with fodder growing.

The developing countries followed a similar pattern, which is still going on, according to Boserup. One of the signs of the technical developments responding to rising population is the green revolution. In Africa, her view is that in the near future it will not be by higher yields, as in Asia, but by extending cultivation to greater areas, shorter fallow and conversion to crop rotation, that agriculture will develop, because of the wider availability of land.

Boserup questions the view of many (see, e.g., Grigg, 1974) that primitive so-called traditional cultivation and pasturing (nomadism) is what the climate and soils of the relevant areas are best suited to, and that more intensive cultivation would lead to rapid deterioration. Her view is that tropical and subtropical African soils could also withstand more intensive cultivation.

Boserup's theory of population-induced technical development is true in many respects. In pre-industrial societies, population growth undoubtedly played an important part in the conversion to more intensive cultivation. But not the exclusive part that she attributes to it.

In the cradle of European culture, the Mediterranean region, for example, sea trade and the continuous wars most probably were among the factors affecting agricultural development. Both increased the demand for agricultural products and both called for development of the science and technology of the time which were in turn absorbed by agriculture (e.g. wheels and iron tools).

Another characteristic example is the ancient irrigated farming system along the Nile and in Mesopotamia, China and India. Population growth may have been the stimulus for irrigation itself. For most of the growing season in dry climatic regions there was no other way to increase production. Development of the technique of irrigation, however, in turn affected agricultural growth. It is no coincidence that in irrigation societies – Indian, Chinese and Arab – science reached such a high level, particularly in mathematics, physics and astronomy. All of these were necessary to develop irrigation works, which brought with it technical progress in agriculture too. Similarly to the Mediterranean countries, these people turned to ploughing, crop rotation, row sowing, cross ploughing, terracing and improvement of strains of plants and animals.

In industrial societies, the effect of general and technical development gives a still greater impetus to agricultural development than in traditional societies. Partly scientific and technical developments induced by economic development (Hayami and Ruttan, 1985) including equipment and materials of industrial origin used in agriculture, partly the growing demand for agricultural produces from sectors outside agriculture stimulate agricultural growth.

In recent times, less developed countries have not remained untouched by these processes. Nowadays the different parts of the world interact closely with each other. First colonization, then the economic ties of neocolonialism, and also foreign trade, capital inflow, scientific and technical transfer, the rise of state involvement in controlling and organizing the economy and many other factors, have played a role in agricultural development in less developed regions. In many parts, industrialization is already under way, as is urbanization, and along with them the need for imports and exports. Rising money incomes and demand encourage agricultural production, just as much as, if not more than, population growth. Modern technology is brought in for export crops, and sooner or later, depending on general development, is carried over to domestic food production, just as experiences of many industrializing countries of North Africa, Asia and Latin America testify.

The above does not deny the fact that population density in many ways influences the intensity of agriculture, including the yield per unit area. Where population is sparse, so that there is a relatively large amount of land per inhabitant, or per agricultural worker, the yields are generally lower. This statement is mostly valid for countries more or less on the same development level, because it is the economic and agricultural technical development which above all determines agricultural production. If we disregard the relevant factors like climate, soil, relief, distance from domestic and export markets etc., we find that yields show a clearly positive relation not only with economic development, i.e. per capita national product of respective country groups, but also with their population density (see table 7.2 and figure 7.1).

The obvious reason for the latter is that where land is plentiful, production can be raised more cheaply by widening use of land than by increasing yields. On unit land area, with given technology and above a certain yield, diminishing returns have to be contended with. Thus yields grow more slowly than the costs of attaining them. Increasing land area, however, if the quality is uniform, does not meet with diminishing returns. Land is usually cheaper in countries with a lot of it than in densely populated countries, and so the relative price of yield-increasing means like fertilizer is more expensive than that of land. This is another incentive to increase the land used. Inhabitants of densely populated countries are not only constrained to increase yields if they want more agricultural production, but have the incentive that fertilizer is relatively cheaper than land.

164

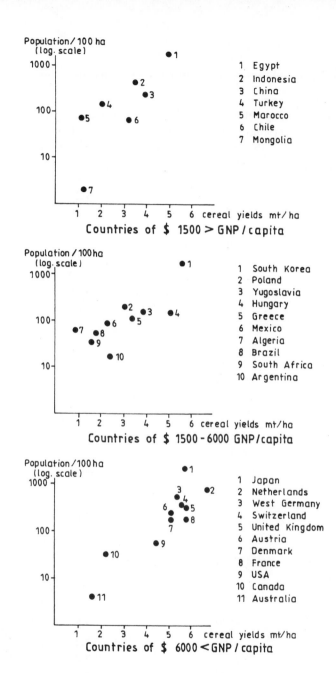

Figure 7.1   The connection between population density and yields

165

Table 7.2
Effect of level of development and population density on yields

Countries according to GNP per capita (1987)	Population per 100 ha agricultural land (1988)	Average cereal yields tonnes / ha (1986-88)
GNP per capita < $1,500		
Mongolia	2[a]	1.3[b]
Chile	71[a]	3.2[b]
Morocco	77[a]	1.1[b]
Turkey	149	2.1[b]
China	266	4.0
India	439	1.7
Indonesia	506[a]	3.5[b]
Philippines	615[a]	1.9[b]
Egypt	2,009	5.0
$1,500-6,000		
Argentina	18	2.4
South Africa	36	1.6[b]
Brazil	58	1.9
Algeria	63	0.9[b]
Mexico	83	2.2
Greece	109	3.4
Hungary	163	5.1
Yugoslavia	167	3.9
Luxembourg	201	3.1
Portugal	314	1.6
South Korea	1,868[a]	5.6[b]
Above $6,000		
Australia	4	1.6
Canada	33	2.2
United States	57	4.4
Spain	127	2.6
France	179	5.8
Denmark	184	5.1
Austria	218	5.2
United Kingdom	308	5.7
Switzerland	326	5.6

Table 7.2 contd.

Countries according to GNP per capita (1987)	Population per 100 ha agricultural land (1988)	Average cereal yields tonnes / ha (1986-88)
Above $6,000		
West Germany	515	5.4
Holland	734	6.7
Japan	2306	5.7

a 1986
b Average for 1985-87

Source: *Nemzetközi Statisztikai Évkönyv (International Statistical
           Yearbook), 1989, KSH, Budapest
           Nemzetközi Statisztikai Zsebkönyv (International Statistical
           Handbook), 1991, KSH, Budapest
           FAO Production Yearbook, 1988, Rome*

Agricultural population and rural population

Whatever the role of population in agricultural development, it is undeniable that economic growth is accompanied by a fall in the agricultural population, as shown by tables 1.3 and 7.3. It is quite clear that the more developed the countries and regions, the smaller the proportion of those working on the land, with the proportion everywhere falling as that of industrial and service employees rises. (It should be pointed out that more people work in agriculture in developed countries than are included in statistics, since assistance from family members is not generally accounted for. Since family farms are based on nearly equal work of husbands and wives, if the wife is not registered the recorded workforce in this category is halved.)

The decline of the agricultural workforce is usually characterised by physical migration away from agriculture, from village to town. This migration, however, was a much stronger characteristic of the past, in what are now developed countries, that it is anywhere today. This type of migration is still important in developing countries today, but even there it is not exclusive. There is significant temporary migration to and from agricultural work, chiefly in Africa. And in the developed countries more people are moving back to rural areas than away from them. The important factor determining the distribution of employment between rural and urban areas in both sets of countries is development of rural industry and of services. The latter is more decisive in the developed countries, but is not insignificant in the less developed either.

Table 7.3
Agricultural employment as a percentage of total employed

Country group	1975	1991
Developed countries	15.5	8.0
North America	4.1	2.3
Europe	16.8	8.9
Oceania	8.1	5.5
Former USSR	22.8	12.4
Others	16.5	7.3
Developing countries	68.4	58.9
Africa	76.2	67.8
Latin America	36.2	25.6
Middle East	53.9	39.1
Far East	71.8	62.9
Others	67.4	53.9

Source: FAO Production Yearbook, 1992

In Asia, non-agricultural workers make up 20-30 per cent of the rural total, and in sub-Saharan Africa 10-20 per cent (Haggblade, Hazell and Brown, 1989). These proportions have shown a growing trend in the last 20 years. Between 7 and 30 per cent of the total number of rural workers are those agricultural workers who are also engaged on a seasonal or part-time secondary activity in rural industry or services. People employed in agriculture in the various African countries, anywhere between 15 and 65 per cent have secondary, non-agricultural work. Families spend 15-40 per cent of their working time on this activity and derive 25 to 30 per cent of their total income and 30 to 50 per cent of their money income from it. The rural industrial and service activities are: food preparation and processing, catering, bakery, oil pressing, tea, coffee and cocoa drying and pre-processing, packaging, repairing, smithing, basket work, sawmills, mines, ceramics, woodcarving, weaving, tailoring and sewing, trade and others. Women in Africa, and even more so in Asian and Islamic countries, work in informal areas and housekeeping – and in Africa trade too – men, on the other hand work in small businesses and occasionally in companies. Rural companies are mainly concerned with processing and trade of export goods. Temporary migration to urban or rural work and to mines and plantations etc. is common among men, especially in Africa (Dickenson et al, 1985). Migration may be periodical or seasonal, but can also last for many years. The typical temporary migration arrangement is for the family to remain in its permanent village home where the women do the agricultural and other work – producing food for the family is the women's task in Africa anyway – while the men send some of their income home, and return themselves from time to time.

In the agricultural areas of developed countries, the bulk of the population is no longer made up of the mostly full-time farmers it once was. The greatly reduced numbers working on the land did so increasingly on a part-time basis, with their main jobs in industry or services (Burger, 1989; Burger, Keszthelyiné, Salamin, 1990; Schmitt, 1989; Pfeffer, 1989). More than half the farms in the US, Austria, Norway and Switzerland and most of those in Italy and Greece are part-time (Alexandratos, 1990). In the EC as a whole, only 23 per cent of agricultural workers are full-time (Eurostat, 1992), and the proportion is even lower in Japan.

The large proportion of part-time farmers indicates that the countryside can now offer enough work outside agriculture to obviate the need for migration to the town.

The move towards the countryside by industry and services began in the US and Western European countries in the 1950s and 60s. The reasons were diverse. Above all, a good business and residential infrastructure in rural areas (roads, transport, telecommunications, trade chain, schools, health care etc.) was already in place. Companies were attracted by the lower cost of labour than in towns and the lower property prices and rents. It was more worthwhile pursuing the desires of a growing economy in new rural areas than in the ever-more crowded and expensive cities. The growing of the rural population and the demands of the new firms attracted new services too. Later the information and computer services also showed an inclination to move to the countryside.

Population began to drift away from the cities, partly to the surrounding areas. In the 1960s and 70s the net migration in the direction of the countryside was higher than in the direction of urban areas (Gilg, 1985). Green belts appeared around the cities. Residents moved out of the city for better air, more pleasant surroundings and cheaper property. Businesses and services moved in their wake. Big stores moved to make use of bigger areas and more parking space. In the USA, some city centres have been rendered 'dead' by this movement.

People moved even further into the countryside for the lower cost of living and even lower property prices than those of the city outskirts and to enjoy the better climate (especially retired people). This also had the effect of making the population of the old agricultural areas increasingly heterogeneous.

Vertical integration

Employment in agriculture, although falling, is supplemented by employment in related activities. If we take into account not only the production of the raw material, but its processing and trade and indeed the materials and equipment indispensable to agriculture and their trade, then we find that agricultural production as a whole takes up rather more of the national economy than we might have thought.

For example, in the USA the food and agricultural raw material system, together with upward and downward complementary sectors, accounted for 17.5 per cent of national product in 1985, compared with 1.8 per cent by the farm sector. In 1986 one quarter of the US counties were classified as agrobusiness counties where farming and farm industries employed a third or more of the labour force (Gale and Harrington, 1993). In the EC 12 countries, 10 million worked in agriculture, 4 million in food processing and 10 million in food distribution and services (Alexandratos, 1990). Table 7.4 shows that although there are significant differences between the countries, depending on development and the importance of agriculture and agricultural industry, the food industry's output is generally approached or exceeded that of agriculture.

According to table 7.5, agricultural processing also plays an important role in the former CMEA countries. Its share of total industrial production is in the range 12 to 23 per cent, and in the more developed former CMEA countries, the number it employs is equal to about two-thirds of the total agricultural sector workforce; in the less developed, one half or one quarter. In Hungary, which was the most important agricultural country in the region, it played a role of corresponding weight (Benet, 1979).

The mutual substitution of land, labour and means of production in raising productivity of land, from the aspect of economic theory

We will now examine theoretically what the preceding chapters said about the necessary growth of intensity connected with population growth and the development of agricultural technology.

As population grows, so the land per agricultural worker diminishes, forest fallow gives way to bush fallow, and subsequently to the three-field system and permanent crop rotation. Intensification begins, with slash and burn cultivation. At this stage, almost the only way of reducing the fallow and increasing the area cultivated every year is the application of more labour supplied by a rising population. The intensity grows rapidly at first, which is to say that the work of the rising workforce substitutes for more and more land. The more intensive the production becomes, however, the less effective the substitution that can be achieved simply by more workers and more effort.

170

Table 7.4
Percentage rates of national gross added value of the agro-food industry in the European Community economies at 1985 market prices

Country	Agriculture[a]	Processing industry[b]
Belgium	2.4	4.1
Denmark	5.5	4.2
Germany, FR	1.8	3.7
France	4.2	3.4
Italy	4.6	2.6
Netherlands	4.5	3.5
United Kingdom	1.5	4.8
Total EC-7	3.1	3.7
Greece	17.1	3.9
Ireland[c]	10.9	7.5
Luxembourg	2.9	3.0
Portugal[d]	8.1	6.3
Spain	6.3	5.1

[a] = agriculture, forestry and fisheries
[b] = food, beverages and tobacco
[c] = 1980
[d] = 1983

Source: Alexandratos, 1990

Table 7.5
Percentage share of food processing industry in 1985

Country	Of total industry[a]	Of employment[b]
Bulgaria	23.2	10.6
Czechoslovakia	14.2	7.8
Germany, DR	15.5	7.5
Hungary	14.4	12.8
Poland	20.5	9.2
Romania	11.7	6.3
Soviet Union	16.7	..

[a] = Not clear whether share of total production or value added
[b] = cooperative and state

Source: Alexandratos, 1990 and from CMEA data.

Let us look at an example.

Assume that in the beginning of shifting cultivation, each producer had 40 hectares, taking fallow land into account, this area getting steadily smaller as the fallow is shortened. The total production is 20,000 kg of grain which is produced on less and less area with more and more producers. The yield per unit area increases with the higher intensity of production but the production per producer falls because of rising numbers (see table 7.6 and figure 7.2). If we divide the decrement of one factor by the increment of the other, i.e. the marginal costs, then we find to what extent the rise of one factor substitutes the fall of the other. In the example one more worker can substitute for the loss of 15 hectares at the beginning, but as the land diminishes, one extra can substitute for less and less land and the corresponding production, until there is no increment in produce from employing more labour.

The optimal rate of substitution is between cases 6 and 7, because until this point one more worker can substitute for more than one hectare. After case 7, a falling fraction of one hectare is all that one producer can substitute for, so that product per producer increases less and less, until the increase reaches zero between cases 10 and 11, i.e. the marginal productivity of the final producer is zero.

This means that product per producer cannot grow further simply through more workpower and new techniques and technology must be introduced to make further progress. It is time to turn to crop rotation and the plough. More developed tools and equipment are called for, and the land must be fertilized. One necessary item for acquiring materials and equipment – especially if we are thinking about modern agriculture, even in backward areas – is money. Thus at least some of the produce must be sold: agriculture must go beyond subsistence and produce commodities.

In the example of table 7.7 and figure 7.3, we examine how far it is worthwhile raising yields at given prices of produce, fertilizer, pesticide, tools and machinery, and at a given level of technology, so that the increase in costs does not exceed the rise in value of production (Burger, 1983).

In the case shown in table 7.7, the least-cost optimum is where yields are between 2,000 and 2,500 kg/ha, since there the marginal value of produce is equal to the marginal cost of production. Before this point it is still worth increasing expenditure, because it grows less fast than the value of the production. Beyond 2,500 kg/ha, a lower value of production results from the corresponding increase in expenditure. The income maximum is at a yield of 2,500 kg/ha (the distance A-A' on figure 7.3) and falls from there on, becoming negative beyond the point where value of product equals production cost (point B). Setting the price at $120/t instead of $100/t shifts point B to point C.

172

Table 7.6
Substitution of land by labour
in the case of 20,000 kg/year total grain production

Case	Land x_1	Reduction of land area Δx_1	Number of producers x_2	Rise in no of workers Δx_2	$\dfrac{\Delta x_1}{\Delta x_2}$ Substitution ratio
1	40		1		
		-15		1	$-\dfrac{15}{1} = -15$
2	25		2		
		-10		1	$-\dfrac{10}{1} = -10$
3	15		3		
		-4		1	$-\dfrac{4}{1} = -4$
4	11		4		
		-3		1	$-\dfrac{3}{1} = -3$
5	8		5		
		-2		1	$-\dfrac{2}{1} = -2$
6	6		6		
		-1		1	$-\dfrac{1}{1} = -1$
7	5		7		
		-0.5		1	$-\dfrac{0.5}{1} = -0.5$
8	4.5		8		
		-0.3		1	$-\dfrac{0.3}{1} = -0.3$
9	4.2		9		
		-0.1		1	$-\dfrac{0.1}{1} = -0.1$
10	4.1		10		
		0		1	$-\dfrac{0}{1} = -0$
11	4.1		11		

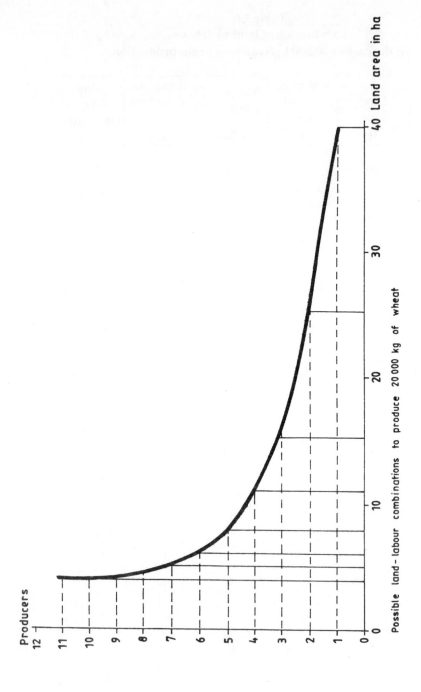

Figure 7.2   Substitution of labour for land

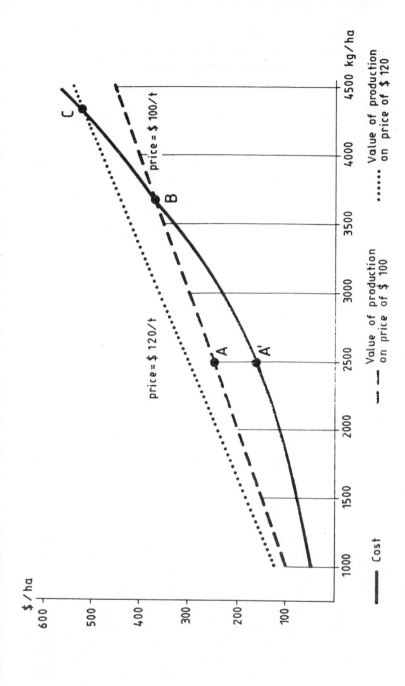

Figure 7.3   Value, cost and income of wheat production

Table 7.7
Values and costs of, and income from, producing wheat
Price of wheat = $100 per tonne

Kg wheat per hectare	Value of wheat $/ha a	Difference Δa	Costs for wheat $/ha b	Difference Δb	$\dfrac{\Delta a}{\Delta b}$	Income $/ha a-b	Difference
1000	100		50			50	
		50		25	$\dfrac{50}{25}=2$		+25
1500	150		75			75	
		50		35	$\dfrac{50}{35}=1.42$		+15
2000	200		110			90	
		50		50	$\dfrac{50}{50}=1$		0
2500	250		160			90	
		50		70	$\dfrac{50}{70}=0.71$		-20
3000	300		230			70	
		50		100	$\dfrac{50}{100}=0.5$		-50
3500	350		330			20	
		20		40	$\dfrac{20}{40}=0.5$		-20
3700	370		370			0	
		30		70	$\dfrac{30}{70}=0.43$		-40
4000	400		440			-40	

In principle, it would be possible to raise yields indefinitely if the value of produce minus cost rose at the same rate as the yields. This is not possible in practice, however. If conditions do not change, sooner or later the law of diminishing returns sets in, i.e. more expenditure is required for the same rise in yields, or the increase in produce is less than the increment of cost. At first costs increase less than yields, but later the two become equal and beyond a point the extra production is of lower value than the extra cost of producing it. This is especially true for agriculture, where the opportunity for applying the same combination of the factors of production for increasing produce is much less than in other industries, and so some of them can make a bottleneck for growth. There is little chance to open up new land, and in a rapidly growing economy, far from rising, the workforce is actually falling. Only in technique and technology is there scope for development. But the main function of new techniques is to substitute for labour and land, not just to increase yields. More modern technology, lower costs or higher producer prices tend to shift out the limit at which increase in returns start to fall and if opposite events occur, shift it back.

As well as costs, yields also depend on the natural fertility of the land. According to the Ricardian theory of land rent, the same expenditure on land of different quality results in different income (rent) and the same yields involve different costs. Better land not only yields more for the same expenditure, but a bigger increment in yield from an equal rise in expenditure. This causes rents to be higher than on worse lands, hence differential rents on land.

This can be illustrated by another example (table 7.8 and figure 7.4). From table 7.8, it can be seen that with $50 cost the less good land produces 1,000 kg wheat per hectare, the better land 2,000 kg. Expenses rose more slowly on the better land up to the optimal combination of production and cost. The optimum is also at a higher level: between 3,500 and 4,000 kg/ha as against 2,000-2,500 kg/ha. Production becomes loss making between 5,000 and 5,300 kg/ha yields compared with 3,500 and 3,700 on the worse land (see point G on figure 7.4). Income at the optimum is $240/ha (F-E on figure 7.4) compared with $90/ha (D-C), i.e. the differential rent at this cost level is $150.

Finally let us examine how far it is worth substituting new land by using more means of production to increase yields on a given area. We have already mentioned that in sparsely populated areas, where land is cheap, it is more worthwhile to bring new land under cultivation than increasing costs on the same piece of land to increase yields. And where the area is more densely populated, and land is expensive, farmers are not only constrained to increase yields, but find it more economic because of the price ratios mentioned above. The question is, how far is it worth substituting land with, say, fertilizer?

In our example in table 7.9, it is desired to produce 25 tonnes of wheat. The annual rent of one hectare is $25 and 100 kg of fertilizer costs $5. To grow the 25 tonnes on 10 hectares, we must produce 2.5 tonnes on each hectare. This requires 100 kg of fertilizer per year. The less land we use, the more fertilizer we have to apply for the same output. Beyond a certain point, the increase in fertilizer needed per hectare is greater than the land that is saved, indicating the onset of the law of increasing relative costs, i.e. greater cost is needed for the same yield on less land.

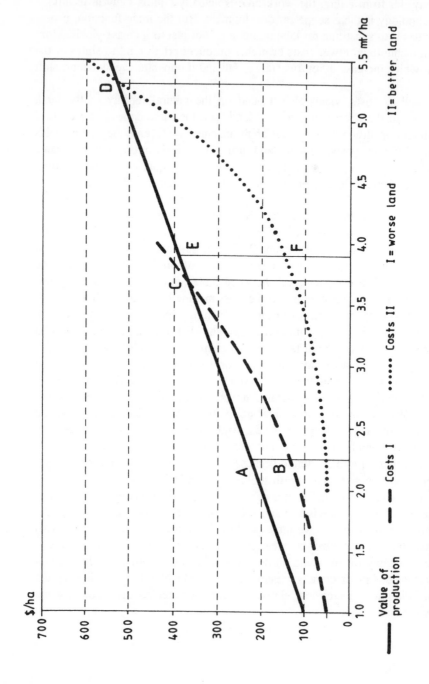

Figure 7.4   Differential rent

Table 7.8
Value and costs of, and income from, producing wheat on better land
Price of wheat = $100 per tonne

Kg wheat per hectare	Value of wheat $/ha a	Difference Δa	Costs for wheat $/ha b	Difference Δb	$\dfrac{\Delta a}{\Delta b}$	Income $/ha $a-b$	Difference
2000	200		50			150	
		50		10	$\dfrac{50}{10}=5$		40
2500	250		60			190	
		50		20	$\dfrac{50}{20}=2.5$		30
3000	300		80			220	
		50		30	$\dfrac{50}{30}=1.67$		20
3500	350		110			240	
		50		50	$\dfrac{50}{50}=1$		0
4000	400		160			240	
		50		90	$\dfrac{50}{90}=0.56$		-40
4500	450		250			200	
		50		150	$\dfrac{50}{150}=0.33$		-100
5000	500		400			100	
		30		130	$\dfrac{30}{130}=0.23$		-100
5300	530		530			0	
		20		140	$\dfrac{20}{140}=0.14$		-120
5500	550		670			-120	

How far is it worth using more fertilizer in order to save on land? As long as, at given prices, more money is saved by reducing land used than is spent on fertilizer. This is the situation in table 7.9 and figure 7.5 between cases 1, 2 and 3. The rise in fertilizer costs becomes equal to the rent saving between cases 3 and 4. This is the point of least-cost optimum, beyond which the extra fertilizer has a higher cost than the saving on reduced land.

cultivated land ha

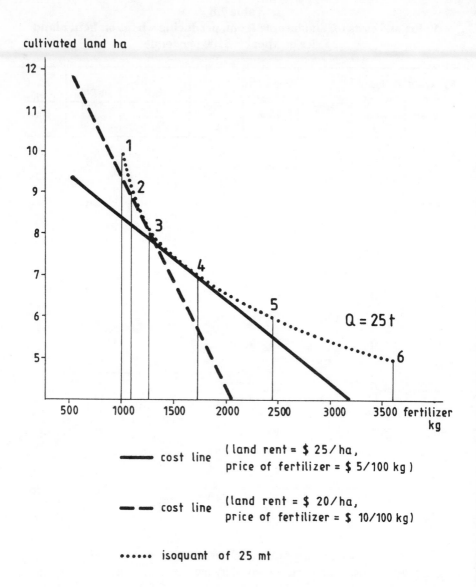

Figure 7.5   Substitution of fertilizer for land

180

Table 7.9
The rate of substitution of land and fertilizer
Annual rent of hectare land: $25
Price of 100kg fertilizer: $5
Total wheat production on the land: 25 tonnes

Cases	Cultivated land (ha) x_1	Rent of land ($) x_1	Reduction in rent charges Δx_1	Fertilizer doses (kg/ha)	Total fertilizer use (kg)	Fertilizer costs on land worked ($) x_2	Increase in fertilizer cost Δx_2	Rate of substitution $\dfrac{\Delta x_1}{\Delta x_2}$
1	10	250		100	1,000	50		
			-25				4	$-\dfrac{25}{4}=6.3$
2	9	225		120	1,080	54		
			-25				6	$-\dfrac{25}{6}=4.2$
3	8	200		150	1,200	60		
			-25				25	$-\dfrac{25}{25}=1.0$
4	7	175		243	1,701	85		
			-25				35	$-\dfrac{25}{35}=0.7$
5	6	150		400	2,400	120		
			-25				40	$-\dfrac{25}{40}=0.6$
6	5	125		720	3,600	180		

In our example it is rational to decrease the land from 10 to 7 hectares and to raise the doses of fertilizer till this point. If price relations change, the point of the least-cost optimum will be shifted. This is shown on figure 7.5, which presents an isoquant curve of 25 tonnes with the possible combinations of costs and cost lines representing different land rents and fertilizer prices. The least-cost combinations are at the tangency points of the isoquant curve and cost lines. This is shown on figure 7.5, in the first case between points 3 and 4 and in the second case between 2 and 3.

Part IV
THE GEOGRAPHICAL LOCATION OF AGRICULTURAL PRODUCTION

8 History of agricultural production

The known history of agriculture goes back about 10,000 years. Around 10,000 years ago, in the Neolithic Revolution, man in various parts of the earth turned from hunting, gathering and fishing to working the land and keeping animals. The indicating evidence of this changeover comes from archaeological findings, fossilized plant and seed remains, cave paintings, agricultural implements found during excavations, as well as comparative linguistics, and research into biology, botany, zoology and, most recently, genetics.

Scientific findings indicate that most domesticated plants and animals had already been brought into use by the second millennium BC. In the middle of the first millennium BC, every domestic crop and animal known today already existed; and all the implements which were basic to agriculture until the middle of the 19th century were in widespread use. Among these were the plough, the hoe, the digging stick, the sickle, the harrow, the axe and the sugarcane knife. Techniques like ox-drawing, fallowing, growing leguminous plants to regenerate the soil, natural fertilization, irrigation, water-lifting, canalization and many others were well established. Some archaeologists believe that the neolithic revolution first took its course in Asia Minor, and South-West Asia (Mándy 1972). This view is based on findings from the Jarmo region and other parts of Kurdistan, the valleys of the Zagros Mountains and the slopes of its foothills and plateaus. Wheat, barley, millet and lentils were found there. The neolithic revolution spread from here to the West, East and North. Moving north, it went first to the Balkans, and then to Middle and North Europe.

In north-east Eurasia, the crops of buckwheat, panic and millet may have originated independently.

In South and South-East Asia (mainly in the subtropical areas of India, China and Japan) greater panic, grain-amaranth, millet, soybeans, jute and cotton were grown. In China silkworms were also kept.

185

According to the archaeological findings, there were four initial centres of plant growing in America.

People migrated from north-east Asia across the frozen Bering straits to America at the end of the last ice age, around 20,000-15,000 BC, migration coming to a halt with the melting of the ice in 10,000 BC. Since they were nomads at the time of the migration, the people only started cultivating the land after the two continents had become isolated from each other. It is therefore likely that the crops they grew and the animals they tended originated in the New World.

In the course of excavations in the hilly region of the Gulf of Mexico's western shore, where the climate is mild an rainy, remains were found of calabash, winter squash, beans and maize. In the dry coastal part of Peru excavations also revealed squash, as well as cotton, various types of bean, berry and canna edulis. In North Columbia and Venezuela manioc, maize as well as stone mortars and cooking-plates were found. These provide evidence that the ancient people made flour. Another centre of domestication was in North America, in the Mississippi valley, where sunflowers, Jerusalem artichokes, goose-foot and amaranth were grown.

The ancient Indians did not have the plough or draught animals and did not make carts (It is probable that the newly arriving migrants killed off all the animals suitable for adapting when they were hunting, during which they burned the forests. At the same time people were beginning to build terraces and irrigate them in dry upland areas).

The prehistory of agriculture was given new impetus by N.I. Vavilov (1887-1942). He set forth his gene-centre theory in a book which appeared in 1926 entitled 'The centres of origin of cultivated plants' (Vavilov, 1928 and 1949-50). This says that domesticated plants emerged where the relevant plant genera or species can be found in the greatest diversity. Here the greatest frequency of the dominant features can be found, and similarly here are most non-mutated genes. The centre of origin is an area where, approaching the edges, the dominant features reduce in frequency and the recessive features appear.

The cultivated species did not stay confined to their areas of origin, but over the millennia diffused great distances. Sometimes, on reaching a distant region – perhaps a different continent – a certain plant species may diversify through time into a rich set of varieties. It may be crossed with related species, or some mutations (hereditarily changed individuals) might be selected in the course of cultivation and propagated. In this way new forms of species arise far from the original gene centre in a new place, called, where there is sufficient richness of new varieties, a secondary gene centre.

According to Vavilov, there were 8 primary centres, or 11 if sub-centres are counted, which were the birthplaces of cultivated plants. All of these, with the exception of the 8th (see table 8.1), lie between 20° and 40°N. Figure 8.1 shows the gene centres, table 8.1 the number of indigenous and cultivated plants in each gene centre, and the more important cultivated species.

Table 8.1
Places of origin of domesticated plants

Gene centre	Number of indigenous species	Number of cultivated species	Important cultivated species
1. China	136	26	millet, panic, soya, radish, cucumber
2. Indian and Burmese			
2a. Hindustani	117	34	rice
2b. Indo-Malay	55	13	sugar cane, banana
3. Central Asian	43	22	wheat, peas lentils, hemp, horse beans, onion, spinach, carrot, flax
4. Middle Eastern	83	27	wheat, barley, rye, oats, lentils, lucerne, vetch
5. Mediterranean	85	33	clovers, sugar beet, hops, lettuce, asparagus
6. Abyssinian	38	17	sorghum, sesame, coffee, castor-oil plant
7. South Mexican and Central American	unknown	23	maize, beans, peppers
8. South American	62	28	tobacco, cocoa
8a. Peru, Ecuador, Bolivia		19	tomatoes, tobacco
8b. Chile		2	potatoes
8c. Brazil		7	groundnuts

Source: Mándy, 1972

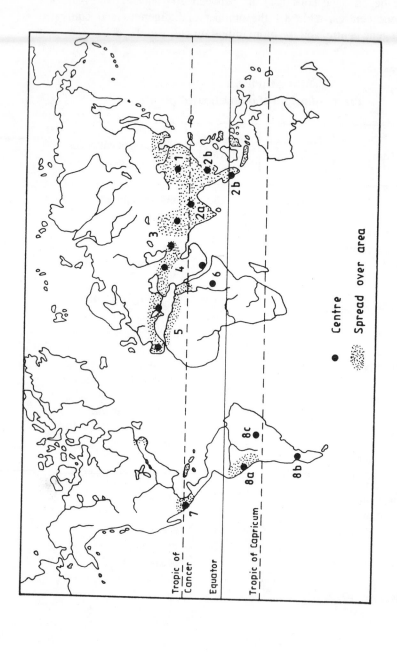

Figure 8.1   Gene centres of cultivated plants (after Vavilov)

Vavilov held that the wild plants from which today's crops derive could originally be found on only 10 per cent of the earth's surface, the plants on most of the planet being useless to man (see figure 8.2).

Grigg, using the work of Vavilov and other researchers, divided the prehistory of agriculture into seed-agriculture and primitive vegeculture, where plants reproduced by vegetative propagation (Grigg, 1974). Seed agriculture set the foundations of the world's major agricultural civilizations and was from ancient time bound up with draught animals and the use of the plough. Primitive vegeculture, however, established itself in tropical belts, in America, Africa and South-East Asia on the fringes of tropical forests and grasslands. The best known vegeculture is found in South-East Asia, which apart from the mainland and the Malay archipelago spread to Assam and South China. The oldest discovered archaeological remains of vegeculture have been found in Thailand and date from 9000 BC.

Vegeculture is usually practised with shifting, slash-and-burn cultivation, alongside the use of the area's perennial plants. The farmers plant roots of the plants, or their tubers among the plant remnants left on the ground after burning. They do not use the plough. The most important agricultural tools are the axe (to clear the vegetation of the forest or bush), the digging-stick and the hoe.

In South-East Asia the main plants cultivated by vegeculture were taro, greater yams and bananas, and among the trees they used were the breadfruit, sago palm, bamboo and coconut. In the vegeculture which developed in the tropical forests and fringes of the savannah of West Africa, indigenous species were yam and oil-palm. In the third centre of vegeculture, South America, the main types were manioc, sweet potato and arrow-root. Peoples engaged in vegeculture usually hunted and gathered too.

The oldest cereal-seed agriculture has been identified by Grigg as taking place in south-west Asia and South-East Asia. The plants and animals domesticated in south-west Asia spread eastward as far as India and westward to south Europe and northern Africa, and later to northern Europe.

It was around 3000 BC that two basic types of agriculture took form in south-west Asia and the eastern part of the Mediterranean. One of them was agriculture without irrigation, probably using shifting cultivation. Its main produce was wheat and barley, and of animals sheep, goats, cattle and pigs. Their implements were the ox-drawn wooden plough, the oxen also providing manure. The other main agricultural type came into being in the flood plains around the Nile and the Tigris and Euphrates. The crops and animals kept did not differ from those of the other type, but irrigation was required because of the extremely low rainfall. The rudimentary irrigation used in the beginning

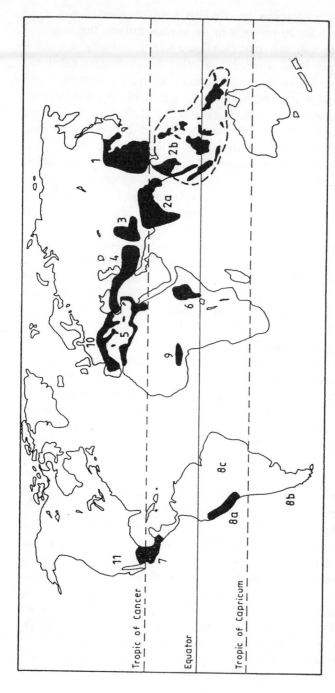

Figure 8.2   Main centres of domestication (after Vavilov and followers)
Source: Grigg, 1974

1 China, 2a India and Burma, 2b Indonesia and Malaysia, 3 Central Asia, 4 Near East, 5 Mediterranean, 6 Ethiopia, 7 South Mexico and Central America, 8a South America (Peru, Ecuador, Bolivia), 8b Chile, 8c Brazil and Paraguay, 9 West Africa, 10 Europe, 11 USA

gave way to water-lifting devices in the fourth millennium BC, embankments were built, canals dug and water was led to distant fields. The first millennium BC saw the appearance of the water wheel and the cerd.

The third society to use irrigation formed between the fifth and second millennia BC in Turkestan along the Kopet Dag and the rivers flowing north from the Hindu Kush. The crops and animals involved were similar to those above.

In Europe north of the Alps, the type of agriculture was that of south-west Asia. Wheat, barley, lentils, flax, vetch and peas came from the south, and millet was probably first cultivated in the Balkans. Oats and rye were indigenous to south-west Asia, but found much greater significance in northern Europe. As agriculture spread north, barley became more important than wheat, and cattle won out over sheep and goats. Wild pigs and bison were probably domesticated in northern Europe.

South-west Asian agriculture also spread to the east. There cotton was independently domesticated towards the end of the third millennium BC (most traces have been found along Indus and its tributaries) and in India sesame and rice were grown.

In northern China the first known farmers grew millet and kept pigs, probably practising shifting agriculture in the loess uplands of the Huangho, the Fenho and the Veiho in the sixth and fifth millennia BC. Wheat, barley, sheep, goats and cattle came here from south-west Asia, and the soya bean, the mulberry tree and pigs were domesticated in the area.

The seed agriculture of South-East Asia was probably mainly made up of rice production. Some historians think that rice was first grown by dry cultivation in the high lands of South-East Asia, and farmers occupied river valleys suitable for flooding in the fourth millennium BC. The earliest remains of wet-rice production are in Thailand, from about 3500 BC. From the swampy land of South-East Asia and the Philippines, rice spread to south China, the eastern part of India, and later south to the Malay archipelago.

Wet rice production in China came into being along the Huangho and its tributaries and along the Veiho and Fenho, and from there it spread to the Yangtse and south from there. Irrigation only became widespread in China from the first century BC.

In Africa there were probably two centres of agriculture south of the Sahara: the western part of the Sudan and the eastern part of Ethiopia. People living along the middle stretch of the Niger grew several indigenous plants, among them various varieties of millet. Between 6500 and 2500 BC, when there was more rain in the Sahara, pastoral nomads domesticated some varieties of millet and sorghum in some parts of it. In the eastern part of Africa, the pastoral tribes kept sheep, goats and cattle and grew some cereals.

The main crops on the American continent were maize, winter squash, beans, manioc, potato and peanuts. They probably also grew cotton, since wild cotton grows in the area. Crop rotation of maize, squash and beans was practised from the River Plate all the way to the Great Lakes.

Primitive vegeculture prevailed in South America, but in Central America and on the coastal parts of Peru sophisticated agricultural civilizations took shape. Corn growing began in Mexico during the sixth millennium BC and by 3000 BC beans, avocados, squash, chilli peppers and cotton were being grown. Tomatoes, peanuts and lima beans were all domesticated in South America. Villages appeared in the third millennium BC in which the inhabitants practised settled cultivation.

The agricultural systems grouped according to Grigg's scheme, which took shape across the world by the middle of the first millennium BC, were the following:

The South-West Asian system and its derivatives

Settled farmers mainly grew wheat, barley, flax, peas, beans and vetch. Among their animals were sheep, cattle, pigs and goats, as well as oxen for drawing their ploughs. The system was divided into four subsystems.

1. *Irrigated agriculture* in the Nile valley, along the Tigris and Euphrates, as well as in Turkestan and along the Indus. In Turkestan and along the lower reaches of the Indus, farmers grew, as well as south-west Asia's most important plants, cotton and rice.

2. *Agriculture without irrigation.* This was the largest sub-type of the south-west Asian system. In the course of the millennium, this succeeded in protecting the moisture content of the soil with the aid of fallowing and cross-ploughing.

3. *Mediterranean agriculture.* Here cereals were grown without irrigation along with fruit, figs, olives and grapes with intensive cultivation.

4. *North European agriculture.* Oats and rye were grown north from the Alps, in addition to the south-west Asian crops. Cattle and pigs featured more strongly than south of the Alps.

The South-East Asian system and its derivatives

This system was divided into two:

1. *Tropical vegeculture* Its most important crops were taro, greater yams, bananas and coconut. Farmers practised shifting cultivation, with the axe and the digging stick their main implements. Among the animals they kept were pigs and poultry.

2. *Wet-rice production.* Rice growing pushed out vegeculture from much of the region. The latter held its place only in interior areas remote from the coast, in high lands and mixed gardens. Vegeculture remained prevalent in Melanesia and Polynesia until the eighteenth and nineteenth centuries. Wet-rice production involved the use of the plough, which was drawn by cattle or buffalo. These techniques, along with the keeping of zebu, spread from South-East Asia to eastern India, southern China and Indonesia.

North China

Along with crops and animals taken from south-west Asia (wheat, barley, goats and cattle) local plants were brought into production: pigs, millet, soya beans and mulberry. The plough was in use by 500 BC. Rice was also produced, but it was not the main crop, and irrigation hardly featured.

Africa

Two subsystems evolved in Africa:

1. *Tropical vegeculture* at the border of the tropical forests and savannahs.

2. *Seed agriculture* in West Africa and the area of the present Ethiopia, which was largely practised through shifting cultivation. The most common types of cereal were sorghum and millet, but rice was also grown.

In the area of Ethiopia farmers were using the plough and fertilizing the soil by the first millennium BC. In the first millennium after Christ, the Kusita people to the south from here (in the area of today's Tanzania, Uganda and Kenya) built terraces, irrigated and used fertilizer. Agriculture was well developed between the 8th and 16th centuries in Sudan in the time of the great states of tribes' alliances (Ghana, Mali and Songai).

America

Here also, two subsystems can be identified:

1. *Tropical vegeculture*, whose main crops were manioc, sweet potato and colophony. It was probably due to the spread of tropical vegeculture that root and tuber culture on the high plains of the Andes and the area around Lake Titicaca developed, in which potatoes, oca, ulluco, quinoa and anu were grown.

2. *Maize-winter squash-beans rotation* was characteristic of a large part of the continent. But tomatoes, chilli peppers, avocados, cotton, agave, peanuts tobacco, papaya and artichokes were also grown.

The Incas practised sophisticated irrigated terrace cultivation, and harvested several times a year. The Aztecs' agriculture, in the Central Plateau of modern Mexico, also reached a high state of development, as did that of the Mayas in the peninsula of today's Yucatan. The plough was not used anywhere, however, and neither were there draught animals, and only the llama, the alpaca and the turkey were domesticated.

9 The regional division of today's agriculture

Agricultural production is distributed according to climate, rainfall, soil, land relief and natural vegetation. Climatic factors significantly affect the crops that can be grown and the animals that can be kept in a given area, but not exclusively. As we saw in the previous sections, each plant and animal originated in a particular area, and was originally raised where the climatic and rainfall conditions, and other environmental characteristics, were favourable for it. A significant proportion of plants and animals, however, spread far from their places of origin, as a result of man's selection, cross-breeding and general improvement of varieties, and thus adapted them to conditions differing from the original ones. One example of this is wheat, which have migrated from subtropical regions all the way to northern regions with their cold climates, and in many cases give better yields than in southern regions, but many other plants are examples of this, like peanuts, soya etc. which also originated in the south. Conversely, cold-resistant plants from temperate zones, like many temperate zone fruit species – among them the berries originally grown in northern regions – have been successfully naturalized in subtropical climates.

Crops' drought resistance can also be enhanced, and many crops originally bred for good soils can be adapted for weaker soils. The traditional techniques of selection and crossbreeding have been joined in recent decades by genetic engineering, by which it is possible to create and propagate permanent mutations and heritably modified variants.

The adaptation of animals can be taken even further, since their requirements can be met beyond what is available from the natural through stabling and providing fodder.

But apart from selection and adaptation of plants and animals to their new environment, the environment itself can be altered through man's efforts. The oldest form of this, and one which is still widespread, is the compensation for lack of rainfall through irrigation. There are many other ways of changing the . Among them are soil conservation, growing crops under glass or plastic in order to maintain the necessary temperature for plant growth and keep out pests, and many other techniques.

Interchanging of plants and animals has been much assisted by discovery of the New World and the upsurge in travelling between continents. It was not only people who migrated, but crops and animals too. Many Old World plants and animals were taken through time to America, Australia and New Zealand, and many others were taken back from there. Developments in transport accelerated the migration of plant and animal species.

The arrival in Europe and Asia the 16th century of the American crops of potatoes, maize, tobacco and tomatoes, and their subsequent naturalization, is well known. But the Europeans took many plants with them, both from their own countries (such as wheat, grapes and citrus fruits) and from Asia and Africa (such as sugar cane) to America, Australia and New Zealand and adapted them there. The animals which now form the basis of the developed modern agriculture in many new parts of the world, like cattle and sheep, were taken from Europe.

Africa was a source of, and destination for, a rich array of plants and animals.

The coffee shrub was indigenous to Ethopia's Kaffa province (*coffea arabica*), the Congo basin (*coffea canephora* or *robusta*) and the coastal country of West Africa (*coffea liberica*). The Arabs spread Ethiopian coffee to the Middle East. From here it was taken to Europe, and later to the West and East Indies. At the end of the 19th century, coffea arabica was taken back to Africa and grown in Nyasaland, Kenya and Uganda.

The groundnut was taken from Brazil to West Africa in the 16th century, and the Portuguese took cocoa to São Tomé island in the 17th century. The rubber tree arrived in West Africa from Brazil at the end of the 19th century.

Bananas and greater yams were probably taken by migrating Madagascar Indonesians to the Bantus, who began to migrate southward and north-eastward from the fringe of the West African rainforest from the time of Christ. The greater yam gave a much better yield than the indigenous yam. As well as having more advanced technology (they knew iron, made iron tools and had iron spears) the superior nourishment of the Bantus also contributed to their being able to defeat, drive out and assimilate the indigenous people that stood in their way.

The Turks brought maize first to Egypt at the beginning of the 16th century, and then to West Africa, the Portuguese also bringing it to West Africa from Brazil somewhat later. Similarly the Portuguese at the end of the

196

16th century brought manioc from Brazil to the island of Sãn Tomé, from which it spread to the mainland in the 17th century.

Maize and manioc became the standard diet fed to slaves. Africa had been considered a source of slaves since ancient times. The demand for slaves was heightened when firstly the Arabs, and then from the 16th century the Turks and the Portuguese needed workers to build ships. The Arabs had traded in slaves for a long time before that.

It was the foundation of plantations in the New World that really set off the demand for slaves. The plantations required workers that could withstand tropical conditions. The Portuguese (followed by the English, French, Dutch and Spanish) zealously supplied the living merchandise. By 1600, 275,000 Africans had been taken to the New World and pressed into slavery, in the 17th century another 1.3 million, in the 18th century 6 million and in the 19th century 1.8 million, 10 million in total. Several times this number died in the course of slave hunting and transportation. Slavery tore apart the African economy, deprived Africa of its most active young workers, and the slave money corrupted the moral structure of slave-hunter tribes in many countries of the continent.

Slaves held for transport had to be fed. They were given manioc before loading on to ships. They yield more than yams, and could be dug up from the ground as required, since the harvest time could be stretched over a long time. They rot quickly after being dug up, however, and so maize was a more convenient food for the voyage. Its yield was also greater than the indigenous African millet and sorghum, the production of which the Portuguese were unfamiliar with in any case, since they were mainly grown in areas occupied by Arabs. Both foods fed to the slaves were rich only in carbohydrate, and lacked the other elements of nutrition.

Thus manioc and maize started out on their way to dominance in Africa. Soon the colonists had spread maize all along the western coast, mainly in Senegal and Guinea. The local population were forced into producing it. Arabs involved in trading slaves from east to west (in Sudan) also grew maize on the slave routes. Soon maize was being grown all the way from Zanzibar through Tanzania, Malawi, Zambia, Angola and the Congo to the western coasts. Slaves in the plantations of the southern United States were also chiefly fed maize.

The advantage of maize was that it was nutritious, could provide two harvests, and compared with sorghum and millet, did not need as much tending, yielded three times the quantity, and was easier to store. However it also accelerated the exploitation of the soil in Africa, since it was grown in monoculture rather than in the American Indians' maize-beans-squash rotation, where the bean contributed to the renewal of the soil as a legume.

Maize made its second conquest during colonization in the second half of the 19th century. It only became the main food in East and South Africa, the Belgian Congo and part of French Africa in colonial times. It was a cheap and nutritious food for those working on mines and plantations, and could be exported to Europe as fodder. It was exported in large quantities mainly during the Second World War. Its growing area in Kenya increased significantly at this time.

Cassava, or manioc, was planted by the Portuguese for slaves awaiting transportation, and it spread first to the western coasts of Africa and then to East Africa. The British, Germans and French promoted it on their colonial territories because of its high yield and nutritiousness.

The second wave of manioc growing came with the foundation of Liberia by slaves freed first by Brazil in 1780. The food shortage during the Second World War and the consequent opportunities for export gave further impetus to its production.

The spread of manioc was promoted by the forced introduction of cotton by the French in the savannah region. Manioc's higher yield meant that it required less land than sorghum and millet, and so freed up space for growing cotton. It also provided cheap food for forced labour brought into the mines and plantations, and for building the infrastructure. Portuguese and British colonists probably also introduced it to islands in the Indian Ocean. It is now the world's second most important food after rice. Its leaves are used as vegetables. It is used to provide shade for coffee, tea and cocoa plants. It also has many industrial applications. As fodder, it is an important export item, with Thailand supplying 95 per cent of the trade, which mostly goes to EC countries (Imfeld, 1986/a).

Despite the large-scale spread of crops and animals, there are even nowadays certain plants and animals which are best suited to a particular type of climate and the associated conditions of temperature, sunlight, rainfall and natural vegetation. The distribution of agricultural production, can therefore be determined according to climatic zones and the types of crops and animals which are characteristic of them (Bernáth et al., 1978).

The world's agricultural zones corresponding to varying conditions of climate are the following:

I. *Tropical zone*
   a) wet equatorial zone;
   b) alternating wet savannah and tropical monsoon areas;
   c) zonal desert and steppe areas; because of the similar agricultural characteristics, the middle-latitude dry areas can be included here.

II *Sub-tropical zone*
   a) wet subtropical areas;
   b) dry summer subtropical mediterranean areas.

III *Temperate climatic zone*
   a) oceanic areas;
   b) long summmer, wet, continental areas;
   c) medium and short summer continental areas.

IV *Cold climate zone.*

Wet equatorial zone agriculture

The original vegetation of the zone was tropical forest. About half of it is still covered by this forest. There is widespread extraction of valuable timber. The high humidity and the uniform high rainfall throughout the year makes permanent cultivation possible.

The zone is the home of various types of palms and bananas, among them the gum-tree, coconut- and oil-palms, bananas, manilla and jute. Vegeculture is widely practised with root and tuber plants such as manioc, yams, sweet potatoes and others. Plantation crops are cocoa, the above-mentioned palms, various spices (vanilla, cinnamon, cloves, nutmeg, ginger etc.). Animal rearing is sparse in the zone because of the prevalence of the tsetse fly.

Agriculture of the savannah zone

Towards the outer extremes of the tropics the dry season gets longer and the growing season shorter. Crops grown in the tropical fringe area of Sudan, are millet, groundnuts, wheat, maize, vegetables, and various types of sorghum, manioc and yams.

In the savannah areas of Madagascar, upland rice or 'dry' rice is the main crop.

In Central America, the main crops of the traditional savannah cultivation are maize and beans. The main plantation crops are coffee, tea, sugar cane and groundnuts.

Characteristic of the dry savannah zone is herding, including pastoral nomadism.

Agriculture of the tropical monsoon zone

Irrigation is the classic form of cultivation in this zone. Irrigated rice growing is the most widespread form in South-East Asia. Irrigation is essential because the summer deluge is followed by such a dry season that soil completely dries out through evaporation, and any crops would wither if they were not watered.

Rice is the crop of tropical and subtropical zones. It requires high temperatures while it is growing (minimum 20°C), and needs dry conditions to ripen. It needs a lot of water in its growing season, a minimum of 1,250 mm or a corresponding amount of irrigation water.

The world's largest producers of rice are in South-East Asia: China, India, Indochina, Bangladesh, Thailand, Vietnam and Japan.

Wet-rice is the most widespread form of production but in some highland regions the much lower yielding upland rice is grown by dry cultivation. Other crops also find a place, however. Dry-cultivated crops are wheat, barley, millet, beans, groundnuts, tobacco and other crops, while irrigation is used for cotton, sugar cane, jute, tea and coffee, and other plantation crops.

The most important animals are cattle and buffalo, mostly as draught animals.

Agriculture of zonal deserts and tropical steppelands, and of middle latitude dry steppelands

The largest deserts of the Earth are to be found in the dry zone, along with arid and semi-arid regions of which small parts are used for irrigated agriculture, the larger parts supporting dry cultivation, albeit with very low yields.

Arid and semi-arid areas are divided between hot and temperate climatic zones (widespread in Africa, South-West Asia and Central Asia). They receive very little rain, with evaporation exceeding precipitation, so that shortage of water is a permanent problem.

In the deserts, the land can only be used using springs or oases with access to underground aquifers.

On the fringes of the desert there are intermediate zones where there is some grass, but still very little rain. One such is the African Sahel belt, where in some years there is sufficient rainfall to ensure satisfactory crop yields and animal grazing, but serious shortfalls in – frequently consecutive – dry years.

The transitional zone adjoins the semi-arid zone, where there are comparatively good natural grazing areas. The natural vegetation of steppe areas consists of short grasses and drought-resistant shrubs.

Dry areas primarily support animal grazing, with crops confined to river valleys and scattered oases. The characteristic plant of the desert areas and their oases is the date palm. The centres of date palm growing are the Persian Gulf and the Oman Gulf.

In warm climate areas of the zone where the rainfall is between 500 and 600 mm, and evaporation is high, millet, sorghum and barley are grown. Cotton, rice, sugar cane and other crops can be grown with irrigation. Due to its relatively short growing period, the originally sub-tropical cotton has adapted well to temperate regions step and semi-desert areas where irrigation is possible. Thus it is grown in large areas of Central Asia along the canals from Sir-Darya and the Amu-Darya (eg the Fergana and Karakum canals), in Uzbekistan, Turkmenia and Tajikhistan.

A still widespread form of animal grazing is the nomadic and semi-nomadic pastoring. The herders follow the rain belts as they migrate with their herds. Nomadic and semi-nomadic herding stretches through the dry areas north and south from the Sahara from the Maghreb and Mauritania in Africa through the Middle East as far as Iran and through Central Asia all the way to Mongolia.

South of the Sahara cattle are favoured, and to the north, sheep, goats and camels. Sheep are the most widely kept animals in the Middle East and Central Asia. Similarly sheep and goats feature most strongly in South Africa's savannah region, but cattle are also kept.

Sheep breeding prevails in the dry areas of Australia, Argentina, Uruguay and New Zealand. The latter countries are also host to cattle in their less dry areas. The world's largest merino flocks are in Australia.

In the dry steppes of the North Caucasus, fine-wool sheep breeds predominate, and course-wool sheep in Kazakhstan. The Central Asian former republics of the Soviet Union, Afghanistan and Mongolia are the home of the karakul sheep or Persian lamb, which was taken from here to South Africa. In the republic of South Africa, merino and karakul sheep are kept, as well as Angora goats.

Agriculture of the wet sub-tropics

The rice-growing of south-east China is the most typical of the monsoon region of Asia. Rice land takes up about 50 per cent the available land of the Chinese plain. Rice is grown in hilly basins, valleys and terraced hillsides in the western part of China. Apart from rice, important crops are cotton, tobacco, sugar cane and fruits in this region.

The other important agricultural area of the wet sub-tropics are the south-eastern part of the United States (Georgia, North and South Carolina, Alabama and Florida), where there is large-scale production of cotton, tobacco, rice, sugar cane and, in Florida, fruits, including citrus.

Another constituent of the zone is the River Plate basin in South America, which is characterized by grain and meat production. The climate of Gran Chaco is favourable for production of citrus, cotton and sugar cane.

South-East Australia is also wet sub-tropical. As well as sheep grazing, there is intensive fruit and grape growing.

Agriculture of the dry sub-tropical zone

It is here that the mediterranean regions of dry summers and wet winters belong.

On the north shore of the Mediterranean, in southern Europe, winter wheat, dry-resistant olive, fig, almond and chestnut are the typical crops. Grapes, fruits, vegetables, rice, sugar, maize, and citrus all grow with the aid of irrigation. Although they originated in South-East Asia, nowadays citrus fruits are most widespread around the Mediterrannean. Irrigation accounts for 10 per cent of cultivated land. Fruit, vegetable and grape growing are, in general, much more prominent around the Mediterrranean (making up about 25 per cent of the total) than in temperate zones, where they usually take up less than 10 per cent of cultivated land.

The southern coastal area of the Mediterranean is host to, in addition to those crops already mentioned, sugar cane, dates and cotton. There is a sharp distinction between dry and irrigated agriculture in this region. Typical of the traditional dry agriculture are the highland berber crop growing and nomadic or half-nomadic pastoralism. Growers of crops normally also keep animals and animal-breeders cultivate land. Cereals – wheat, barley and millet – are grown by dry-land cultivation. The most commonly kept animals are the sheep and goat, and for draught, the donkey and the mule.

Irrigation is found primarily in Egypt and a few North-African and South-West Asian oases, and used to grow rice, maize, cotton, vegetables and sugar cane, winter crops grown without irrigation being wheat, barley and fodder plants (clovers).

Another area with a mediterranean climate, central and southern California, is America's vineyard, fruit orchard, and vegetable garden. Today the wine-growing areas of California (the most well-known being the Napa and the Sonoma valleys) supply most of the wine for the United States. Wheat and cotton growing are in decline, but still go on. Two-third's of California's cultivated land is irrigated.

The Cape area at the south-west tip of Africa is another mediterranean-climate region, where there is also large-scale vegetable, fruit and vine growing. In Chile's mediterranean central region, there is rather less fruit and vegetable growing, with cereals more common. A similar situation holds in Australia's mediterranean south-west areas.

Very few animals are kept in mediterranean regions, since pasture dries up very quickly in summer, and forage production is of low productivity. What livestock there is, is mainly composed of sheep and goats. Dairy and beef cattle may also be found, in the coastal areas.

Agriculture of temperate zone

The temperate zone falls between the subtropical and sub polar zones, between 35° and 70°. It extends further in the northern hemisphere than in the southern. Its climate is characterised by four well-defined seasons and changing weather. The polar border is defined by the isothermal line where the temperature of the warmest month is +10°C, which coincides with the edge of the northern forest belt. Annual rainfall near the oceans is above 1000 mm, and decreases moving into the continents.

Natural vegetation adjacent to the subtropical area is steppe grass, in oceanic climates temperate deciduous forest, which increasingly gives way to forest steppeland towards the interior of the continents. Towards the poles, the forests first become mixed and eventually coniferous taiga.

About one-quarter of the dry land of the earth falls in the middle latitudes, and one-third of the cultivated land. More than 40 per cent of the world's arable land is found here.

In Europe arable land occupies a proportionately greater area of the total in countries with flat land: in Great Britain the proportion is 77 per cent, in Hungary 74 per cent, in Denmark 70 per cent, in Poland 62 per cent and in the Netherlands 60 per cent. On the arable land, mainly cereals, root crops, industrial and fodder crops are grown. Animal breeding is also important.

The zone may be divided into three parts: oceanic, long-summer wet continental, and medium- and short-summer continental areas.

Agriculture of the oceanic areas

Much of Western Europe, some of western coastal North America, in Latin America the central and southern part of Mexico and the southern part of Chile, and New Zealand fall into this category.

Typical of the region's arable production are wheat, rye, barley, oats, flax, potatoes and fodder, and the characteristic forms of animal rearing are pasturing, mainly of cattle, and keeping of swine and poultry indoors. Towards the south, sugar beet is more widespread (in the Flanders region and Paris basin of France, and in southern Germany), as are fruits, grapes, wine-making and vegetables. The Netherlands is Europe's greatest producer of under-glass vegetables, mostly tomatoes, and of ornamentals. In more northerly countries – chiefly where population is less dense (Britain, Ireland, northern Germany) – there is widespread cattle grazing. In more densely populated countries fodder growing and indoor animal breeding is favoured over pasturing. The Netherlands, Belgium, Ireland and Denmark have the highest stocks of cattle in Europe. Next to cattle, swine and poultry are kept in the greatest numbers.

Dairy cattle, sheep breeding and intensive pastures and meadows are prominent features of New Zealand's agriculture too. It is among the highest exporters of meat and dairy products in the world.

Agriculture of long-summer continental areas

In Europe the countries along the Danube, South Ukraine, the Crimea, the lower Don region, ie. all of the southern lands of the former Soviet Union as far as the Caspian Sea, belong to this category. In Asia, the largest area in this zone is in North-East China. In the United States the corn and soya belt of Mid-West belongs here (Ohio, Indiana, Illinois, Iowa, Wisconsin and Minnesota), with the associated livestock-fattening, and from here to the West, where rainfall is lower, the spring wheat belt (Montana, North and South Dakota, stretching into Alberta and Saskatchewan in Canada) and the more southerly winter-wheat belt (Kansas, Oklahoma and Texas).

Precipitation throughout the region is variable, but generally sufficient for cultivation. The most prominent soils in the Eurasian steppe are the deep chernozom rich in nutrients, and in North America the almost equally fertile, slightly alkaline prairie soils.

The region stretching from Europe into Asia is the location of the main wheat and maize-growing areas. The area is known as the wheat-corn belt of Europe. These two crops provide 60 per cent of arable land production in the Hungarian Plain, the Bachka, the Morava Valley and Croatia, the Transylvanian basin, the Banat and Wallachia. There are also important maize-growing areas in Moldova, southern Ukraine, the northern Caucasus and Georgia.

Other important arable crops of the area are legumes, hemp, sunflower seeds and sugar beet. There is a lot of fruit and vegetable growing, swine-keeping based on maize, and cattle and poultry rearing.

In North-East China around the 40^0 latitude, where there is a continental influence, wheat, maize, legumes and millet predominate. In Manchuria to the north wheat and millet are the main crops, and to the south, in the Huangho basin, maize and soya. There is large-scale swine-keeping throughout the region.

Agriculture of the medium- and short-summer continental regions

In the wet areas on the northern side of the temperate zone towards the North Pole, the summer is short but the average July temperature is around 20°C. Winter is long and hard. The soils are mostly poor and there is little arable land. There is, however, good quality meadow and pasture, and hay production is highly developed in many places.

By far the most common feature of the region's agriculture is intensive cattle-breeding and dairying. The northern-European milk-belt (Scandinavian countries, Finland, North Germany and the Baltic states) make up part of the region. The short summers and long winters favour spring wheat, and rye, oats and barley are also grown. Also of significance are potato and flax growing.

In the United States and Canada, the North American milk belt is on both sides of the Great Lakes. Here too, the main arable crops are spring-sown wheat and hay.

The Eurasian and North American forest belts also stretch into this zone, the world's largest connected forest area. Forestry and timber-extraction are well developed. Fishing is important on the coasts.

Agriculture of the cold climatic zone

The sub-arctic regions which adjoin the northern border of the temperate zone, and the neighbouring tundra are constituents of this zone. The climate is extreme continental, with long winters and very short summers. Rainfall is very low (200-300 mm), but evaporation is so slight that the land can still become marshy. Plants of the tundra are mostly moss, lichen and scattered, moisture-favouring grass.

On the southern fringe of the cold zone fast-ripening varieties of potato, some vegetables (cabbage and root vegetables) and some fodder crops are grown outside. Further north it is only possible to grow produce under glass. An important activity is reindeer-herding, which supplies milk and meat locally, and is a source of raw material to the leather industry.

Agricultural zones changing with altitude

In mountainous areas, the temperature falls with altitude. Climatic zones in these areas thus lie vertically above each other, and correspond with agricultural zones.

The agriculture of tropical highland areas manifests most clearly the variation according to climatic zone. In Tanzania, for example, tropical crops (sisal, rice, cashews, coconuts, beans etc.) are grown on the plain and up to an altitude of 800m. Up to 1500m the sub-tropical cotton, sugar-cane, soya and maize prevail. Coffee and bananas are grown on the plateaux between 1500 and 2000m, and between 2000 and 3000m temperate zone crops: wheat, potatoes etc. (Németh, 1984).

Production according to zone is shown on table 9.1 and figure 9.1, and the major growing countries of the main crops on table 9.2. Comparison of table 4.5, which shows the world's main exporters of each product, and table 9.2,

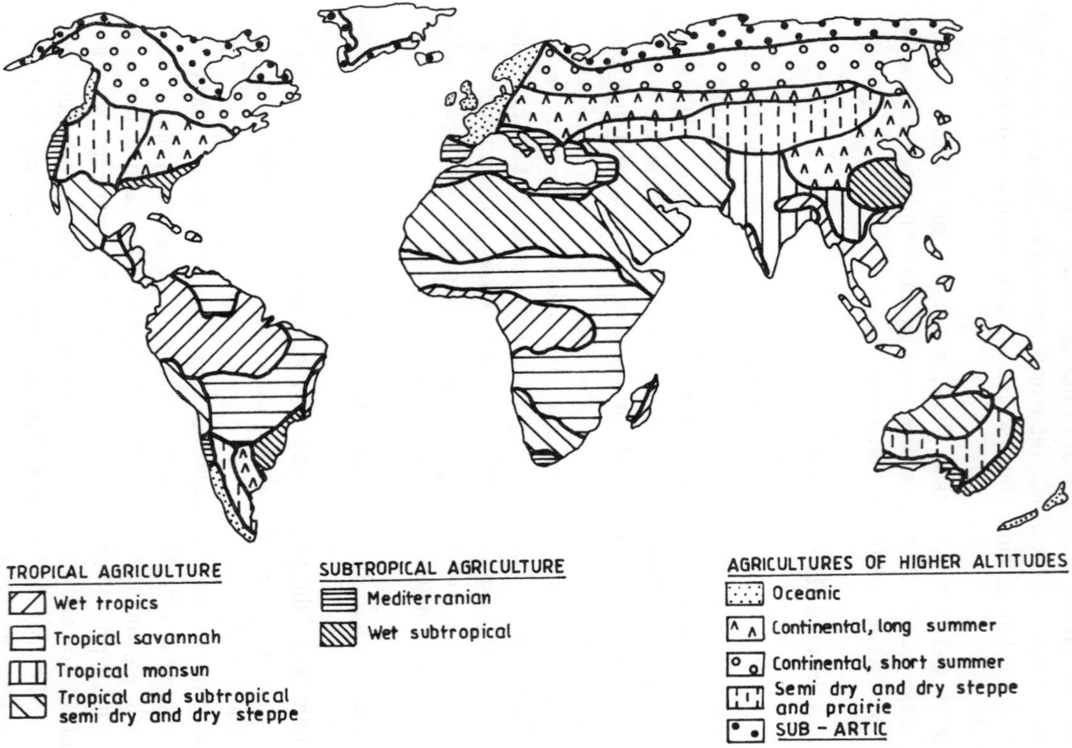

TROPICAL AGRICULTURE

- ▨ Wet tropics
- ▤ Tropical savannah
- ▥ Tropical monsun
- ▨ Tropical and subtropical semi dry and dry steppe

SUBTROPICAL AGRICULTURE

- ▦ Mediterranian
- ▨ Wet subtropical

AGRICULTURES OF HIGHER ALTITUDES

- ░ Oceanic
- ⋀ Continental, long summer
- ○ Continental, short summer
- ▤ Semi dry and dry steppe and prairie
- • SUB – ARTIC

Figure 9.1   Principal agricultural zones of the world

shows that the highest producer of a particular commodity is not always the same country as the highest exporter. The conditions which allow exports to be significant are that production be more than enough to satisfy domestic demand, and that the trade infrastructure be well developed. Some of the greatest producers in the world (such as the former Soviet Union in several commodities) are constrained to import, whereas some of the lower-ranking producers of the world (such as Italy in rice, and the Netherlands in tomatoes and meat) are exporters of significance.

Table 9.1
Agriculture typical of climatic zones

Climatic zone	Natural vegetation	Main regions	Agricultural production
Wet tropical			
Permanently wet, median temperature 25-27°C, rainfall 1500-2500 mm.	Tropical forest approximately 50% of the area	Amazon basin, Congo basin, Indonesia, South-East Asian peninsulas and islands	Caouchouc, oil and coconut palm, banana, manilla, cocoa, batata, manioc, yams, spices, tropical timber
Tropical savannah			
Spring or summer rain, followed by dry season, 20-28°C, rainfall 700-1500 mm	Open, high grassland, bush and tree savannah	Areas on the fringes of African forest, South American campos and llanos.	Millet, sorghum, wheat, maize, rice, groundnut, sugar cane, coffee, tea, pasturing (where there are no tsetse flies)
Tropical monsoon			
Rain from July to November, median temperature 20-28°C, rainfall 1500 mm.	Deciduous monsoon forest	South-East Asia	In the cooler, dry period: wheat, barley, dry-resistant oil crops. Rainy period: rice, jute, sugar cane.

Table 9.1 contd.

Climatic zone	Natural vegetation	Main regions	Agricultural production
Low and middle latitude desert and surrounding dry steppe			
High maximum summer temperature, cool when sun is low. In middle latitudes warm summer, cold winter, rainfall 50-500 mm.	Sandy and rocky desert, dry-resistant shrubs, grass.	Sahara, South-West Asia, Central Asia, Central and West Australia, dry and desert areas of North America	Date palms in oases. Animal pasturing (camel, goat, sheep, cattle), millet, sorghum, sisal. With irrigation: cotton, rice, grapes, fruits.
Wet subtropical			
Eastern sides of continents, 25-35^0 latitude. Long, hot, rainy summer, cooler, drier winter, in South-East Asian monsoon type, rainfall 700-2000 mm.	Deciduous and evergreen forest.	South-East China, the south-eastern part of the USA, the River Plate area of South America, South-East Australia.	Growing season of 7-11 months, 2-3 harvests. In autumn, wheat and barley sowing, in Spring rice, cotton, sorghum, maize, soya, tobacco, sesame, castor oil, poppy. Plantations: sugar cane, cotton, tobacco, tea, tung tree, citrus.
Subtropical dry summer mediterranean			
35-45^0 latitude, west sides of continents, median temperature 15-18^{0}C, rainfall 400-700 mm.	Evergreen dry-resistant shrubs and trees.	Mediterranean area, South-West Australia, California, central Chile, South-Western Africa.	Olives, figs, vines, citrus. Without irrigation: cereals and clovers. With irrigation: rice, cotton, maize. Few animals because of dry summer, mostly sheep and goats.

Table 9.1 contd.

Climatic zone	Natural vegetation	Main regions	Agricultural production
Temperate oceanic			
Climate of western sea coasts in middle latitudes. Cool summer: 12-17°C, mild winter: 5-10°C, rainfall: 600-2000 mm.	Deciduous and mixed forest, grass.	Western Europe, West Coast of North America, southern and middle Mexico, south Chile, south-western part of Argentina, New Zealand.	Wheat, barley, rice, oats, sugar beet, flax. Meadow and pastures, beef and dairy cattle.
Temperate continental, long wet summer			
Summer 4-5 months, warm, rainy. Rainfall maximum at start of summer, rainfall 500-1000 mm.	Grassland steppe and forest steppe.	Central North America, Middle and East Europe and southern European former Soviet Union, in Asia the areas along the Huangho and in Manchuria.	8-9 month growing season. Chernozom soils predominate. Wheat, maize, hemp, soya, sunflower, sugar beet, tomato, peppers, fruits, vines. Mixed animal breeding.
Temperate continental, medium and short summers			
Short summer (July average temperature 20°C), long, hard winter, rainfall 400-600 mm.	Mixed and needle-leafed forests (taiga). Forest belt of Eurasia and North America.	Scandinavia, former Soviet Union, northern parts of USA, southern Canada.	Fodder, dairying (milk belts) forestry and timber, spring wheat, rye, barley, oats, potatoes, flax, sugar beet.
Sub-Arctic areas			
Short summer, long cold winter (limit of production 55-60°N, 44-55°S)	Tundra, moss, lichen, scattered grass.	Northern part of former Soviet Union, northern Canada, northern parts of Scandinavia, Alaska.	60-90 day growing season. Fast-ripening cereals (barley), some varieties of potatoes, some fodder crops. Greenhouse and some outdoor vegetables. Reindeer herding.

Table 9.2

Production of the major agricultural products in quantity and percentage of the world's production (1989-91 average)

Wheat			Maize		
Country	1000 MT	%	Country	1000 MT	%
China	94,681	17	USA	194,177	41
Former USSR	93,969	17	China	89,922	19
USA	61,273	11	Brazil	23,505	5
India	52,827	9	Mexico	13,036	3
France	33,203	6	France	11,804	3
Canada	30,036	5	Former USSR	11,235	2

Rice, Paddy			Cattle		
Country	1000 MT	%	Country	1000 head	%
China	187,036	36	India	197,067	15
India	111,070	21	Brazil	148,051	11
Indonesia	44,742	9	Former USSR	117,867	9
Bangladesh	27,559	5	USA	98,374	8
Viet Nam	19,216	4	China	79,308	6
Thailand	19,172	4	Argentina	50,054	4

Pigs			Tomatoes		
Country	1000 head	%	Country	1000 MT	%
China	357,914	42	USA	10,845	15
Former USSR	77,533	9	Former USSR	6,877	10
USA	54,572	6	Turkey	5,983	9
Brazil	34,005	4	Italy	5,756	8
Germany (FR+NL)	33,350	4	China	5,573	8
Poland	20,056	2	India	3,373	5

Lemons and Limes			Apples		
Country	1000 MT	%	Country	1000 MT	%
Italy	713	11	Former USSR	6,000	15
USA	705	11	China	4,555	11
Mexico	682	10	USA	4,452	11
Spain	577	9	France	2,225	6
India	560	8	Italy	1,922	5
Brazil	429	7	Turkey	1,917	5

Table 9.2 cont.

Wine			Sugar (Centrifugal, Raw)		
Country	1000 MT	%	Country	1000 MT	%
France	6,284	22	India	10,951	10
Italy	5,812	21	Former USSR	9,148	8
Spain	3,437	12	Brazil	8,101	7
Argentina	1,802	6	Germany (FR+NL)	7,966	7
Former USSR	1,767	6	Cuba	7,882	7
USA	1,542	5	France	4,539	4

Coffee, Green			Tea		
Country	1000 MT	%	Country	1000 MT	%
Brazil	1,497	24	India	710	28
Columbia	793	13	China	562	22
Indonesia	407	7	Sri Lanka	229	9
Mexico	361	6	Kenya	194	8
Viet Nam	255	4	Indonesia	149	6
Côte d'Ivoire	254	4	Turkey	132	5

Cocoa Beans			Bananas		
Country	1000 MT	%	Country	1000 MT	%
Côte d'Ivoire	728	29	India	6,370	14
Brazil	364	15	Brazil	5,546	12
Ghana	297	12	Philippines	3,562	8
Malaysia	228	9	Ecuador	2,862	6
Indonesia	160	6	Indonesia	2,317	5
Nigeria	142	6	China	1,788	4

Cotton Lint			Wool, Scoured		
Country	1000 MT	%	Country	MT	%
China	4,563	25	Australia	572,667	30
USA	3,283	18	Former USSR	278,333	15
Former USSR	2,580	14	New Zealand	266,933	14
India	1,766	9	China	121,837	6
Pakistan	1,735	9	Argentina	76,567	4
Brazil	662	4	Uruguay	61,000	3

Part V
AGRICULTURAL LAND

10 Land tenure and use

As a means of agricultural production, land has a greater than usual significance. Land is a gift of nature: it cannot be reproduced; although its fertility can be enhanced. Since its size is limited, its ownership is monopolistic in nature, and so ever since private ownership started, the landless have claimed rights to it, and their political leaders have fought to obtain it. The struggle was especially keen when agriculture accounted for most of production, and land was the source of both the wealth and power. Land ownership was at the root of many slave and peasant revolts through history. The conflict received ideological support with the rise of the middle class. Feudal land rights stood in the way of free enterprise and free trade, and was at odds with the new way of thinking. Serfdom hindered the supply of labour for the emerging industry and with it the formation of low wages, feudal ownership prevented the free buying and selling of land which could enable free enterprise, and the feudalistic split of countries stifled the free movement of goods. Many liberal ideologists, followed by the Marxists, advocated nationalization of land.

In Europe, family farming spread with the gradual decline of the feudal system, and the agricultural workforce considerably contracted with the development of industry. In North America, Australia, and New Zealand, wide areas of land became available, relieving the scarcity. The further reduction of the agricultural population, and the shrinking share represented by land in the total productive capital, served to make the problem of land ownership less significant.

Its significance did not, however, become any less significant where capitalist development was slow, where large numbers still worked on the land, and where certain features of feudalism remained, such as large estates, sharecropping and smallholdings, accompanied by landlessness. This was the

215

situation in many East and some South European countries up to the end of the Second World War, and still is in those Latin American countries where despite the wide availability of land, large estates and sharecropping became the norm, and large numbers of smallholders worked a tiny proportion of the land, not to mention the large numbers of landless workers. A similar state of affairs holds in many of the world's other developing countries where the rural population is large and there is insufficient land for everybody. In these countries only radical agricultural reforms and land redistribution could, or indeed can, help alleviate the chronic land shortage.

Since the Second World War there has been land reform in many countries. Many Eastern European countries redistributed land in 1945, but this was soon followed by collectivization. After the fall of communism there are once again moves to land reform in these countries. Land reform also took place in Italy after the Second World War, and in Portugal in 1977 and 1984. After decolonization, many developing countries also carried out land reforms, but implementation was often not consistent, and because of rapid population growth and rising agricultural population, the land question still remains unsolved.

Here we discuss the question of land use from the points of view of
- size of estates
- land use, or technical aspects of farming
- land tenure, or the social aspects of farming.

Size of estates

The definition of large and small estates is relative. Classification as large or small depends on what can be considered average size for the relevant area and means of cultivation. In India, for example, around 40 per cent of farmers own less than 0.2 hectares, on Java half of the farms are less than 0.4 hectares and one-third less than one. In Brazil, estates of more than 5,000 hectares take up 20 per cent of agricultural land, holdings of less than 2 hectares, making up 20 per cent of the total number of farms, only occupy 0.3 per cent of the land (Dickenson et al, 1985).

According to the FAO, 65 per cent of Latin America's agricultural land is taken up by estates of more than 100 hectares. In Africa and the Far East, however, estates of more than 10 hectares are considered large, and only make up 22 and 12 per cent respectively of the total land (see table 10.1).

The size of estates is partly a result of historical and social circumstances, and partly due to the amount of land available in the area. In South America, the Spanish and Portuguese monarchies applied their accustomed feudal scheme in awarding large estates to the conquistadors, who also unilaterally occupied much of the plentiful land there. Population is still small over large parts of South America, but in spite of this there are more and more people excluded from land ownership, or have very small amounts of land.

Table 10.1

Proportion of small and large estates in the 1970s, as a percentage of total land area

	Latin America	Africa	Middle East	Far East
Small holdings [a]	3.7	22.4	11.2	21.7
Large holdings [b]	65.0	22.0	34.0	12.0

[a] Small holdings are those less than: 10 ha in Latin America, 5 ha in the Middle East, and 2 ha in Africa and Far East.

[b] Large holdings are those greater than: 100 ha in Latin America, 20 ha in West Asia, 10 ha in Africa and East Asia.

Source: Agriculture: Toward 2000, FAO, Rome 1981

By contrast, the high rate of population growth and a series of land reforms in South and South-East Asia has led to the subdivision of land into smaller and smaller holdings.

In Europe, the average size of farm at the end of the 1980s varied between 4 hectares in Greece to 51 hectares in the United Kingdom. The average in the United States at this time was 187 hectares, but this included holdings of a few hectares in the North-East coast as well as western ranches of hundreds, thousands or hundreds of thousands of hectares.

In Australia the intensive farms of the coast are of 150 to 300 hectares, but in the arid livestock farming lands of the interior they can be between 2,000 and 600,000 hectares. In 1977-78, 18.7 per cent of the farms were smaller than 200 ha, and 18.1 per cent were larger than 2,000 ha (Rural Industry in Australia, BAE, 1983).

Even greater extremes are to be found in South America. In Brazil, more than half the farms are of less than 10 hectares and account for 3 per cent of the land, and one per cent of the proprietors are absentee city-dwellers owning 45 per cent of the land in extensively-cultivated estates of greater than 1,000 hectares. In Argentina there is a similarly unequal distribution of land, although there the size of both large and small holdings is larger. Holdings of less than 50 hectares make up 50 per cent of the total and take up 2 per cent of the land, the 1 per cent of owners with more than 5,000 hectares owning 50 per cent of the land. Estates of between 10,000 and 100,000 hectares are not uncommon. A significant proportion are in the hands of companies (Mészáros et al, 1987).

The size of most of the farms in New Zealand (54 per cent) is between 40 and 250 hectares and that of 1 per cent more than 2,000. The latter occupy about 40 per cent of the land (Balázs, 1978).

Forms of land tenure

Land can be owned commonly or individually. These two basic forms of ownership and land use divide into various sub-categories and intermediates.

Common land may be ancient communal land, traditional or modern state ownership or cooperative property, and no matter what form it takes can support both common or individual farming. The latter may be through allocation or tenancy.

Individually owned or used land can give rise to family and capitalist farming, as well as transitional capitalist types of farming incorporating elements of the feudal or old Asian farming systems. Typical of these last two forms are the employment of sharecropping and paid labourers, the latter being usual on extensively farmed large estates. The form of tenure does not exclusively determine the size of the estate: family farming can take place on half a hectare as well as on 1000 hectares, capitalist farming on 100 hectares or 100,000.

Communal land and shifting cultivation

Communal land is the oldest form of land tenure. It was the starting point for modern agriculture too. Communities moving to cultivating the land and keeping animals from hunting, gathering and fishing everywhere did so on commonly owned land. More precisely, the land was common, but farming only partly, and ever less so in the course of time.

The traditional method of farming on communal land is slash and burn. The forest is communally cleared and burned, following which the head of the community allocates land to families who then work their own parcel and take the produce themselves. After the fertility of land has been exhausted, the community moves on, and only after the land has regenerated do they return to the same patch. With population growth, the return period, and hence the fallow, gets progressively shorter. Forest fallow turns to bush fallow and grass fallow, and gradually permanent cultivation becomes the norm. Nowadays shifting cultivation is often in a transitional state, so that the people live in a

218

settled community, permanently working the land around the village, but practising shifting cultivation in areas further afield. On being turned to permanent cultivation, the land becomes permanently used by the same family, and this right often becomes heritable. Permanent use can be transformed into family ownership. In large parts of Africa and Asia, and among South American Indians, even today most land constantly used by the same family is still not titled to it. In some Asian countries, however, a tenancy or quasi-ownership large-estate system has come to dominate on communal land owned by the crown, i.e. the state (as in the past, for example, in India and Iran, and even today in Saudi Arabia and Oman).

In 900 AD, forest still covered a large part of the land of Europe. Enclosure of the land began in the 13th century in England, but half of the country's arable land was open fields as late as 1700 (Grigg, 1974). The process of enclosure was completed in 1820, when the right of the villagers to graze animals on the common pasture was revoked. Enclosure was carried out in Denmark, Finland and Sweden at the end of the 18th century. The collective rights over land use held by Normandy's rural communities were revoked by 1850.

Slash-and-burn cultivation remained alongside permanent cultivation in Europe up to the 18th and 19th centuries, and in the forest areas of Scandinavia and Russia it was the norm until the 16th century, and could still be found in some places up to the 19th.

East of the Elbe, remnants of common land tenure like the system of communal pastures remained until the 20th century. After the emancipation of the Russian serfs in 1861, only 10 per cent of land held by the peasantry was in the hands of individuals, the rest being communal village land, the *obchina*. The head of the village community, the starosta, periodically redistributed the land between the villagers.

Communal land and shifting cultivation can still be found in some parts of Central America, Columbia, Peru, Ecuador, along the Amazon in Brazil, often among settlers as well as Indians. It is still exists in South-East Asia, the Philippines, Malaysia and the more remote islands of Indonesia. In 1945, 21 per cent of the cultivated land in the North part of Vietnam was communal, and 29 per cent in the central region (Árvai, Éliás and Szarvas, 1984). One-third of the land in Laos is cultivated by slash and burn to produce rice (Árvai, 1985). Shifting cultivation is most widespread in Africa, chiefly in sparsely populated rainforest and wooded savannah areas. For example, in Angola 60 per cent of arable land is cultivated through tribal communes, as is half of Mozambique's and much of Zaire's (Németh, 1987/a and 1987/b). Even part of North Africa's arable land is common, as, for example, in Morocco, where communal land is redistributed from time to time.

Slash-and-burn shifting cultivation is not exclusive to commonly owned land. Coffee plantations in Brazil, cotton plantations in the USA and cocoa plantations in Nigeria were extended by the slash-and-burn method as long as land was plentiful.

Pastoral nomadism

Nomads also graze their herds on common land, but the animals themselves are private property. They typically live in patriarchal extended families, between which there are large differences in wealth. People living by shifting cultivation are not usually able to produce more than needed to cover their own needs, and so have no wealth. Pastoral nomads, however, find it possible to generate surpluses. The richer families can keep servants and slaves, through whose labour they acquire large amounts of wealth.

Wealth largely consists of livestock. Often, however, they can augment it through war and raids. Many nomads are well-armed. Camel-drivers were for centuries the wandering traders of the Sahara and Arabian desert (the Bedouins), who traded in gold, ivory and slaves. They defended their merchandise against bandits with arms. Other nomads were forced to take up arms so that they would not be taken into slavery (Imfeld, 1986/b). Also nomads were the Huns, and later the other migrating horse-riding people who set off from the desert fringes of China and Mongolia seeking better grazing fields and thereby conquered lands.

Today's nomads have been forced off the good grassland areas onto the drier savannah and steppe country by the spread of settled farming. They normally graze their herds as they move along routes following the rain, and go to permanent markets to sell animals and skins and buy items they need. However, they often acquire what they need by raids and robbery.

Since animals constitute wealth, they often strive to build up their herds more than is necessary. Nowadays the increasing numbers of nomadic people and their animals is subjecting the weak pasture of, for example, the African Sahel belt, to overgrazing. Anticipating the large-scale dying out of their herds in dry years, herders attempt to build them up, in the hope that if they start with more, more will survive. This sets off a vicious circle: too many animals increasingly overgraze the pasture, which ever further reduces the chances of their own survival. Millions of people and animals die of starvation in the years of drought. Some authors suggest that the tendency to overstock could be a result of modernization. They say that today's generation lacks the livestock-breeding expertise that in the past was passed down from father to son, and helped to determine the size of the herd (Imfeld, 1986/b).

In colonial times, there were attempts to settle the nomads in order to counter the apparent threat arising from the difficulty of keeping them under supervision because of their mobility, and their habit of carrying arms. After independence, the new governments also aimed to settle them for similar reasons, as well as in the interests of improving their cultural situation and state of health. In spite of this there are still many nomads, mainly in the northern and southern desert and dry savannah areas of Africa. Among the better-known are the Fulbe living mainly in Nigeria but wandering in the whole of North Africa and the Masai, who live chiefly in Kenya. All of them keep cattle. The number of Masai is put at one million. There are also nomads in countries of the Arabian peninsula, in Iran and Afghanistan, and in Inner and Outer Mongolia, the latter surviving attempts to settle them and force them into ranching collectives.

Many nomads nowadays are semi-nomadic. The herders' families – women and children – live in settlements, work land and keep animals. Animals for milking are kept on permanent sites, the young and non-dairy animals moving with the men.

One form of semi-nomadic pastoralism is transhumance. This is primarily typical of the Mediterranean area, but is also found elsewhere. In the Maghreb countries the Berber herders of 4,000 years ago grazed their livestock in a similar way that their descendants do today. They drive their sheep and goats herds to the slopes of the Atlas Mountains in summer, and to the rainy Moroccan coast and the perimeter of the Algerian Sahara in the winter. The practice of grazing sheep and goat flocks in upland areas in the summer, and on the plains in the winter, used also to be widespread in the European Mediterranean coastal areas, and had started before Christ. This can still be found sporadically in Greece, Italy, Albania, the former Yugoslavia and Spain. Similar transhumance went on in Central Asia, where sheep flocks were driven to different areas to escape dry periods and the winter cold, as for instance from the valley of the River Tshu to the Siberian plain and back, and even in the Slovak mountains, where shepherds spent the summer with their flocks on the mountains and the winter on the plain. Transhumance is also found on the slopes of the Andes in South America.

State-owned lands

State holding of land is another form of common ownership. There are ancient and modern forms. In the irrigation societies of Asia, the land belonged to the state, or rather to the king, emperor or other ruler (for example in China, India, Iran, Arab countries etc.), and those using it paid taxes to the state. In the course of time the tax collectors acquired much land for themselves and became large estate holders. British colonial powers usually regarded them as having rights of ownership over the land. Remnants of the system still remain in a few places.

221

English settler colonies were from the beginning the property of the state, or the British Crown. In the first New England settlements in North America, land was granted to the colonising companies, who later divided and sold it. At first the forests and pastures were used communally, but later these were also enclosed. As settlers made there way West, they took land into their possession. It was possible to acquire land very cheaply, but even so much of the land was occupied without buying it. The Preemption Act of 1841 allowed those already occupying land to buy it for 5 dollars per hectare. The Homestead Act of 1861 allowed occupation along with instalment purchase of 64 hectares at a discount. Many people, however, acquired much larger holdings by various means. The ranchers on the High Plains and the foothills of the Rocky Mountains, up till the Taylor Grazing Act of 1934, used crown land for free, and for a long time even after that paid not more than a nominal fee for it. On the Western part of the High Plains much of the land is still rented from the state (Grigg, 1974). Private ownership became dominant over much of North America, however.

Land tenure was different in Australia. In the beginning, pastoralists squatted Crown lands unilaterally. Sheep shepherding took up ever-increasing areas of land. The state charged only trivial amounts for grazing until 1847. An Order in Council of 1847 introduced a lease system of up to 14 years in New South Wales. From the 1860s onwards it became possible to make land claims. Only a minority of land became privately owned, however, the greater part remaining tenanted from the state. Today only 12 per cent of agricultural land is in private hands, mostly in the intensively cultivated coastal regions. More than 50 per cent is on long-term 30-50 year leases, the rest being state reserves. Most of the latter is desert land, national parks and land reserved for the aboriginal population.

In New Zealand it was still possible to buy land in the 1840s, but in the 1850s the letting of Crown lands on licence was introduced. In the 1970s Crown lands accounted for 42 per cent of agricultural land, and four-fifths of it was leased by farmers. 50 per cent of the land was privately owned, and 8 per cent on perpetual lease (Balázs, 1978).

Nationalization of private land is also a common occurrence. In 1917 the revolutionary government issued a decree nationalizing all of the land in Russia. Partial or total land nationalization was also common in countries freed from colonization. In the African and Asian countries the white-owned plantations were usually nationalized. In Latin America, nationalization of plantations was part of some land reforms. In Iran, the woodland, pasture lands and water sources were taken into state hands in the 1960s. Tanzania nationalized its entire land area in the 1960s, as did Mozambique after winning independence in 1975.

State farms

State farms are usually set up to serve the preferred aims of the government. These can be:

1. Military aims (for example, in former times, military stud farms);
2. Development and dissemination of higher yield varieties and modern technology (demonstration farms);
3. Shouldering the costs of investment in soil improvement and irrigation on created farms (for example out of desert or sodic soil areas);
4. The establishment or maintenance of plantations or the safeguarding of other efficient large farms when they go out of private ownership (for example, after the expropriation of intensive holdings of colonists or other large landowners), chiefly to protect exports.
5. Protection of species (conserving ancient species in danger of extinction, such as the Hungarian grey cattle and racka sheep);
6. Environmental protection (national parks, forestry etc.).

State farms, then, are not necessarily products of the state socialist system, although they are most commonly found in such countries. In the former socialist countries, especially in the Soviet Union (and subsequently in Bulgaria up till 1986) the prevalence of state farms and the conversion of collectively-owned cooperatives into state farms was seen as an important goal since the former were not held to be fully socialist forms of ownership (and not easily put under central control), in contrast with full state ownership. The situation was similar in Cuba. Whereas in Hungary state farms worked only 15 per cent of agricultural land, and existed in a form roughly in line with those mentioned above, they made up more than 50 per cent of the Soviet Union's in the 1970s and 80s. The proportion was relatively low in Romania at 18 per cent of the land area; 19 per cent in Poland and higher in Czechoslovakia at 31 per cent. In Albania, however, it was 74 per cent (Agricultural Outlook, February 1992). In Cuba after the 1959 land reform, state farms were set up out of part of the former large estates, mostly from livestock farms and rice plantations, with sugar cane plantations mostly becoming production cooperatives. In 1962, the latter were also made into state farms. From the middle of the 1960s considerable pressure was put on individual peasant farmers to integrate into the state farms (Árvai, 1987).

Third World countries also contain state farms. In Egypt, state farms are set up in desert reclamation projects. Many of them are divided into parcels after reclamation and sold to private farmers. Demonstration farms based on irrigation have been established in Kenya's northern province, Turkana, with FAO support. Similarly, many demonstration cattle farms have been set up, with foreign assistance, in India. Sweden and Germany have provided technical support for setting up state farms in Ethiopia to serve as demonstrations of

223

cultivation techniques to the local peasant farmers. Sudan's 1 million hectare cotton-producing irrigated Gezira project, tenanted in 17 hectare parcels, and Mali's similar state irrigation project, controlled by the Office du Niger and covering 85,000 hectares are also worth mentioning here.

Farming cooperatives

One of the modern forms of common farming is the production cooperative. Members of the cooperative farm on land that they either own themselves, or is owned by the cooperative or by the state.

Many great thinkers wrote about the advantages of common households and production. Thomas More (1478-1435) in his book 'Utopia' envisaged the creation of households in which 40 men and 40 women would live on, and cultivate, land allotted for them. The Italian Jesuit monk Thomas Campanella (1568-1639) advocated such ideas in his work 'Civitas Solis' or 'Sun State', and set up a communal-farming, communist-style state in South America among the Indians until it was closed down by the Catholic Church. Later the theme was taken up by the utopian socialists, such as Charles Fourier (1772-1835) and Robert Owen (1771-1858). Fourier's 'Theories of Four Movements' and 'Essay on Agricultural and Household Cooperation' discussed phalanstery, the common houses of people cultivating the land communally, and Owen's writings described 'home colonies'. Owen also set up a short-lived commune in North America, as did Etienne Cabet (1788-1856), who called his own communist colony 'Icaria' after the title of his theoretical work. At the time when they were formulating their ideas, agriculture dominated the economy and so common production meant by and large common farming. Communal ideals were aimed at freedom from exploitation by landlords, and later by capitalist tenants, and the hope of a better life, and not least probably from nostalgia for an ancient communal way of life, which seemed a legendary golden age.

The socialist thinkers put the ideas of common farming on a more rational basis, and stressed the importance of efficiency. One of them, the socialist politician and historian Louis Blanc, in 1839 came out in support of peasants forming themselves into cooperatives, and following this Marx and Engels, in the 'Communist Manifesto' and the 'Critique of the Gotha Programme' referred to the desirability of cooperatives. Kautsky, at the end of the century also stressed the benefit of large-scale agriculture to socialism (Kautsky, 1899).

The most developed country of the 19th century was Britain, where capitalist leases prevailed in agriculture. It appeared to the Marxists that all capitalist countries would follow this path of development. The voluntary peasant cooperative appeared as an alternative to the large capitalist farm.

They held that cooperative farming was necessary not only to escape from exploitation, but to increase efficiency too. They argued that abandoning peasant farming in favour of common use of land and machinery and working together would lead to more rational agricultural production and greater efficiency. Common farming, as they conceived it, would be similar to the large capitalist farms, but without the exploiting landed aristocrat and rentier, where the benefit of the surplus value would go to the producers rather than be withdrawn as rent. The idea of common households also appears in some of Marx's works, which would be more economical than small households because of savings on kitchen space, cooking facilities, heating fuel etc.

The German Karl Ballod – who grew up in Russia and studied there – wrote in his 1898 book 'The Future State' about machine stations, agricultural towns and the advantages of reorganizing the 5.7 million small German farms into 100,000 large farms each of area 200 hectares. His book was at that time also printed in Russian. Following Ballod's scheme, 36,000 large farms were set up in 1919 in the Weimar Republic (Weber, 1987/88). There were similar aims in the Hungarian Soviet Republic of 1919, where land was nationalized and plans set out for organization of cooperatives begun, but because of the short life of the Soviet Republic they never came to fruition.

Socialist production cooperatives

Lenin (Lenin, 1975) intended that in post-revolutionary Russia the peasants should be gradually and patiently persuaded to set up agricultural cooperatives voluntarily. The agricultural ideologist Bukharin supported Lenin's views on cooperatives, but at the start of the first Five Year Plan in 1928 he opposed the enforced industrialization and collectivization (Bukharin, 1988).

At Stalin's command, rapid and total collectivization was enforced in 1930-32. Land nationalized in 1917 but remaining in the hands of village communes and individuals was taken away from the peasants and drastic measures were employed to force them into collectives and bring with them their animals, land and tools. These measures ranged from depriving the peasants of food – which they had produced – to imprisonment, banishment and execution. The compulsory delivery of produce in force at the time required every last grain to be taken from the peasants, partly because of shortages in the cities due to falling production, but partly also because they thought that starvation would bring them round to the idea of joining the collective farms, the kolkhozes. In the three years of the collectivization, millions died of starvation and further millions died in prisons and labour camps. Much of the country's livestock also perished, since despite being prohibited from doing so, the peasants slaughtered them. Of course, this unauthorised slaughtering brought on another wave of reprisals.

The great suffering was not made up for later. Soviet agriculture was at a lower level in the 1970s and 1980s than in Tsarist Russia, which was still backward compared to the rest of Europe. One of the chief causes of this backwardness was the policy of enforced industrialization and the associated subjection of agriculture to large-scale capital withdrawal, which was mainly carried out by compulsory purchase of produce at extremely low prices. This withdrawal prevented the collectives from making the necessary investments, changing varieties and buying enough fertilizer. The state provided assistance for the kolkhoz farms and assisted their mechanization, firstly by setting up machine and tractor stations and later by direct subsidy, but the value of the subsidies was always much less than the withdrawals.

The other factor inhibiting development of Soviet kolkhozes and state farms was the bureaucratic central control and the lack of interest of the workforce. The farms were not allowed to organize their own farming and could not direct production according to local conditions of climate, soil, environment and workforce. Their work was directed by central planning directives, which often forced them into irrational actions. There was also a lack of motivation to make an effort. Wages were also set centrally to be low and egalitarian.

Agricultural development was unable to keep pace with demand to such an extent that the system of compulsory deliveries was maintained throughout the entire 70 years, although in the last two decades took the form of compulsory contracts.

The dire state of Soviet agriculture and the country's increasing demand for grain sooner or later forced the Communist Party into action. Khruschev started experiments in the 1960s to improve the agricultural situation by providing more capital, but mainly by bringing more land under cultivation: moving into virgin lands and increasing the maize area. This had little effect. Later, from the second half the 1970s, central investment in agriculture was greatly increased. But even this was of little help under the circumstances. Over the years of collective farming, the productive potential, the morale of the labour force and the farming expertise had decayed too far. With the farms on the point of collapse, the higher flow of capital into agriculture was in vain.

The greater opportunities for investment were not accompanied by changes in the rigid central planning system, and nor was there any improvement in the system of incentives, which could have offered some hope of progress. In the second half of the 1980s, Gorbachev experimented with improvements in the incentive system. The party and government set out guidelines for the forming of groups within kolkhozes which would rent the land and equipment, and after settling accounts with the collective, would have a share in the income. There were also improved opportunities for growing on household plots and selling of produce by individuals. These proposals came up against resistance from central and local bureaucracy, and the from kolkhozes themselves, whose incompetent leaders had long lost the habit of taking initiatives, and succeeded in undermining the reforms.

Gorbachev set up several initiatives for introducing private farming and even for privatizing land. He failed to have land privatization accepted by the Supreme Soviet, and the promotion of individual land use was stifled by the local bureaucracy and the leaders of the kolkhozes, but after so many years working together, the plans raised little enthusiasm even among the members of the collectives themselves.

The Soviet Union did not remain alone with its the historical experiment with agriculture. After the Second World War, countries in the Soviet sphere of influence in large part followed its example, partly from Soviet pressure, and partly because these countries' leaders had associated themselves with the Soviet model of farming. After the Second World War, the East-Central European countries carried out radical land reforms, dividing the large estates and making individually-owned small farms the norm. In most countries, however, shortly after the peasant farmers had received land through redistribution, the authorities began to force them into cooperatives, in many places using the harsh measures previously employed in the Soviet Union. Thus production cooperatives and state farms became dominant in the 1950s in Bulgaria, and in the other European socialist countries, with the exception of Poland and Yugoslavia, by the beginning of the 1960s.

Most of these countries made the same mistakes as the Soviet Union, in all the areas of central control, large-scale withdrawals and lack of incentive. In the GDR and Czechoslovakia large resources were committed to agriculture from the 1970s onwards, so that yields became satisfactory, but because of the poorly performing incentive and control system the structure of production did not adapt to the requirements and there was no corresponding rise in efficiency. Low yields and permanent food shortages were common in Romania and Albania.

Hungary was the only country where despite enforced collectivization, in 1960-61, agriculture achieved significant successes. This was mainly due to the economic reforms which were carried out first at the end of the 1950s and latterly from 1968. The most significant was the ending of the central planning directive system which, although it was replaced by a many-layered, complicated regulatory system limiting the freedom of enterprises, still allowed them – including farms – a much higher freedom of action than in any other socialist country. The reforms raised incentives for both enterprises and workers and were accompanied by large-scale investment and subsidies between the mid-1960s and the mid-1970s, leading to surpluses of agricultural production. From the end of the 1970s, as mentioned in Chapter 2, the highly concentrated state farms of average size 7,000 hectares and production cooperatives averaging 4,000 hectares were largely decentralized, many smaller, independent farm units were set up, labour-intensive production was put out to contract on small private plots, and on land equipment was rented. The development of production cooperatives into mixed production and service cooperatives could have been rounded off by the handing over of titles to land and property to the cooperative members and making cooperative membership voluntary with rights of withdrawal.

Politics, however, stepped in once again. After the change of political system, the Hungarian coalition parties decided that cooperative members who had not owned land in the past would only be entitled to 1 or 1.5 hectare each as well as a share in the cooperative's property and of whatever land remained after compensation. The majority of the land could be purchased by the former owners and their heirs with their compensation vouchers. Cooperative members and those claiming compensation could decide after the compensation was made, and the property allotted, whether to work the land individually or cooperatively.

It should be pointed out that most of those claiming compensation no longer work on the land and it is unlikely that most of them wish to start farming again. The situation is made more complicated by the fact that – considering that the original 10 million hectares of agricultural land has fallen by about 1 million since collectivization (through urbanization, industrialization etc.) – in some places there is not enough land to compensate all of the claimants.

The laws of land and property have caused great uncertainty among the cooperative members and their leaders. They cannot plan for the future because they do not know whether enough land and property will remain to carry on farming. On the other hand, because the compensation and property allotment is taking so long to carry out, private farming is not reviving. Neither are their any subsidies, nor low-interest credit, to assist the process. Falling production and rising unemployment is becoming a hallmark of the transitional agriculture.

New land reforms in former socialist countries

After the collapse of the European socialist systems all of the former socialist countries are carrying out new land reforms, and have started the process of privatization and reprivatization. The purpose everywhere is to revitalize private farming and change over a significant proportion of the land area to private ownership.

Czechoslovakia intends to restitute land confiscated between February 25 1948 and January 1 1990. Former owners or their descendants may claim back a maximum of 150 hectares. Excluded from the scheme is land which has been built on, where perennial crops have been planted, or which are used for military or mining purposes, or are national parks or memorial parks. The reforms are currently in progress.

In *Bulgaria*, the law of February 1991 provides for land up to 20 hectares to be returned to the original owners, and 30 hectares on hilly and mountainous regions. If it is not possible to return the original land, then the owner has the right to the same area of land of equivalent quality.

In *Romania*, the land law of February 1991 allows up to 10 hectares of land appropriated for production cooperatives to be claimed back. In the case of land taken by state farms, the former owners are entitled to shares in the new agricultural companies.

In *Albania*, according to the law of May 1991, land occupied by production cooperatives and state farms also has to be redistributed among its former owners or their heirs. Most of the land area is already in private hands (Agricultural Outlook, February 1992).

In *Hungary*, four compensation laws - Act XXV of 1991 (Magyar Közlöny, 1991 no 77), Acts XXIV, XXXII and IL of 1992, and the transitional cooperative law of January 1992 (Magyar Közlöny, 1992 no 6) prescribe that compensation bonds must be given for confiscated property, including land. Compensation bonds may be used by the former owners to claim vouchers for bidding for land held by production cooperatives at compulsory auctions. Since the value of compensation bonds falls far short of any property taken by nationalization, or otherwise, in the case of land the state offers subsidies for up to about 50 hectares provided that the buyer undertakes to use the land for agricultural purposes for five years.

Cooperatives have been required to set up various kinds of land funds. One-third of the land they used remained in the name of their members, or people who have retired from them. Their rights of disposal over the land have been re-established. About two-thirds of the land of cooperatives was owned by the cooperatives. Fifty per cent of this is to be turned over to the cooperative's members, employees and former members with property claims, or these peoples' heirs. The other fifty per cent goes to the compensation fund, which the Compensation Offices sell by auction to voucher-holding former landowners or their heirs.

The First Cooperative law of 1992 and the Second Transitional Cooperative Law of 1992 also provide for 100 per cent of non-land property belonging to agricultural and industrial cooperatives to be given over to private title by December 31 1992. These shares of the cooperatives are assigned to working and retired cooperative members and former members. The latter do not have membership rights in the cooperative. Allotment of the cooperative property was decided by the general assembly of the cooperative. If the assembly decided to discontinue the cooperative, the entire property was divided. If groups or individuals wished to leave, then they had to put in their claims for the particular assets which they wanted to take out from the cooperative by the date of the assembly dealing with the allotment of property at the latest. The groups splitting off first decided on the division of assets separately and afterwards collectively in the general assembly. Concerning individuals, the assembly either agreed with requests of those wishing to leave to withdraw particular assets, or put the items up for auction. If an item which a member wished to withdraw was worth less than 10 per cent of the total property of the cooperative, a court might be called on to effect the distribution.

In the *new German Lands*, the 1990 law to adapt agriculture to a market economy restores private ownership of land (in the GDR, land belonging to production cooperatives remained throughout in individuals' names), made provision for allotment of producer cooperative property through a two-thirds vote of members and prescribed the transformation of producer cooperatives or their dissolution and specified the basis on which family farms may be established.

In general, land restitution has not yet achieved its stated aim of privatizing farming. In most countries the old producer cooperatives have re-established themselves under the new laws in the form of new cooperatives or some other form of company. In many cases the new cooperatives are smaller than the old ones and within the cooperatives smaller groups have formed (for example limited liability companies). Household and part-time farming now account for more of the land than they did in the past. In Romania, where, as in Albania, the government dissolved the producer cooperatives in 1991, some associations of producers re-established themselves and large-scale enterprises were working 47.7 per cent of the land by summer 1992 (Vincze, 1993). In Bulgaria, where most producers also chose to follow cooperative farming and few owners claimed their land back (by 1993 25 per cent, mostly in highland areas), the government recently dissolved the cooperatives by decree and ordered them to distribute their assets between their members. Members, however, reestablished many agricultural cooperatives after dissolution, mainly in cereal growing areas, (Kopeva and Mishev, 1993). In the rest of the East-Central European countries private farming is limited to between 10 and 20 per cent of the land. Neither has the number of private farmers been boosted by state farms, whose privatization – like that of industrial enterprises – has been subject to protracted delays. Even in the new German Lands newly-established production cooperatives and other newly-established companies farm 75 per cent of the agricultural land (Wagner, 1993).

The producers have probably been induced to choose farming for the following reasons:

– Although producer cooperatives were forcibly created several decades ago, today's generation is used to cooperative farming. Large farms - primarily those in Czechoslovakia, Hungary and the former GDR - provided security and a relatively high standard of living for their workers, with an income equal to or higher than that of industry. This income was also supplemented by household farming. In Hungary, a series of reforms during the 1980s gave rise to the majority of labour-intensive production being carried out by contract with members of the cooperative, either on their own smallholdings or on land and with machinery rented from the large farm. In many producer cooperatives only the cultivation of highly mechanised arable crops remained common, and the producer cooperatives became combinations of production, purchasing, contracting, marketing and service cooperatives. Reforms increasingly strengthened democracy within the enterprises.

– New private farmers do not have sufficient equipment available to them. Most of the equipment consists of large farm buildings and high-powered machinery, which are not divisible. The producers have little capital for new equipment and buildings and receive little government support or low-interest credit.

– Most farm workers do not have the necessary expertise or experience for full-time farming.

– Most of the land obtained through division of large farms is so small that it is not feasible to carry on full-time farming on it.

According to data from the Hungarian Ministry of Agriculture (Heti Világgazdaság, vol. XV, no. 40, 1993), by the end of 1992, 4-6 per cent of existing cooperative members had broken away in groups and 8-9 per cent individually. Of the estimated 15-26 thousand people who withdrew individually, about 60 per cent also farm on their own on land totalling about 150,000 hectares, so that each farmer has 5-10 hectares. After compensation, estimates indicate that three-quarters of a million new and a quarter of a million existing landowners will share approximately 5 or 6 million hectares (Varga, 1993). (At the end of 1992, land used by the production cooperatives totalled 5,389 million hectares, that of state farms 2.08 million and that of individuals 450,000.)

The average land received by the 70,000 land claimants in the Czech Republic will be less than 2 hectares (The Economist, September 1993).

– At present the infrastructure necessary for private farming is lacking: systems for procurement, trade, contracts, and production orders, a proper information system etc.

– The demand for agricultural goods is small and falling. Both the domestic demand and exports are dropping. The difficulty of selling produce means that the risks of farming are very high.

– In circumstances of the general recession, the difficulty of finding a job, and rising unemployment, cooperative farming still seems more secure then private farms. This is, however, increasingly illusory, because the cooperatives and companies running the farms and the state farms are also reducing their workforces (in Hungary, for example, the agricultural workforce has fallen by half since 1990) and do not offer the social services to their workers that they used to.

Although production cooperatives and associations of producers have lasted longer than expected after the land reforms, their survival is fragile. Their fragility is partly due to their financial situation. Bringing down subsidies has put farms in a difficult situation since, although prices have been liberalized, input prices have risen much more than output prices. The income-generating industrial and service enterprises which once operated as part of the large farms, and supported agricultural production from within, have closed down or been split off. Most farms are in debt, and many have gone bankrupt. Interest rates are so high that their agricultural income is seldom enough even to cover the interest payments, and badly indebted farms do not get further credit.

There is another factor putting the future of cooperative agriculture in doubt, however, and that is the uncertainty surrounding ownership. With land going into private hands, farming is separated from what is being farmed. Most landowners do not cultivate the land either individually or commonly. In Hungary, it is estimated that the land area of the reestablished production cooperatives and associations will be cultivated by only one-fifth of people owning land in the cooperatives. The other owners are either retirees or outsiders who acquire land through their own or inherited rights. Most of these have no desire to become farmers.

The situation is similar with regard to property. Only 40 per cent of producer cooperative property remains in the hands of active cooperative members in Hungary.

The result of uncertainty of ownership and unviability is that part of the land area remains uncultivated and large farms hardly use any fertilizer or pesticide, improved seeds seldom, and do not replace obsolete machinery, not to mention the lack of new investment. The few private farmers are in no better a position, having neither money nor means for proper farming.

Economic sense would have suggested privatization of land and property to the benefit of active agricultural producers rather than on a compensation basis. They could then have decided democratically whether to continue farming together or individually or combining the two.

The countries of the former Soviet Union still do not seem resolved on the question of privatization. Although there are various laws and decrees providing for private farming, and the monopoly of kolkhozes and sovkhozes (state farms) has been broken, private production is still limited to very small areas. Its expansion is inhibited partly by the same factors as apply in East-Central Europe, such as agricultural workers fear of change and the lack of a suitable basis for it, and partly by the unchanged institutional system and the conservative bureaucracy. It should be pointed out that in the Russian and Ukrainian Chernozom region there is no real tradition of private farming – in contrast to East-Central Europe and China – since before collectivization the communal *obchina* land system held sway.

Since 1990 there have been several government laws and decrees promulgated to advance land privatization and break down prohibition of land ownership. In December 1991 a presidential decree announced the need to speed up land reform and the encouragement of private farming, and the obligation on the kolkhozes and sovkhozes to be reorganized. There was a decision in 1992 to allow private ownership, inheritance and, within certain limits, the buying and selling of land. A presidential decree of October 1993 announced the same thing. Similarly, a decree was put out in 1992 requiring kolkhoz and state farms to re-register themselves. They had to state whether they were remaining in their old form or were restructuring.

By 1 January 1993 more than 77 per cent of farms had registered. 35 per cent had stayed with there previous form of organization, 43.3 per cent became limited companies, 8.4 per cent agricultural cooperatives, 3.8 per cent associations of peasant farms and 1.7 per cent share companies (Epstein, 1993).

The area occupied by private farms has risen comparatively quickly in the last three years, but private land use – including the small fruit and vegetable gardens and reregistered associations of private farms – still constituted less than 10 per cent of the agricultural land area of the Russian Federation in mid-1993. The largest rise is among the formerly strictly limited household plots and part-time farms. It is now almost exclusively these farms which produce vegetables, fruit and potatoes.

The average size of full-time farms is about 38 hectares, so private farms are relatively large (David, 1993; Kartali, 1992; Heti Világgazdaság, vol. XV, no. 40, 1993).

In the *Ukraine* the government in 1992 expressed a wish in principle to hand over 3 million hectares to individual farmers. This constitutes 10 per cent of arable land. For farmers to gain the right to buy land they have to work it for 3 years, and can only become owners after a further 3 years. They may not employ outside labour, and fruit orchards and vineyards may not be owned privately (Szabó, 1992).

Socialist cooperatives outside Europe

Socialist countries outside Europe also followed the Soviet example, or in some cases went even further along the road of communist agriculture. Examples of these are China and Vietnam.

China instituted land reforms in 1952 which gave rise to family farming among 100 million people on an average land area of 1 hectare. Then between 1953 and 1956 Soviet style cooperatives were established. Peoples' communes were brought in after 1958, which were not only industrial and agricultural entities, but served local administration, military, financial, trade, cultural, educational and social functions as well. The communes were founded on communist principles, dispensing with material incentives and money wages, and putting in their place egalitarian payment in kind. The commune system gave rise to large-scale falls in production and starvation. The problems were compounded by the chaos of the Cultural Revolution between 1966 and 1976. Real incomes in 1977-78 were no higher than in 1955-57, and grain production per capita was no higher either.

1978 saw the introduction of the 'family responsibility system' and the use of the communes' land was divided between families. Each family received on average 0.81 hectare. (It should be pointed out that the communes' low level of mechanization meant that even in the past their production was based on families and households: to work the commune's 1500 hectares, the 1300-1500 households were organised into work groups, and the work groups into brigades. Each work group worked 20 hectares, and each brigade 140-150 hectares.)

The reform extended to 95 per cent of households by 1983. Many Chinese provinces made possible long-term leases or even sub-leases of land, and in a few, rights to use the land were made heritable (Rui-zhen, 1987).

In the period since then, conservative forces have often threatened to reverse the reforms. So far, however, private farming has been a success in China, although its development has lost its early impetus. Grain production in particular has ceased to grow sufficiently. Production has shifted in the direction of non-staple foods because of the lifting of price restrictions on these and the ending of compulsory deliveries. From the mid-1980s, China once again had to import wheat. The government reverted to administrative measures to increase grain production. The austerity measures and price increases in 1989-90 led to large grain surpluses and helped set the stage for new economic reforms.

The Chinese government has introduced reforms of the way staple foods are distributed. Those of 1991-92 included abolition of direct price subsidies for grain and edible oils for urban residents and of rationing coupons for edible oils. In addition it has liberalized foreign trade in some respects by reducing import restrictions and relaxing the monopoly previously retained by the state trading agency (Webb, 1993).

Vietnam's route to development has been similar. North Vietnam collectivized agriculture between 1958 and 1961. During the war with America between 1964-74, a Chinese-style commune system and a military-communist way of distribution were brought in. Decline in production was exacerbated by the destruction of the war.

The core of the 1979 reform here, too, was the institution of a contract system. Land was divided up for use by families, who made contracts with the government for a certain amount at a fixed price, the rest being left to themselves to dispose of as they wished. The government halted the organization of cooperatives they had started in the South. Between 1980 and 1984, the production of rice rose by 34 per cent in the North and 24 per cent in the South. The annual rate of growth was 2.8 per cent between 1982 and 1984. During the 1980s, further reforms were put into effect to liberalize the economy in general (Fáyné, 1990).

In 1988, trade in rice was privatized, input supplies decentralized and households granted long-term leases on their land with intergenerational transfer rights.

Prices were decontrolled in 1989 and subsidised rice sales to government employees brought to an end. Inflation was forced down and the currency devalued. Policy reforms have led to improved technology of production. Fertilizer use has increased, and there has been a greater use of high yielding seed varieties and more investment in irrigation (Levin and Giordano, 1993).

Laos and Cambodia, where communes were also founded during the war with America, followed a route similar to that of Vietnam. In Cambodia, the destructive acts of the Khmer Rouge regime of 1975-79 included serious damage to the agricultural situation, doing away with the money economy and bringing in military communism. After the reforms in Vietnam, the two countries also started down the road of reforms towards private farming.

The need to return to private farming has now become clear to the countries of East and South-East Asia, with the exception of North Korea. The high agricultural population density, the small land area available to each household of less than one hectare on average and the low level of mechanization denies even that efficiency advantage that was theoretically open to the European socialist countries in the field of mechanized large scale cultivation of major arable crops. With the economies of scale not being open to them, only by the increase in intensification – by the use of irrigation, fertilizer, high-yielding varieties and better techniques of tillage – can yields be increased. The best way to encourage labour-intensive cultivation, however, as borne out by both European and Asian experience, is through individual farming.

In other socialist countries outside Europe and Asia, the movement towards collectivization was, with the exception of Cuba, less widespread than in China and Vietnam.

The African countries following the Soviet model aspired to collectivization, but with little success.

Tanzania's government brought in the 'ujamaa' system (village associations based on common land use) on nationalized land in 1967. The system had two aims: firstly to bring people into cooperative villages, where there would be better infrastructure than scattered settlements, and secondly to introduce production cooperatives. Ujamaa was put into effect during the 1970s. By 1976, 90 per cent of the population (more than 5 million people) had been brought into Ujamaa villages, but less than 8 per cent of production had successfully been made collective, on cooperatives averaging 40 hectares. Bringing people into villages did not reach its desired aim either, since through lack of money the villages did not develop adequate infrastructure (Deere, 1984).

Ethiopia tried to organize production cooperatives and state farms after the land reform of 1975. This was only partially successful. In 1983-84 only 1.5 per cent of the agricultural population worked in cooperatives. The 10 year plan aimed at having 53 per cent of the rural population in cooperatives on 52 per cent of the land in agricultural use by 1993-94, but this unrealistic goal was anyway nullified by the changes in the political system (Woldemeskel and Getachew, 1989).

Angola has 4.7 million of its 8 million agricultural hectares as tribal lands. After gaining independence in 1975, land was nationalized and a large part of the 3.3 million hectares of Portuguese-owned farms were expropriated. The larger farms were reorganized as state farms, and the smaller ones as producer cooperatives. In the following period the area covered by plantations and the level of production dropped considerably (Németh, 1987/a).

Mozambique also nationalized the land after independence in 1975. Tribal people were allowed to continue to use their common lands, and the commodity-producing large farms (which covered about half of the land in colonial times) were theoretically available for rent, but in practice their former owners in large part returned to their countries of origin and the farms were reorganized into state farms. A plan envisaged the formation of communal villages, each of one thousand families, who would then farm the land collectively. A few collectivized farms were accordingly set up along the Limpopo valley, but their reputation caused such alarm among the farming people that both there and elsewhere agricultural production declined (Németh, 1987/b).

Since the mid-1980s, both of these countries have given up enforced collectivization, and have even started reprivatizing some of the collectives.

Algeria nationalised the expropriated lands of the former colonists and set up so-called self-ruling producer cooperatives, and divided lands formerly belonging to domestic large landowners between the peasants. Production cooperatives were set up out of peasant lands and public lands. Most of these combined collective and private farming. At the beginning of the 1980s, 2,000 agricultural cooperatives and 6,000 state farms were in operation on the majority of the agricultural land, but 60 per cent of the produce originated from the private sector (Árvai, 1983). Since 1988 along with a more liberal economic policy there has been some reorganization and greater support for private farming. The state farms were relinquished and reorganized as collectives where individual farming has also got under way.

Production cooperatives in other developing countries

The producer cooperative movement has not been restricted to socialist or socialist-leaning countries.

The first model of cooperative farm was the *kibbutz* started by the first immigrants to Israel. Kibbutzes were founded on communist principles. Members of the kibbutz, apart from personal items, have to give up all their property and there is no personal income in money. Work is done collectively. The kibbutz takes care of their food, clothing, housing and the communal upbringing of children. In recent years they have also taken on industrial and service activities to increase their income.

Today there are still many kibbutz's in Israel, although the movement never became the norm, and they attracted fewer followers than the founding settlers hoped for. It is no coincidence that many of the original settlers at the beginning of the century migrated from Russia, where the ideas of collective agriculture were very strong.

A more widespread form was the *moshav* cooperative, where the land is divided into parcels which are then worked individually by members. The law only allows them to pursue agricultural activities, and they may not legally employ people for wages. The produce is sold by a common organization. Moshavs are closer to purchasing, selling and service cooperatives than to production cooperatives. Both the kibbutz and the moshav encompass the whole community in which they work, and include rural administration, cultural and social functions. In both cases the land is nationalized.

Mexico introduced the *ejido* communal village system during the revolution of 1911-17. The peasants, gathered into cooperatives, were allowed to work the common land individually or collectively. Most ejido members are private farmers. After the land reform of 1936, about one-third of the land became common. By 1977, a further 60 million hectares had been expropriated in several stages, and now half of the country's agricultural land belongs to the ejidos.

The ejido sector remained poor, farming being practised at a low level. It attracts little capital, one important reason being that common land cannot be used as mortgage security, and so banks will not give credit. In the North of the country the private sector is better equipped and is more prosperous. The

237

irrigation system was also developed there. The government of President Salinas announced plans in 1992 for the privatization of the ejido sector to allow credit to become available and thereby stimulate agricultural production. In 1993 the prohibition of selling and buying the land ceased and a large amount of ejido land was bought up by big landowners.

Bolivia also gave some of the expropriated land to Indian village communities, during its land reform which started in 1953, but a much smaller proportion than Mexico (Morgan, 1978 and Griffin, 1987).

Experiments with cooperatives of the communal Indian village type, similar to those in Mexico, also appeared in other South American countries.

Peru, for example, in the course of the land reforms of 1968-75 set up producer cooperatives on the haciendas which had been expropriated and divided among new owners. In addition cooperatives for regrouping smallholders (consolidating their farm plots) and servicing agricultural cooperatives were organized for old and new landowners, and cooperatives for livestock grazing. Membership of the consolidation cooperatives was compulsory above a certain landowning level. In such cooperatives, the members could keep 1 hectare for their private use, and were required to hand over the rest for common use (Zádor, 1986).

This experiment with cooperatives in Peru met with little success. It satisfied neither the former colons, sharecroppers who were deprived of the land allotted to them during the land reform, nor the Indian communities, who had already been farming individually on . Bureaucratic central control of the cooperatives and low wages contributed to the poor results. Reaction to the new cooperatives soon after their imposition involved spontaneous land-seizure and uprisings.

Since 1981 the different Peruvian presidents have variously strengthened and dissolved the cooperatives. After coming to power in the military coup of 1981, President Belaunde announced a return to private land ownership. At that time about 75 per cent of the cooperatives were dissolved. Agricultural productivity rose, but the schools and doctors' surgeries which the cooperatives had provided disappeared. The social democrat president elected in 1985, Alan Garcia, tried out both reform and counter-reform measures. The result was confusion and a fall in production. Remaining cooperatives are raided and pillaged by the Shining Path guerrilla movement among other troubles, and many are forced into growing cocaine through which the movement obtain money to support their activities.

In other parts of the world, many countries gaining independence from colonial rulers after the Second World War also set out to follow the Soviet model by nationalizing their industry and encouraging cooperative farming. Many of the independence movements were politically oriented to the Left, and their new leaders were attracted to the Soviet system by its apparent economic successes.

India's governing Indian Congress Party announced in a decision of 1959 that the way to improve the condition of the poor rural people was through cultivating land in cooperatives. The First Five-Year Plan aimed at establishing producer cooperatives. In fact very few of these were set up, and many of them broke up. The remainder, sometimes owned by absentee proprietors were often worked by sharecroppers or by employed labour.

North Africa's cooperative farms were not confined to Algeria: Morocco and Tunisia also organized producer cooperatives on some of the former colonial plantations which had been expropriated.

Apart from those mentioned, many countries linked land reforms with the setting up of producer cooperatives and state farms to prevent the break-up of efficient large farms and plantations. This is covered in more detail in the discussion of land reform.

The producer cooperative movement suffered retreats all over the world in the second half of the 1980s. The upswing they experienced after the Second World War was followed by disillusion, neglect and decay brought about by unfulfilled hopes. Perhaps we may later witness a new upswing in their fortunes based on the voluntary formation of associations between private landowners who see the benefit of working together without any kind of imposition of government will or central control.

Private and individual farming

Lands held privately or individually can range from large estates to small, family holdings.

Classification of large and small, however, can be seen to be a relative concept, with the scales varying in different parts of the world. A 100-hectare farm is a smallholding in America, but a large estate in East Asia. Large estates are usually established even where small ones predominate, but there are countries where one or the other can be said to be characteristic. Among the large-estate countries are Brazil, Argentina, Uruguay, and in Asia, Saudi Arabia and Oman. Australia and South Africa can also be included here.

These countries resemble each other only in respect of the size of their holdings, but the form of possession can vary significantly. In Brazil, for example, a significant proportion of the farms have city-dwelling absentee owners. Extensive cultivation is the norm on these lands, which are frequently worked by sharecroppers. Argentina and Uruguay have many estates owned by companies, while in the Arabian Peninsula an ancient sharecropping system remains from ancient times. Australia's farms are partly family-owned and

239

partly in the hands of companies, while in South Africa capitalist farms are in the majority.

More variable than property relations are the land use, both between and within countries. We will look at two types of private commodity farming which are usually associated with large estates and whose activities differ from those of the usual 'mixed farms' which include both arable and animal-rearing. The first type is the ranch, and the other the plantation.

Ranching

The ranch is an extensive livestock farm. It usually takes up a large area, since – especially nowadays – it is situated in dry grassland with weak soil. Extensive livestock farming in some respects resembles nomadic herding, but in respect of both social and property considerations is different. Ranches are mostly established on settler countries, and ranchers graze their herds either on their own or on rented land, with their animals staying on their allotted territory. Livestock is kept for commodity production.

Today most ranches are in the Western part of the United States and in the areas across its borders in Canada and Mexico, as well as in the Venezuelan llanos, the Brazilian sertao, the northern pampa of Uruguay, Argentina's South-East pampa, Chaco and in Patagonia, and in Australia's semi-desert interior regions, New Zealand's South Island highlands and in the savannah highlands of South Africa, including the Karoos. Ranches can have areas from a few hundred up to several hundred thousand hectares.

Ranching began in the southern part of the Iberian peninsula. It was Columbus who first took cattle to the West Indies, where they multiplied and many became wild. From the West Indies, ranching spread to Mexico and then to Texas, southwards to the Venezuelan llanos and the Brazilian sertao, and then to the pampas along the River Plate. Ranching was the major economic activity in Mexico and Cuba up to the beginning of the 18th century, and ranches had started up in California, Arizona, New Mexico and Texas by the beginning of the 18th century. Vast cattle fazendas were founded in Brazil at the end of the 16th century. In the wet pampas of today's Argentina and Uruguay, wild cattle were hunted until the large estates annexed the land and the hunters turned to cattle herders.

Until the end of the 19th century, cattle hide and wool were the main commodities produced by the ranches. In the second half of the 19th century not only were European markets opened up to foreign meat, but refrigerated railway waggons and ships made its transport possible. In the United States towards the end of the 19th century, cattle were driven North from the southern ranches, and later were taken to the Chicago slaughterhouses by train. With the spread of agriculture to the West, ranching moved to the High Plains, first to the Central and Northern parts, and later to the West.

In Argentina and Uruguay, merino sheep took their place along with cattle. The end of the 19th century saw the beginning of a demand for beef and mutton in these countries too. Meat was mainly taken to Britain. In the 1880s, most of the Argentinian and Uruguayan pampa was taken up by enormous ranches. In the last decade of that century Italian and Spanish immigrants rented land on the estancias, where they grew wheat for themselves for a few years and then, according to the terms of their contracts, planted lucerne and moved on to other land. It was in this way that wheat became Argentina's main produce, and sheep and cattle herding was pushed out to the drier perimeter regions of the pampa: to the South-East, to Patagonia, Chaco and North Uruguay. Later, other crops took their place alongside wheat.

The first merino sheep arrived in Australia in 1797. By 1870 sheep breeding and the wool industry had leading roles in the country. Livestock grazers took up more and more of the land. Starting in the 1860s, the open grasslands were enclosed and livestock farming became intensive. At the end of the 19th century, when meat and wool prices were low, the rainier areas were turned to wheat production, and later to mixed farms of producing both wheat and sheep. Now ranching is only found in the driest areas.

A similar process took its course in New Zealand where, until the end of the 1860s, nearly the whole country was one giant ranch. In the 1870s wheat-growing started on the Canterbury Plain. Frozen mutton and dairy products were transported to Britain starting in the 1880s. On both islands, extensive sheep-grazing gave way to intensive dairying and sheep farming. Nowadays extensive sheep farming remains only on highland regions of South Island and dry areas of North Island.

In South Africa the Boer settlers founded the first large livestock farms in the Little Karoo region. Their animals were sheep and cattle. Outside the Karoo there were farms among the mountains. Most families had two free holdings, grazing their herds on the arid Karoo in winter, and on the uplands in summer. After the British captured the Cape area, land became the property of the Crown, and after 1831 land had to be bought at auction. This was one of the reasons why the Boers started off on their Great Trek northwards to the grazing lands of the High Veld. The Karoo and the fringe of the Kalahari desert remained mainly a sheep area, with cattle-breeding moving southwards. The karakul sheep brought from Central Asia turned South Africa into a large exporter of astrakhan fur. Angora goats yielded mohair for export. Ranching is widespread in the other southern African countries, including Namibia, Zimbabwe and Zambia (Grigg, 1974).

Plantations

The plantation is a farm for producing of certain tropical or sub-tropical perennial crops for the market. Plantation crops are usually play an important part in the countries' exports. Plantations are monocultural, and usually need large amount of labour. They are not necessarily on the same scale as ranches, and indeed small farmers often produce plantation crops, but the idea of a plantation is associated with that of large farms.

The classic plantations of the past were for sugar cane, cotton and tobacco. These were the crops which were first capable of being processed or transported over long distances.

Nowadays the most important tropical plantation crops are: cocoa, bananas, coconut, jute, sisal, hemp, rubber, coffee and oil palm. The subtropical crops are: sugar cane, cotton, tea, peanuts, citrus fruits and tobacco. Of lesser importance but also widely grown are many others such as the spices pepper, cloves, vanilla and cinnamon, and the pesticide pyrethrum.

It was the Portuguese who founded the first plantations, on the Canary and Cape Verde Islands off the West African coast. Sugar cane was the crop that they grew there, and they also set up sugar refineries to process it. From here they introduced sugar cane to the West Indies. The first sugar plantation on Hispaniola was set up in 1503.

American plantations depended on slave labour. The first African slaves were transported by the Spaniards to Hispaniola in 1501. The practice of slave cultivation spread from Latin America to the South of the United States where slaves worked on the tobacco and cotton plantations. Slave labour flourished up to its abolition in the middle of the 19th century whereupon many plantations ceased, or were divided up and sold to smallholders or put out to rent to sharecroppers. Large plantations employed wage labourers.

It is worth examining some examples of the spread of American plantations.

Sugar cane plantations

At the beginning of the 16th century, sugar cane growing shifted from Hispaniola to the North-East part of Brazil. Share-tenants cultivated six-hectare plots on the large estates with 20 slaves on each plot. In the 18th century, production started on a large scale in the British and French Antilles, and later in the Dutch Barbados, Guyana and Martinique islands. The Little Antilles led the sugar trade at the end of the 18th century. In the 19th century the centre of sugar production moved to the two Spanish islands Cuba and Puerto Rico. More than half a million slaves were transported to Cuba between 1810 and 1870 to work on the sugar plantations. Slavery was only abolished in Cuba in 1886. Cuba maintains its lead in sugar exports to the present day, but after the United States broke its connection with it following the revolution, Peru also came to prominence in sugar production.

Cotton plantations

Cotton plantations in the United States started in the 1790s in the South, in the states of Georgia and South Carolina, spreading to North Carolina and Virginia and later westwards to the Lower Mississippi Valley. The cotton area was at its highest in the 1920s, when the whole of the South grew it, and irrigated production began in Arizona, New Mexico and California.

Abolition of slavery did not stop the expansion of land sown with cotton. Contraction only began in the 1930s owing to the spread of boll-weevil and the low prices of the 1930s. This period saw farmers of the cotton belt turning to peanuts, tobacco, soya beans, sorghum, maize and other crops as well as cotton, so that the region lost its uniform identification with cotton.

Following the freeing of the slaves, land was divided among sharecroppers. Many of these, however, migrated North with the rise of industrialization and the consequent demand for labour. After this, many of the holdings became either family farms or large plantations worked by hired labour.

Banana Plantations

Bananas arrived in the Americas from the Canary Islands in 1516, but was only produced in significant quantities from the end of the 19th century, with the introduction of rail transport and refrigerated ships. Banana plantations appeared in Costa Rica, Nicaragua and Panama in the 1880s, and even earlier in the Caribbean coastal areas of Jamaica. Honduras, Guatemala and Mexico soon caught up with these. The plantations were owned by large companies. The largest plantation owner was the United Fruit Company (now United Brand). This company not only ran the banana plantations, but held sway over the politics of the so-called 'banana republics'. As the unofficial representative of the United States, it brought down governments and put others into power. The banana boom lasted until the 1920s. Between the two World Wars, some diseases of the bananas, worn-out soil and political tensions moved the United Fruit Company to close down many of its plantations in the banana republics and the greater part of production was taken over by smallholders. The centre of production moved to Ecuador after the Second World War.

Coffee plantations

Coffee became one of South America's most important plantation crops. It was brought to the Antilles in the 18th century and was already growing in the Rio de Janeiro area by 1774. From here it spread first to the humid inland areas

243

beyond Santos and Rio de Janeiro, afterwards to the Paraíba valley and the interior of São Paulo, and then northwards towards the Rio Grande and westwards towards the Paraná River. At first slaves produced the coffee on large estates. After the freeing of the slaves in 1886, Spanish and Italian migrants were employed in the state of São Paulo to clear the forest and plant coffee trees. These people also usually grew their own food. After five years, on the appearance of the first harvest, they moved on to another fazenda. Smaller landowners also took part as the coffee-growing area spread westwards. Even today, the area around Santos is one of Brazil's main coffee growing regions, and coffee is shipped from the port of Santos. Nowadays, however, much of the former coffee-growing land is worn out and other crops grow there, and indeed ranching has become important as labour has become more expensive.

Rubber

The demand for rubber grew significantly in the second half of the 19th century. Goodyear invented vulcanization in 1839, and shortly afterwards Dunlop the pneumatic tyre. The manufacturing, chemical, motor and electrical industries all had a great need for rubber.

The rainforest of the southern coast of Amazonia was the original home of the *Hevea Brasiliensis* rubber tree. There, rubber tapping and the export of latex began. 1850-1910 can be called the Brazil's rubber period. Rubber caused a bigger boom than gold. The population along the Amazon grew by 20,000 a year and new cities (Manaus, Obidos, Santarém) sprung up. After a while, however, the rubber tappers had to venture ever further into the rainforest and their task became more and more difficult. They worked further and further from the River Amazon, which was the only transport route. Latex became more expensive. In 1876, the English smuggled out the rubber seeds which had been preciously guarded by the Brazilians. The saplings were grown at Kew Botanical Gardens in London and then taken to Ceylon, Malaya and Sumatra. The transplanting was a success. Between 1910 and 1913 the British Firestone company set up plantations, and were followed by French and Dutch companies. These accounted for 90 per cent of the world's production by 1924. The British plantations were in the Malayan Peninsula, Ceylon and South India, the Dutch in Sumatra and Java, and the French in South-East India. Nowadays the main producers are Malaysia, Indonesia, Sri Lanka and Thailand. The centre of the rubber trade is Singapore. The significance of rubber declined in the 1950s with the increasing use of synthetic rubber, but made a comeback as a necessary constituent of steel radial tyres and other products.

Asian plantations

In Asia, the British and Dutch East India Companies had for a long time bought spices, coconuts, tea, indigo and other commodities, and taken them to Europe. Small farmers produced the export commodities alongside food crops, and were often forced to do so by measures such as compulsory deliveries and taxation. The colonial period at the end of the 19th century saw the setting up of plantations, but only in sparsely populated regions, because Asia, unlike the settler countries, was densely populated and in the densely populated areas every last piece of agricultural land was worked. In setting up new plantations, rubber had the greatest momentum, in order to supply the growing demand for it from the rapidly-industrializing Europe. Other than rubber, tea plantations became significant, and there were others: coffee, tropical fruit, spices.

The Asian plantations tended to be larger than the American, and were controlled by large companies with owners in London, Paris and Berlin. Since the plantations were set up in sparsely populated regions, they had to bring in labour from outside. Thus tea was picked in Ceylon by Tamils taken there for the purpose, and rubber tapped by Biharis in Malaya and Assam, and by Chinese in Sumatra.

In addition to European industrialization, the Asian plantations were given a further lift by the partial decline of the American plantations after the abolition of slavery.

Most plantations were in the coastal regions, from where the goods could easily be transported. Following the end of colonial times, local landowners, as well as Indians and Chinese, took them over, or they were occupied by squatters, as in Sumatra. Nowadays many plantation crops are actually produced by small farmers.

African plantations

A good proportion of the African plantations also started in the second half of the 19th century. Although the Portuguese had for a long time grown sugar cane in the Cape Verde, Canary, São Tomé and Fernando Poe Islands, these had declined since the focus of sugar planting and processing moved to Brazil in the 16th century. Until the colonization of the 19th century, Africa was considered not so much a source of commodities as of slaves. There were few indigenous crops, and there were difficulties of transport, since there were hardly any navigable rivers, and in the estuaries, mangrove swamps hindered the harbouring of ships. Rainforests and various tropical diseases prevented the penetration of the interior.

Plantation crops eventually made headway in Africa, as in Asia, when they received the encouragement of rising European demand and declining

American plantations. Despite this, not many plantations appeared in Africa because white settlers were put off by the hostile climate. In addition, capital was mainly attracted to South-East Asia at the end of the 19th century. Labour was also difficult to find, because the local population were generally unwilling to work as employed labourers. In the first decades of the 19th century, the by now unsaleable slaves were put to work on local plantations (for example in the Sultanate of Zanzibar, Dahomey and Angola), and although slavery did not continue into the second half of the century, labour was still in many ways forced, and those working on the plantations themselves did so under conditions of semi-slavery.

The most well-known plantation land in the latter part of the 19th century was the Belgian Congo, where the Belgian Free State was first claimed for the Belgian King Leopold by the explorer H.M. Stanley, and later, in 1908, taken over by the Belgian government when international protests against the ruthless exploitation, physical punishment, imprisonment and other oppression of the local population became too strong. Many concessions were given for founding plantations in the Belgian colony.

In North Africa, the French and Italian colonists started up plantations, mainly for citrus fruits, vines and cotton. Included among plantation countries were the former German colonies of Cameroun, Togo and Tanganyika. In East Africa, Kenya, having been taken over by the British, there were many plantations in the so-called White Highlands. The number of plantations in West Africa was much smaller due to the unattractiveness of the climate for would-be white settlers and bans on plantations by the French, and, for some time, by the British too. There were also plantations in those parts of South Africa and Rhodesia populated by white settlers, and also, mainly in the 20th century, in the colonies already held for many centuries by the Portuguese, Angola and Mozambique.

As in Asia, small farmers were made to produce plantation crops. This was mostly done through compelling deliveries and imposing taxes, but they were also given assistance with seeds, advice and other services, as well as with purchase of their produce.

The plantation crops of North Africa are mainly cotton, citrus fruits, dates, other fruits and vines. In East Africa, coffee, tea, cloves, and pyrethrum are most prevalent. Widespread in West Africa are oil palms, bananas, cotton, cocoa and rubber (see figure 10.1). Liberia has enormous rubber plantations owned by the Firestone Company. In Ivory Coast, besides cocoa, there is significant coffee growing. Cotton is important in Nigeria and Mali. The loose

Figure 10.1   **Major production areas of Africa**

Source: Sebes, T., 1969, *Africa*, Móra Könyvkiadó, Budapest

soils of the Sahel countries are well-suited to peanuts, one of the largest producers being Senegal. Zaire is a producer of oil palm, coffee, cotton, cocoa and bananas. Guinea Coast is noted for its extraction of high-value rainforest wood. In Angola, coffee is the most important plantation crop, and in the countries of southern Africa along the coast of the Indian Ocean there are sugar cane, tropical fruit and tea plantations. The most valuable crop of the settler farms in the highlands of Zimbabwe is Virginia tobacco (Grigg, 1974).

The number of plantations reduced after decolonization. In North Africa, plantations were either allotted to smallholders or turned into state and cooperative farms. In Kenya a large proportion of the plantations of the White Highlands were divided up (according to the law 400,000 hectares, but in the end actually 570,00 hectares, from an original 3.1 million hectares) into farms of 10-15 hectares, with the owners receiving long-term compensation. Many of the new owners were unable, however, to pay the instalments on the compensation and were forced to sell. In this way, some of the plantations were reconstituted by black, Indian and white owners. Many plantations still have English owners (Hecklau, 1989). In Tanzania, some plantations were turned into state farms or shareholder companies with joint foreign and Tanzanian ownership. In Kenya it is the European-owned coffee plantations which are significant, in Tanzania the sisal plantations. There are still many plantation areas in Liberia, Zaire, Zambia and Zimbabwe.

The family farm

Small farms which are managed and largely worked by the members of a family, with at most 1 or 2 permanent, and a few more seasonal employees fall into the category of 'family farms'.

The family farm does not aim to maximise profit, as does a capitalist farm, but to maximise the consumption of the family members (Chayanov, 1966). In family farms the output optimum will be reached at level when the drudgery of the marginal labour expenditure of the working family members will equal the subjective evaluation of the marginal utility of the sum obtained by this labour. The subjective evaluation of the values obtained by this marginal labour will depend on the extent of its marginal utility for the consumers of the farm family. Family farms do not strive to maximize the net profit as capitalist enterprises do, but their net product (gross income minus outlays on materials), i.e. demand satisfaction per unit labour. If there is an opportunity for family farm labourers to work outside the farm in crafts or trade the wage payment of these occupations will be regarded as opportunity cost of . In this case labour will fully be applied on the family farm only if the agricultural net product is higher than, or the same as, the wages earned outside the farm, otherwise it will be divided between all the working opportunities in such a way that the highest payment per labour unit should be reached. According to G.H. Schmitt (Schmitt, 1989) farming becomes part-time because the farmers cannot reach the desired net product maximum in low-income agriculture and are forced to take on outside work. This is true not only for developed Western agriculture, but – as mentioned in Part I – to a certain extent in the developing countries too. There, home-produced crafts are the most common secondary activities, but there is some outside employment too. In Africa, for example, 25-30 per cent of the family income and 30-50 per cent of its money income comes from non-agricultural activities either within or outside the farm.

The family farm may be privately-owned or tenanted. In the United States the two are often found in combination. Wheat- and corn-growing farmers often rent at least as much land as they own. Of medium sized farms, about 60 per cent are on partly rented land (Reimund, 1991).

The size of family farms – as with land holdings in general – varies considerably in different parts of the world. The average sizes for Europe are shown in table 10.2. There is a wide distribution around the averages. In the former West Germany in 1987, for example, 46 per cent of farms were between 10 and 50 hectares and only 8 per cent larger than 50 hectares. At the same time in the United Kingdom the number between 10 and 50 hectares was only 38 percent, and 31 per cent were larger than 50 hectares. In the United States the 'small' family farms range in size between a few hectares to several thousand. There is a similarly large spread in Australia.

In Argentina and Brazil the small family farms are overshadowed by the large estates. More than half of Brazilian small farmers work farms of less than 10 hectares (Handelsblatt, 1990).

Family farming either developed directly out of ancient common farming with the rise of population and agricultural intensity – as in a large part of Africa – the land becoming permanently used by one family, sometimes by becoming its property, or arose from historical events. The historical route in Europe was firstly the working of land by slaves and later by serfs, and in England tenanting, whereas in Asia it was through sharecropping on the royal estates or their large tenants. In the southern part of North America, and in Central and South America, capitalist and family farms also grew out of a process which started with slavery and changed later to sharecropping.

The historical routes culminated with the evolution of family farming, or by radical land reform, and in some parts of the world have still not finished.

History can be said to have been kind to those settler countries where family farming took root right at the beginning, such as the northern part of the United States, New Zealand and Australia. The first English immigrants in these countries did not have to cope with the remains of a feudal system, like the one they had left behind, while at the same time they were already well

Table 10.2
Size of farms (1987)

	Belgium	Denmark	FRG	Greece	Spain	France	Ireland	Italy	Luxem-bourg	Nether-lands	Portugal	UK
Average area in ha	14.8	30.7	19.4	4.0	13.9	28.6	22.7	5.6	30.2	15.3	4.3	51.5
%-age of farms of size												
<5 ha	23.5	1.9	29.7	51.2	45.7	16.9	16.1	48.1	17.3	22.4	35.4	12.6
5-10	15.4	16.7	16.6	14.8	16.3	10.9	15.2	12.0	9.1	16.4	5.7	11.6
10-20	20.8	26.0	20.3	5.6	10.6	17.8	29.1	6.2	11.4	23.0	2.4	14.3
20-50	20.3	38.9	25.8	1.8	8.1	30.5	30.7	3.3	29.8	25.8	1.1	23.8
50+	5.0	15.3	7.8	0.3	5.2	16.8	8.9	1.4	24.0	3.9	0.9	31.2

Source: Europe in Figures 1989/90, Eurostat, 1992

acquainted with the incipient capitalist farm and, for their time, advanced technology and ideas of enterprise. It was among them that the 'enterprising farmer' originated, which became associated with the world's most efficient agriculture. It is worth comparing the way that the family farming systems of Europe and the New World came into being.

The development of family farming in Europe

Capitalism first evolved in Europe, in its most developed country, England. Feudal property relations came to an end as a direct result of capitalist development first in Western and later in Eastern Europe. In Western Europe the family farm became prevalent, but the large capitalist estates of Eastern Europe were marked with the remnants of feudalism, which disappeared only after the Second World War.

The winding up of feudalism started first of all in England. The manufacturers in Flanders and later in England needed more and more wool, which stimulated the growth of sheep breeding. Enclosure of common land started in the 13th century and became widespread from the end of the 15th century. Sheep farming was good business for the landed gentry, and they let out large areas for this purpose. In the 15th century they started to mark out and consolidate sections of what had until then been common fields as belonging to one particular farm. Farms received proportionate measures of meadow, pasture and fallow. Grazing access to common lands and to arable lands after the harvest was thus stopped. Much of the enclosed land became the property of the lord and was leased. The newly enclosed lands of the peasants were often worse than their old ones, and since their ability to raise animals was limited by the fencing off of the common pastures and the ending of their right to graze on the stubble, they became even poorer. They were often obliged to sell their lands to the lords. Some became tenant farmers on the large farms, but the poorer ones and the landless farm labourers left the village and became industrial workers or reserves of manpower for industry.

Enclosures started as individual acts of coercion, but received legal confirmation from parliament at various times between the 18th and 19th centuries. In the 19th century English agriculture was characterised by capitalist tenanted farms of a few hundred hectares. In the second half of the 19th century, when overseas competition in wool from Australia and New Zealand started, and when the creeping agricultural crisis made land ownership and rental less and less profitable, increasing numbers of large estates were broken up and became the property of family farmers. In this way family farming gradually took its place in England, similarly to other European countries.

251

Up to the time of the Revolution in France, only a small part of the land was in the use of feudal landlords. A large proportion of the land was farmed by tenants with perpetual or limited leases. The perpetual leases could be inherited, let out or gifted. The tenants paid rents to the landowners, taxes in kind and fulfilled various duties of service. There was already a class of rich peasants, who rented land along with their own farms, and of course beneath them were the small peasants and the landless class.

In 1789 the national constituent assembly abolished the landlord's jurisdiction and some other feudal rights. In 1793 all feudal rights were discontinued and the Convent upheld the peasants right to take possession of the land they used without compensation. The richer peasants were also given the opportunity to buy land confiscated from the Church in 1789. Where there were no public lands to distribute, the landless and poorer peasants got plots of land from confiscated Church or landlords who had fled. France thus became a nation of smallholders.

In most of Europe's Latin countries, and in the Low Countries, Switzerland and the western part of Germany, feudalism was dismantled by the victorious Napoleonic armies or by local liberals in sympathy with or in league with the French. The French armies announced the immediate ending of priests' tithes, vassalage and landlords' rights in each country they occupied. By 1799 feudalism had legally ended in all of France's eastern neighbours, in North and Central Italy, and in 1808 in South Italy and between 1811 and 1813 in Spain. Political changes and restorations inhibited further reforms in South Italy, Sicily and the Iberian Peninsula. In Sicily, 90 per cent of the land area remained in the hands of nobles.

Feudalism had already ceased in Denmark in the reforms of the 1780s. The beneficiaries of enclosure were in this case not the landed nobles, but the peasant tenants and farmers. The great estates were divided up and sold to the sitting tenants. This process was effectively complete by 1800. By 1865 Denmark had become a nation of peasant landowners. A similar process took place in Sweden. The traditional common cultivation died out in the second half of the 19th century. The feudal provinces were assimilated into the rest of the country, where the free peasantry had always been dominant. There was a broadly similar story in Norway, which belonged to Denmark until 1815, and then to Sweden.

In Eastern Europe, where feudalism had become established somewhat later than elsewhere, capitalism was also slow in coming. Instead of giving way to a landholding peasantry, the farmstead of landlords became even larger. With Europe becoming capitalist, its rising demand for agricultural produce and the consequent high prices and export opportunities prompted the landed gentry to extend their farmed estates by occupying the land of serfs, and producing grain through feudal forced labour. The governments which represented the magnates and the gentry confirmed their feudal rights and prolonged feudal property relations. All this naturally held back industrial and urban development. The movement to capitalism in the wake of the West led, therefore, not to the smallholders' agriculture but to the transformation of the great feudal estates into capitalist farms. East of the Elbe, the all-pervasive process of agricultural development was the 'Prussian Course', by which feudal lords became capitalists, and serfs wage-labourers.

Prussia abolished serfdom between 1807 and 1809, and put an end to feudal privileges, but a royal decree of September 14, 1811 refused to recognize the rights of peasants to own land, and in fact required them to hand part of their plots, one-half or one-third, to their lords in exchange for their freedom, or pay them its value. Buying land was only open to the better-off peasants. The landowners manœuvred to join the untended lands and most of the peasants' lands to their estates. By the middle of the 19th century, Prussia had become a country dominated by great capitalist estates.

In the countries belonging to the House of Habsburg, the earliest land reforms date from the end of the 18th century, but the final abolition of feudal property relations and the granting of land rights to peasants, with compensation, only took place after the revolutions of 1848. Great estates also took hold in Hungary, and in Galicia 50 per cent of the land belonged to large manors at the time when peasants were granted the right to own land. Peasant ownership prevailed in varying proportions in a majority of the Habsburg Empire's other countries, such as Bohemia and Moravia.

In Russia serfdom only ceased after the Tsar's decree of 1861. By the terms of the decree, the peasants should have been given land. The size of the plots depended on agreement between the peasants and the landowners. The land to which the peasant gained access to remained the property of the noble. In return for its use, the peasant was required to give certain services to the lord. The decree also provided for redeeming of land, but gave no deadline for this measure. However it allowed the peasants to change their rent to money two years after the issuing of the decree. Most of the land remained great manorial estates.

In the Central, Northern and some Novisibirsk Provinces, land was not given to individual peasants, but to the whole community, which had to fulfil the duties towards the overlords collectively. Individual purchase of land was made possible by a separate law. Among the noble's privileges which remained after abolition of serfdom were the right of 'protection' of his peasants, and the power of policing them. Only a small proportion of the total peasant land belonged to individual peasants, the rest being available to the community at large, which from time to time shared out the land between members of the community. The peasants could only leave the commune after paying for their plot of land, and this only the better-off peasants were able to do. The duties towards the lord an the state were carried out by the community, the *obchina*, and its council, the *mir*.

Feudalism persisted even longer in South-East Europe. Serfdom only ceased in Romania in 1864, and the large estates remained. Most of the peasantry worked on the large estates or rented land in exchange for labour.

Serbian peasants were allowed to obtain land from the beginning of the 19th century. In the rest of what later became Yugoslavia it was only after 1848, and in Macedonia just before the First World War, that the process of land redistribution began. Large estates featured strongly in Yugoslavia, too. As a result of the 1919 land reform, the former tenants of the former Turkish large estates were granted the rights of ownership in the southern and western parts of the country. The estates continued in the North, although they reduced in size (Land Reform, 1974).

The only country in Central Europe where a small-landowning peasantry took hold was Bulgaria. During the Russian-Turkish War of 1878, the peasants organized a mass land redistribution of the estates. Afterwards the land distribution was given official blessing on payment of compensation, and the peasants also received the rights to the remaining Turkish lands without compensation. In newly independent Bulgaria almost the only large estates which remained belonged to the monasteries (Ciepieleski et. al., 1985 and Hobsbawm, 1988).

Small family farms, therefore, were the end result of developments in most of Western Europe. In Southern Europe many large estates broke up, and the power of the great landlords was also brought to an end in Italy by the post-war land reforms, and in Portugal by the land reform of 1977, followed by the more thorough reform of 1984.

In Eastern Europe changes had to wait for radical reforms. Russia nationalized land in 1917, and divided it for use by the peasantry in such a way that the right to part of the local communal land – including the household plot, arable and meadow land – was titled, and the parts used commonly – pasture, rivers, wasteland etc. – remained untitled. In the Russian Federation in 1927, 95.4 per cent of peasant land was still cultivated by the obchina communities, (Tanka, 1988). In the other countries of Eastern Europe, the land reforms after the Second World War put a family farm system into place, but this was soon swept away by collectivization along 1930s Soviet lines. The only exceptions to this were in Poland, where 77 per cent of the agricultural land remained in private hands (4 per cent became production cooperatives and 19 per cent state farms), and Yugoslavia, where collectivization stopped as a consequence of the break with the Soviet Union in 1948 and the economic reform of 1965. In 1991, 81 per cent of the area of Yugoslavia was being cultivated by individually-owned farms and 19 per cent by cooperatives. Private and collective agriculture was integrated in the form of agrobusiness combinates handling processing and distribution and working with the multitude of small farms through contracts.

Poland's agriculture, despite remaining largely small peasant farms, did not fare any better than other socialist countries' collective agriculture. Among the reasons for this was the break-up of farms through heritage and the central restrictions such as the prohibition of buying, selling and renting land and limiting the employment of labour. In addition agricultural prices were low, withdrawals high, and state subsidies lacking. Polish farms for the most part remained poorly equipped, and many of them did not rise above subsistence level.

Family farms in Europe

The formerly diverse livestock-breeding and crop-growing so-called mixed farms of Western Europe gradually became specialized. Some specialization was already well-established in some regions (in South Europe fruit, vegetables, wine, sheep and goats, in Southern France wine, in Northern France and Southern Germany sugar beet, in the oceanic countries cattle-breeding, in Scandinavia dairying etc.) but most farms in these regions also produced all or most of their own food requirements too. It was mainly a result of developments after the Second World War that farms in the most developed countries devoted themselves exclusively to one or two commodities in either livestock farming or crop growing or a combination of the two. Specialization of farms was usually accompanied by specialization of regions, so that certain areas became primarily associated with cereals, cattle, vegetables and ornamentals (the latter two especially in Holland). The specialized farms now confined themselves to producing commodities, the farmers meeting their food requirements through the market, like workers in any other industry.

Specialization of farms was not paralleled, however, by their concentration. The average farm size in the 10 member states of the EC grew from 12 hectares in 1960 to 14 in 1985 (Europe in Figures 1989/90, 1992). Only in Belgium and Luxembourg did the number of farms fall by as much as a half over the quarter of a century, in Germany, Holland, France and Denmark the reduction was by 30-40 per cent, and in the other countries 10-20 per cent or even less (see figure 10.2).

There were two main reasons why there was so little concentration: firstly, high levels of subsidy maintained otherwise unviable small farms, and secondly, part-time farming became widespread, where the farmer's main income was not agricultural. According Europe in Figures 1989/90, only 23 per cent of those working in agriculture in the EC were employed on a full time basis. (It should be pointed out that among the part-time farmers were those with no

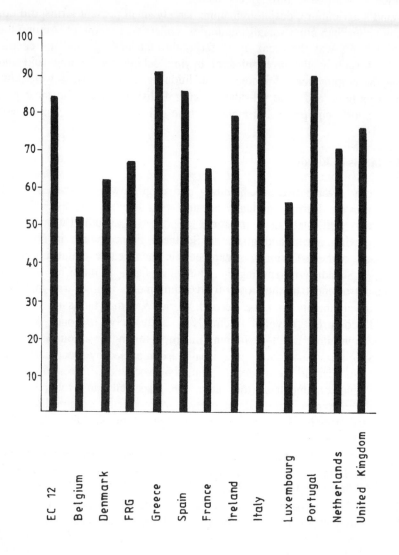

**Figure 10.2   Decrease in the number of farms from 1970 to 1986
(1970 = 100)**

other occupation, and so were part of the hidden unemployed.) In 1983, full time farmers constituted 44.4 per cent of the total in West Germany, 55.5 per cent in France, 11.6 in Italy, 74.9 in the Netherlands, 64.6 in Belgium, 72.1 in Luxembourg, 63.1 in the United Kingdom, 61.9 in Denmark, 45.9 in Ireland and 10.2 in Greece (Alexandratos, 1990). The smaller the farms (see Southern Europe), the more part-time farming. This part-time farming, as mentioned previously, is widespread in such other developed countries as Japan and the United States.

Although most commodity production, around 2/3 or more, is due to a small number of full-time specialized large farms, part-time farms are also highly specialized except in Southern Europe's more backward regions. Part-timers, having less time, tend to fully mechanize and simplify their farming as much as possible. (The situation is different in kitchen-gardens around houses or spare-time allotments, but these are of little significance in agricultural production.)

Part-time farming is one of the causes of a new phenomenon, the feminization of agriculture (Pfeffer, 1989): most male members of the family work outside agriculture; the women are at home and look after the farm.

Family farms in North America and Oceania

Specialization got under way in North America long before it did in Europe. The first settlers on the East Coast chiefly farmed for their own needs, but those occupying the lands toward the West produced for trade from the beginning (Hobsbawm, 1988). Mechanical harvesters made their first appearance in the first half of the last century (the Hussey in 1833 and the Cyrus McCormick in 1834), and the agricultural entrepreneurs used them to substitute for scarce and expensive labour. The plentiful land, relatively large farms and small workforce forced the earlier family farms, too, into simplifying production and concentrating on one or two crops with mechanical assistance.

It was a different story in the South where there were a lot of slaves to do the work. Specialization here was not based on the family farm but on the plantation. After abolition, the land was worked by squatters, i.e. sharecroppers and wage-labourers. More and more black workers went North to take part in the rapid industrialization in the North. At the end of the 19th century and the beginning of the 20th, the southern Cotton Belt also took on a different character with the plantations first being broken up and sold off, and later larger mechanized farms taking shape.

In the North at the end of the last century, agriculture's westward spread gave rise to the wheat and corn belts, whose function was partly to provide fodder to fatten cattle headed for Chicago's slaughterhouses. The higher income-producing corn – later in rotation with soya beans – pushed the production of wheat to drier areas further to the West. This gave rise to the spring-wheat belt in Montana, North and South Dakota and across the Canadian border in Alberta and Saskatchewan, and the autumn-wheat belt in Kansas, Oklahoma and Texas. As cultivation moved to the West, it grew more extensive and the farms larger. This was due to the abundance of land and the increasing possibilities of mechanization on one hand, and these regions' drier climate and weaker soils on the other. More intensive farming supplied the cities from the earliest settled states in the North-East and around the Great Lakes, from Maine to Minnesota and in the milk belt stretching up to Canada, where Swedish, Irish, Swiss and Dutch settlers, with their dairying traditions, gave rise to the city-supplying and fodder-producing areas (Mészáros et al, 1987). As the wheat belt was pushed westwards, so extensive ranching went even further on the High Plains as far as the Rocky Mountains. It was mainly companies that set up the ranches on these dry-climate, weak-soil areas. The one-time cotton growing state of California became the United States' supplier of fruits, vegetables and wine, as well as growing cotton, rice, sugar cane and other crops, and Florida became the major citrus-growing region. Labour-intensive production in southern areas is mainly undertaken by foreign migrant workers, in particular from Mexico. Figure 10.3 shows the main production zones of the United States.

Family farms in the United States and Canada are in general larger than in Europe, and the same is true for company farms occupying a smaller part of the land. Smaller farms are to be found in the densely populated areas in the Eastern coastal states and the areas adjacent to the Great Lakes, but even there are usually bigger than 50 or 60 hectares. Most part-time farmers also live in the city belts, where opportunities for ment outside agriculture are greater. In 1987, 46 per cent of farmers' main occupation was outside agriculture and more than 50 per cent of farm incomes came from outside (Reimund, 1991).

In 1991 only 12 per cent of the average farm household income was earned from farming operations. Only 18 per cent of farm households obtained more income from farming than from elsewhere (Gale and Harrington, 1993).

In the corn belt it is hardly possible for a farm to be viable on an area of less than 500 hectares. There are many farms which are partly owned and partly rented. Concentration has also been faster in North America than in Europe, especially in recent decades. During the deep recession at the beginning of the 1980s, there were mass bankruptcies among farms which were already in debt and unable to pay the rising interest, so that they passed into the ownership of other farmers.

Development in Australia and New Zealand was in more or less the same direction that it was in North America. The Australian farmers first started the wool industry, and later on the wet areas combined merino breeding with

258

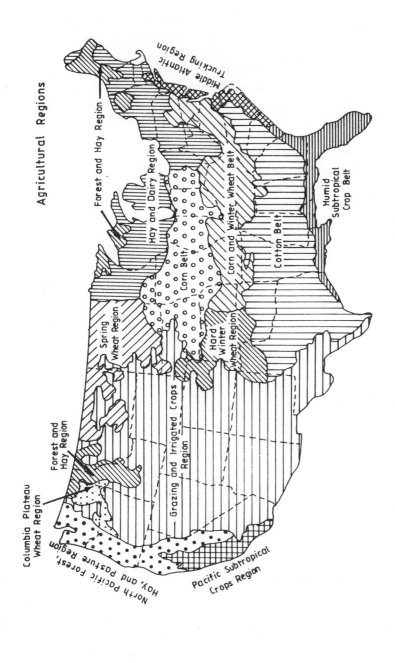

Figure 10.3 **Main agricultural regions of the United States**

Source: Walter Sullivan, *Landprints*, Times Books, New York Times Book Co., 1984

wheat production. Production became mechanized here, too. In 1843, John Ridley invented the 'Stripper', a horse-powered harvesting machine, which revolutionized wheat production. Harvester-threshers were in widespread use from the 1890s. There was an attempt by farmers in the tropical coastal region of Queensland to grow sugar cane on plantations using semi-enslaved Kanaka labour imported from Melanesia, but this was prohibited by the British Government in 1901. After this, the plantations broke up into what became family farms. Sheep farming and wheat-growing are still Australia's chief agricultural activities, except in the coastal areas of the East and South-East, where sugar cane, bananas, tobacco, cotton, citrus, vines and fruits grow over a wide area, and beef cattle and dairy cattle are bred.

New Zealand's agriculture was also built on pastoral merino breeding. Later, chiefly on North Island, cattle and dairying became widespread. Livestock farming is still the leading sector of New Zealand agriculture, and provides much of the country's exports. For domestic consumption, cereals, potatoes, other temperate zone crops, fruits, vegetables and vines are also grown. Most farms are of the family type, and more than 50 per cent of them are of between 50 and 500 hectares (Balázs, 1978).

11 Land reforms in the developing world

Many developing countries carried out land reforms after the Second World War. The reforms concerned the basic interests of the biggest population group, the peasantry. Before the reforms, the agricultural sector in these countries was typified by an extreme ownership structure. A small number of large estates occupied the greater part of the cultivable agricultural land, and the large number of tiny farms only a small percentage. The masses of sharecroppers, smallholders who could not make a living from their own land, and unemployed, provided labour to work the great estates. The condition of sharecroppers in many countries was close to serfdom. They were paid in kind, had to hand over most of what they produced, and in addition on the great landowners' estates and houses were also obliged to work their rent and discharge various other services. This was the case not only in the traditionally feudal-style Latin American countries, but in Asia and in many African countries where much or all of the common land had been appropriated and made quasi- or actual private property by royal tax-collectors, or granted by the king to other high-ranking officials and soldiers in recognition of their services. The colonial authorities often recognized the quasi-proprietor as the true owner. The tension between small and large landowners was further aggravated by the colonial settlers acquisition of land to start plantations.

The land reforms had both social and economic goals. The social aim was to eliminate or moderate the social inequalities of the village. Land reform was one of the principal claims of the independence struggle, and the mainly left-wing leaders who came to power had already promised to carry it out. But even the remaining conservative élites could not get out of meeting the demands of the popular movements. In Latin America the widening guerrilla movements, the peasant uprisings and spontaneous land occupations led to

261

revolutionary situations which only land reform appeared to give hope of alleviating.

The economic goal of reforms were usually to lift agriculture out of its backward condition. The feudal-style estates were normally worked extensively with low yields. Yields were typically higher on lands of small and medium landowners. The reforms thus promised the raising of agricultural intensity.

The desire to raise efficiency lay behind the linking of many land reforms with the setting up of producer cooperatives and state farms, and was the main consideration of governments in North Africa, Angola, Mozambique and some other countries in their unwillingness to divide up the plantations abandoned by the colonists. Economies of scale were also cited as grounds for reunifying the redistributed land through setting up cooperatives.

From a wider economic point of view, one of the hopes of land reform was that by granting land to landless labourers would absorb some rural unemployment and diminish the drift to the cities. Industrial capitalists' hope was that the rising buying power of landowning peasants would lead to an increased demand for industrial goods and give a stimulus to industrial development.

Most land reforms were carried out in such a way that they made use first of all of abandoned land (for example, lands abandoned by colonists after independence was proclaimed, or those of people fleeing revolutions, coups d'état, and other changes of regime, or of enforced emigrants) and also of public land and unused or badly cultivated areas. In the case of radical reforms, this was followed by expropriation of cultivated privately-owned land. Less radical reforms did not usually go as far.

In countries where sharecropping was widespread, the first priority of land reforms was its abolition, or the reduction of rents, increase of security of tenants, and generally widening and codifying tenants' rights. In many countries, land reforms started this way and continued with land redistribution. There were countries where the process got no further than this stage. Radical tenant reforms granted to the tenants exclusive rights of use, or even of ownership, over the land.

We will now look at the more significant land reforms of the three developing parts of the world – Latin America, Asia and Africa. Land reforms generally take their place within wider agricultural reforms which include institutional reform, modernization measures, promoting intensification and productivity, raising yields, building infrastructure and others. Close interaction between land reform and some of these other elements is therefore also mentioned where appropriate.

Latin America

Latin America is the region of extreme property relations. The Spanish and Portuguese colonists left a legacy of extensive large estates with their exploitative sharecrop tenancy system, and a large number of very small holdings on a small minority of the land area. Scarcity of land and rural poverty are still burning questions in most Latin American countries. Some kind of land reform has been forced on nearly every country through rural uprisings, land occupations and various peasant movements. How effectively the laws were enforced depended very much on the governments and those who wielded political power. There have been alternating periods of dictatorship and democracy in many Latin American countries. In the democracies there were attempts to solve the land question by legal democratic means. Legality in many cases was accompanied by inertia and inconsistencies due to taking the interests of all concerned parties into consideration. Among the dictatorships, the extreme radicalism of the Left – typified in many cases by forcing peasants into cooperatives – alternated with the inclination to restrained reforms or even counter-reform of the Right. After the fall of some dictatorships in the mid-1980s the new democratic governments moved against the measures of their predecessors either by trying to eliminate radicalism (as in Peru) or by taking up land reforms which had been abandoned in the past (as in Brazil).

Mexico

Latin America's very first land reform took place in Mexico during the Revolution of the 1910s. In 1910, 1 per cent of the population had possession of 97 per cent of the agricultural land, and 92 per cent of the rural people were landless.

It was the demands of guerrilla leader Emiliano Zapata and his followers which gave rise to the Mexican land reform. Zapata led the armed revolutionary campaign in the years after 1910. Among those who took part in the uprising were Indians who were fighting to regain lands taken from them for the great haciendas. The revolutionary Congress of 1917 adopted a new constitution whose 27th paragraph, in response to a demand of the Congress's peasant generals, included a law of land ownership and reform.

The law provided for expropriation of estates over a certain size (above 100 ha of irrigated land, 200 ha arable, 150 ha irrigated plantation, 300 ha non-irrigated plantation and 5,000 ha poor-quality land in mountainous regions), and prescribed the setting up of Indian-style communal villages, the so-called *ejido*s. Under the terms of the law, all holdings within 7 kilometres of a new ejido and over the set size limit could be confiscated and made part of the ejido. Ejido land was to be communal, and worked in the form of cooperatives or individually.

The first laws concerning ejidos, of 1920, 1922 and 1925, had little effect on the overall transformations, and it was the agrarian reform laws of 1934 and 1942 which put in place the organization which have governed the form of ejidos up to the present day. They allow the setting up of an ejido with a minimum of 20 people – usually heads of families – who thereby obtain the right to land. The structure of the ejido is laid down in the law too. Large-scale expropriations and mass organization of ejidos followed the land reforms of the 1930s.

The early ejido laws gave priority to collective farming, and such ejidos were the main aim of efforts up to 1940. Collective farming gradually ceased after this, however, and now most members of ejidos work individually.

As mentioned before, approximately 50 per cent of Mexico's land belongs to the ejido sector, but mostly in the less fertile and unirrigated South of the country. Ejidos did not provide the hoped-for solution to the problem of rural poverty. Yields on most of them are low, as are the incomes of their members. Neither is there much opportunity for development (Progress in Land Reform, 1970; Tai, 1974; Morgan, 1990). Their reprivatization is now in progress.

Bolivia

An agrarian reform programme was adopted under pressure from the peasant trade unions during the revolution which broke out in 1952. The peasants had occupied several large estates in the economically most important part of the country, Cochabamba, and the organizing movement threatened to continue the process in the rest of the country. After trade unions were set up all over Bolivia, their influence led to legal recognition of the spontaneous land occupations, and the party which gained power in 1952 accepted the reform programme. The redistribution which began in 1953 led to approximately 500,000 families receiving land. Some divided large estates also became communal villages, but these were of much lesser significance than in Mexico (Progress in Land Reform, 1970).

Guatemala

The land reform of 1954 provided for the expropriation and division of the large estates, but the military junta which came to power a few months later prevented it from being put into practice in a consistent manner. The reform was primarily directed and granting the right of sharecroppers to permanent use of their land. The number of families who did receive land was about 26,000 (Progress in Land Reform, 1970; Fleszar, 1974).

Venezuela

Along with those of Mexico and Bolivia, the Venezuelan land reform is considered to be the most successful in Latin America. Before the reform got under way in 1958-60, 2 per cent of the landowners held 80 per cent of the agricultural land.

Even in the 1940s there had been peasant syndicates who had successfully pressed for certain reform measures, such as the leasing of public land at low rents to 80,000 families. The ban on the syndicates by the military government of 1948 to 1958 only led to the movement's growing even stronger during this period. After the fall of the military government in 1958, peasants made 500 land occupations, mainly on lands which had been given back to their former owners during the regime. The new government passed the land reform law in 1958, by which the government bought from the landowners, at market prices, land which was then redistributed. Venezuela's oil incomes were what made this process possible. The National Agrarian Institute distributed 3.6 million hectares (1.7 million private and 2.1 million public) to 145,000 recipients over the period 1959-1967. It also set up cooperatives to provide services to the new landowners and offered them financial assistance (Progress in Land reform, 1970).

Cuba

Land reform occurred in Cuba after the Revolution, in 1959-63. The great estates were broken up. The upper limit for domestic landowners was first set at 400 hectares, and for sugar and rice plantations at 1,300 hectares. The 1963 agriculture law reduced the limit to 67 hectares. The land distribution between 1959 and 1963 brought into existence a large smallholding sector, which accounted for about 37 per cent of the cultivated land.

The smallholders were obliged, however, after the end of 1960, to sell or lease their land to the state farms, or to produce in accordance with the plans of the state farms. Hiring of outside labour was banned on private farms, as was selling produce privately. Central control was moderated at the beginning of the 1970s, and employing wage labour and private trade were permitted. Pressure on the peasants to work on state farms or to produce according to state farm plans was also reduced. The number of peasant associations integrated into the state farm planning system fell by half between 1973 and 1977.

At the First Party Congress of 1975, Fidel Castro offered two courses to the farmers: integration into state farms or setting up agricultural cooperatives. Although the Party still considered state farming to be a higher form of socialist agricultural organization, cooperatives also became eligible for full state support. Their number consequently multiplied. Cooperatives covered 53 per cent of privately-held land in 1983 (Deere, 1984). Pressure for nationalization, however, was reasserted from the mid-1980s.

Columbia and Ecuador

To stop the spread of the Cuban Revolution of 1959, the United States encouraged the countries of South America to institute agrarian reforms. They saw the causes of increasing mass discontent as the extreme inequality of the land ownership structure and the wide inequality of income distribution. In 1960 the South American countries and the United States met in Bogota to agree on certain reform measures. The agreement (Alliance for Progress) clarified and elaborated on the Punta del Este Charter. The participating countries agreed to make reforms, but did not set the form that they were to take.

In the wake of the agreement in 1961, Columbia put an agrarian reform law into effect with the purpose of putting to an end the remaining after-effects of the civil war-like conflicts of 1948 and the invasions of large estates.

In Ecuador, a reformist military government came to power in 1963 which represented United States interests. It put out an agricultural reform decree in 1964, and followed it up with a supplementary law on colonizing public lands.

In both countries reforms were partial and did not go a long way to solve the extreme disparities between latifundios and minifundios. However, they did give to the sharecroppers a part of the land they worked in return for compensation, and cleared up some hitherto badly-defined tenancy rights regarding length of lease, maximum rent, and the rights and duties of tenant and landlord. Uncultivated large estates or the unused or badly-used parts of estates were expropriated with compensation and redistributed. In addition, some public land was shared out.

The organization charged with implementing the Colombian reforms, INCORA (Columbian Institute of Agrarian Reform), also set up 'colonization' areas, where along with small farms there were established demonstration farms, schools, health centres and agriculture service stations. From 1970 onward production cooperatives were also organized, according to the Peruvian and Chilean model. However, only 2 per cent of agricultural land was redistributed. Instead of the annual target of 30,000 new farms, between 1962 and 1972 a total of only 20,000 farms were set up.

Of the 170,600 new farms planned in Ecuador for the period 1964 to 1974, only 13,700, or 8 per cent, actually appeared. It should be noted that a large part of the 'new' farms were not really so, but simply cases of share tenants becoming owners. Other cases involved legalizing earlier occupations of public land.

Following the passage of the land reform laws, Columbian landowners gave up a large part of their sharecrop tenancies in order to forestall privatization and the obligation to grant longer-term leases.

One definite positive aspect of the land reforms was that a great many large estates divided up their smaller holdings (by sale or transfer etc.) in fear of expropriation. The smaller farms started to be more intensively worked, since the laws also provided for the confiscation of land left fallow or neglected. In both countries there came into being a modern, capitalist, commodity-producing agricultural sector (Progress in Land reform, 1970; Tai, 1974; Mertins, 1979).

Chile

Of the 691,900-strong agricultural workforce in 1965-67, an estimated 28.1 per cent were permanently ed, 21.5 per cent landless, 26.7 per cent family members and 23.7 per cent smallholders. The number of sharecroppers were already in decline in favour of wage-labourers in the modernizing large estates.

The 1967 Agrarian Reform Law, brought in during the Christian Democratic government and Frei presidency, empowered the government to expropriate all estates larger than 80 standard hectares. (The standard hectare was based on the very fertile land of the Maipo valley near Santiago, and lands of different fertility were adjusted according to it by various multipliers.) Owners were compensated depending on the level of cultivation of the land taken from them, with local officials having considerable influence in fixing the compensation. Ownership of this land passed to the implementing Agrarian Reform Corporation, CORA.

The Agrarian Reform Law required the recipients of land to form cooperatives (*asentamiento*). Members of the cooperative could keep 1.5 hectares for their own private use in the most fertile Central Valley, and more in the less fertile southern parts, along with unlimited grazing rights.

The government was committed to cooperative farming, even though the 1967 agrarian reform law gave precedence to private farming, stressing that it was only setting up collective organizations (*asentamientos campesinos*, or officially *Sociedades Agricolas de Reforma Agraria*) for a transitional period and only if the new owners so wished. As long as the asentiamento system lasted, private plots coexisted with the collective. In 1970, about 20 per cent of cultivated land was collectively worked. A large proportion of the collectives were neglected and worked at low productivity, due to the fact that the producers left to themselves on their own land were more highly motivated to produce. An average of about 20 (varying between 9 and 35) per cent of the collectives were worked individually. The total reformed sector accounted for about 30 per cent of agricultural land.

The Unidad Popular coalition government of Salvador Allende, which came to power in 1970, committed itself to developing agriculture along socialist lines. It accelerated the expropriations. As a result production on the remaining large estates declined and investment came to a halt. By 1972, most of the confiscated lands were officially termed production cooperatives (Comités Campesinos), but in fact were still operating as asentiamentos. Other farms effectively became state farms. These were set up on farms which the state took into its control, if not its ownership, because of conflict between workers and owners, or land occupation.

In this way the government had, by 1972, taken over all of the land which the law of 1967 allowed it to do. The Frei government had expropriated 1412 properties over 6 years, compared with the Allende government's 3278 in 2 years. It was not only heads of families who were members and had land rights in the cooperatives, but every family member aged over 16, who were also entitled to their 1.5 hectares of land. Thus, although there were more than twice as many beneficiaries during Allende's period of office than during Frei's, there was only 50 per cent more irrigated land available for expropriation, and so the problem of land-hunger remained. The government was, however, unable to change the Agrarian Law because of its lack of a majority in the Congress.

The reform sector under Allende still only spread to 41 per cent of the agricultural land area and to 10-15 per cent of people ed in agriculture. Since the 1967 Agrarian Law allowed landowners to retain about 40 standard hectares, a large number of the old landowners had divested themselves of parts of their holdings and concentrated their machinery and capital on what remained. In this way the development of a modern, well-equipped middle-sized holding sector had been set in motion since the start of the Christian Democrat government.

20,000 people received land under the Frei government, and the number reached 75,000 in 1973 under Allende, when the land reform process reached its conclusion. The latter number is equal to one-third of the number of permanent workers on the large estates in 1965. Land redistribution primarily affected permanent workers and hardly touched the situation of temporary workers and smallholders.

After the military takeover of 1973, the government broke up the asentamientos and their lands, either handing them back to their former owners or allocating them to individual farmers. Altogether 35 per cent of the reform sector, including the state-controlled farms, went back to their old proprietors. The remaining land was awarded to the new owners mainly on the basis of political reliability. In 1979, only 36,746 of the original 75,000, i.e. 49 per cent, were left with newly-received land, of average parcel size 10 standard hectares.

One positive result of the reforms was the practical disappearance of estates larger than 80 standard hectares. Whereas formerly they had made up 55.4 per cent of the land area, this proportion fell to 6.1 per cent after the reforms. Their former property passed not to the smallholders, but to middle-sized landowners. In place of the great haciendas, a capital-intensive medium-sized farms became the basis of agriculture (Castillo and Lehmann, 1985).

Peru

The military government decided on large-scale land reform in 1970. They set out to take possession of 41 per cent of the agricultural land (15,000 estates and 9.7 million hectares) and distribute it among 39 per cent of peasant families, some 365,000. The programme should have been finished by 1975-1976, but its implementation fell behind plans. By 1979, however, 15,826 estates had been taken over (10.5 million hectares), but only 7.7 million hectares had been distributed among 337,662 families.

Much of the land (62.3 per cent) became completely collectivised (Agrarian Production Cooperatives, CAP) or partly collectivized (Agrarian Society of Social Interest, SAIS, farms), containing 45.2 per cent of families awarded land. In fact a large part of the new owners, despite being organized into the various types of collective, continued to work the land individually, against the government's wishes. Although only 6.7 per cent of the expropriated land (expressed in standard hectares) was in private hands, 48 per cent was actually worked individually.

Sharecropping persisted outside the reformed sector, as in the upland haciendas, and the capitalist private estates on the coast continued to work their lands using hired labour. The new collective farms were run in a manner taken from the old private estates. Many of the members of highland cooperatives cultivated their land in individual parcels, while along the coast, private cultivation continued on only a small number of the cooperative farms. More land was distributed in the highland areas, and that among village communities who had traditionally worked their land individually.

The military government's collective-based reforms met with little success in the field of raising production or reducing conflicts. One land occupation followed another (as for example in mid-1974 in Andahuaylas, where 40,000 peasants occupied 78 haciendas, demanding their expropriation and redistribution). Cooperatives failed to live up to the hopes they were invested with. Many of them worked inefficiently, and the collective spirit failed to take root. The CAPs only partially achieved their aim of working entirely collectively. The transitional cooperatives (SAIS's) did not succeed in developing into the 'higher' collective form either (Kay, 1985). President Fernando Belaunde returned to power in 1981, having earlier been overthrown

269

by the army. As mentioned before, he announced a privatization programme, and during his time in office 75 per cent of the collectives were broken up.

Nicaragua

Land reform in Nicaragua started in 1979, with the confiscation of lands belonging to the Somozist officials and military officers. Many estates had already been occupied by peasants after the Sandinist victory. These estates were taken into state ownership. In 1982, the state sector covered 23 per cent of the land.

The second phase of the reforms fell in the period 1983-84. The 1981 decree on land reform made uncultivated, or not appropriately cultivated land liable to confiscation. In 1983-84 many undercultivated lands came under the management of production cooperatives (Sandinist Agricultural Cooperatives, CAS). By 1983, the CAS' share of land had reached 5 per cent. Most of this land came from nationalized sector, and only a very small part (1 per cent) from expropriated land, mostly from extensive cattle ranches.

In addition to the state and cooperative sectors, many peasants registered in their own names land which they had earlier occupied in virgin land in the country's interior.

From 1985, after the spontaneous land occupations began in the Masaya region, the government brought down the previously-agreed 350-hectare limit of private land ownership, and, where necessary, expropriated farms above the limit. After the UNAG smallholders' alliance firmly insisted that the peasants be able to choose for themselves in which form they wanted to farm, they also began to distribute land to private farmers. Between January 1985 and July 1986, four times as many private farmers were granted land as in the previous period.

In the former war areas, the returning families also received grants of land. This land redistribution affected about 18,000 families.

By 1986, the CAS sector took up 10 per cent of the agricultural sector, and the state sector 13 per cent (Peek, 1985; Bastiaensen, 1988).

Brazil

In accordance with the 1961 Punta del Este accord, other Latin American countries (Brazil and Argentina) also went some way towards reforming their agriculture, but they did not go beyond some measures for in settling sparsely populated or unpopulated regions, titling already-used land, and compulsory purchase, for substantial compensation, of unused but privately owned land.

In Brazil, for example, the new military regime under President Humberto Castelo Branco (1964-67) announced the following measures in the 1964 Land

Statute: 1. expropriation, with compensation, under certain conditions; 2. regulation of tenancy conditions; 3. taxation of land property. Tax was increased in proportion to the size of the holding and the extent to which its land was not used productively.

The law on expropriation could only be applied in areas where there was serious social tension and unrest (the coastal areas of Paraíba and Pernambuco states, the federal district of Brasilia, and in the states of Rio de Janeiro, Rio Grande do Sul and Ceará). The National Institute of Colonization and Agrarian Reform (INCRA) was entrusted with the agrarian reform. Its responsibility was the colonization on public lands and regularization of squatters occupying public lands after 1964. According to the Statute, a squatter who lived for one year on public land was to be given preference in buying it, while a squatter for ten years who had a dwelling on the land and cultivated it could claim title to it.

Although legally all the conditions of the agrarian reform were put in place, it led to few results in practice. Between 1964 and 1978 according to INCRA statistics the government granted titles to 196,500 squatters and an additional 55,000 families benefited from the agrarian reform (they received credit, technical assistance, seeds and cooperatives were developed) and 50,000 participated in public colonization projects.

The problem of the landless was made more serious by the layoff of many agricultural workers who formerly lived on the fazendas. The 1963 agricultural employment law granted farm workers equal rights to those in other sectors: they could not be paid in kind, and the landlords had to pay social insurance for them. After sacking many of the workers for this reason, the consequent labour shortage prompted many plantations (such as coffee plantations) to turn to cattle grazing. A large proportion of former agricultural workers became unemployed and the increased mechanization of the large and medium farms released even more labour.

In response to rising unrest, which had been further inflamed by the bad harvest due to drought in the North-East, in the South West Parana and in Minas Gerais, the government, under President Emilio Garrastazu Médici (1969-74), decided to resettle one million agricultural workers, share tenants and smallholders from Ceará, Pernambuco, Paraíba and Rio Grande do Norte to land along the Amazon. There were about 5 million square kilometres of nearly uninhabited land available there. Opening up of the region began in 1970 with the building of the Transamazonica and Cuiabá-Santarém highways. The first settlements were on a 64,000 square-kilometre area between Rio Xingú and Rio Tapajós. Every settler family received 100 hectares of land, of which they could cultivate 50 per cent.

By 1973 it was clear that the settlement plan had not achieved its objective. Even though the original target of one million families had been reduced to

100,000, only 7,500 had actually moved in by 1977. Of these, only one-third were from the most seriously affected North-Eastern region.

The reason for the lack of success lay primarily in organization: settlers were badly selected, the farm areas were badly assigned to settlers, the soil was not properly prepared for cultivation so that production fell off very rapidly, the credit that was offered was based on optimistic assessments of yields, there was a lack of specialist advice and marketing opportunities, tropical diseases made their appearance and in addition to all of this, there was an unchecked, spontaneous flood of incomers into the region. The project had also failed to take account of the consequent rapid drop in forest soils' fertility or of erosion.

The failure of the plan led to its abandonment by the government, and now that the land has been shown to be of low fertility and unsuited to intensive cultivation, today only spontaneous cattle ranches are appearing in the area (Kohlkepp, 1979).

Later, the government of João Figueiredo (1979-85) granted 670,000 land titles. In addition 115,000 families participated in public colonization projects and 38,000 families in agrarian reform.

Despite the series of reforms, minifundios in 1982 represented 60 per cent of total holdings, but only 7 per cent of the land area. On the other hand, 1 per cent of the landowners had 45 per cent of the area. Latifundios covered 67 per cent of the land, and only one-third of that area was productive. Rural enterprises making economical and rational use of rural properties constituted just 10 per cent of holdings and 19 per cent of the land.

In the wake of the political opening of 1974, many political and social groups took up the cause of land reform. The most active of these was the Catholic Church.

The democratic elections in 1985 brought to power President Tancredo, who was followed after his early death by José Sarney. They set the issue of land reform in motion once again. A modified version of the Land Statute was drawn up under Sarney's presidency, whose main points were: 1) colonization of public lands; 2) agrarian reform on private land 'located in already occupied regions' where grave distortions and social tension prevail; 3) eliminating progressively the latifundios and minifundios.

The plans allowed for 409.5 million hectares of private land and 71.7 million of public land to be granted to 7.1 beneficiaries. 1.4 million families should have received land between 1985 and 1989.

The organizations and lobbies on behalf of the great estate owners prevented the plan from being passed in Congress and only a modified, softened version went through. References to 'areas of social tension' disappeared, sharecroppers and renters were excluded as beneficiaries, a distinction was made between productive and non-productive latifundios and only the latter could be subjected to expropriation. In the final version of the

272

reform bill, general reforms were de-emphasised in favour of regional reform plans and overall the reform process was shifted in the direction of regional solutions.

The land reform plan has fallen far short of its original aims, and there has been no pause to land invasions and clashes between peasants and the landowners' armed guards (Sanders, 1987).

South and South-East Asia

In contrast to South America, the population density in South and South-East Asia is very high and the average land holding small. Here medium-sized holdings are of 2 hectares upwards, and anything above 10-20 hectares can be regarded as large. Despite there being insufficient land available to base land reforms on, the exploitative sharecropping system, large-scale landlessness and extreme fragmentation of small holdings all led to strident demands for reform.

The first and most radical land reforms took place in Japan, Taiwan, and South Korea.

Japan

The reform of 1868 brought to an end all feudal rights in Japan. Feudal lords lost their feudal privileges, and tenants' rent in kind was changed to money, paid from then on direct to the state budget instead of to tax-collecting landlords. After the reform, the government committed considerable expenditure to modernizing agriculture, repairing its infrastructure, introducing new crop varieties, providing credit, promoting education and extension. Agricultural productivity rapidly grew, but there was hardly any reduction in the inequality of rural incomes. The sharecroppers' burdens grew even heavier, and during the agricultural crisis at the turn of the century many smallholders lost their farms and became landless.

After the Second World War, on the initiative of the occupying US authorities, new land reforms were carried through between 1945 and 1950. All landowners had to sell their holdings over 1 hectare to the State at low prices. Former share tenants gained title to their land for a small amount of compensation. About one-third of land under cultivation was thereby transferred to tenants. The land reform statute forbade landholdings by non-farmers and the sale of land. It also outlawed the renting out of more than one hectare.

The number of farms tilled by tenants fell from 46 per cent in 1945 to 10 percent in 1950 and 5 per cent in 1965.

The radical reform considerably reduced the inequality of agricultural income and raised the purchasing power of agricultural workers, which in turn had a substantial effect on Japan's industrial boom. However it also prevented the concentration of land necessary for modernization. The average holding in 1950 was 1.01 hectare, and although the regulations on renting were to some extent liberalized in the 1970s, this figure hardly grew over the years (Land Reform, 1974). Japanese farmers have tackled the problem of the low earning potential of their farms by working them on a part-time basis and securing most of their income from activities outside agriculture. This now applies to 80 per cent of farmers.

Taiwan

Rents were lowered in 1949, followed by the distribution of public land. The reforms were extended by the 1953 law, which changed leases of property into titles. The proportion of land leased fell from 41 per cent to 16 per cent and the proportion of farm-owning families rose from 33 to 59 per cent (Land Reform, 1974).

South Korea

Before land reform, 19 per cent of landowners had title to 90 per cent of the land and 50 per cent of farmers were sharecroppers. After the reform, 69 per cent of farmers became owners of the land they worked, 24 per cent became part-owners and only 7 per cent remained tenants.

After the Second World War, the proportion of produce paid as rent fell from 40-60 per cent to 33 per cent. There was also land redistribution, firstly in 1948, of land which had been confiscated by the occupying Japanese, and then of Korean holdings of more than 3 hectares, between 1950 and 1953. 1.6 million farmers, about 70 per cent of the total number, were granted property rights over 25 per cent of the agricultural land (Land Reform, 1974).

China

The 1952 land reform distributed half of the cultivated area, about 46.6 million hectares, among 300 million landless or near-landless peasants, constituting 60-70 per cent of the rural population. This was followed in 1953 with the organization of production cooperatives, and by 1956 agriculture had been more or less completely collectivized (Rui-zhen, 1989).

North Vietnam

Land reform was carried out between 1954 and 1956. Great estates were expropriated and redistributed so as to keep each holding roughly the same size. After the reform, middle-level peasants ended up with on average 0.161

hectares, poor peasants 0.144 and formerly landless labourers 0.141. Collectivization started in 1958 and made universal by 1968 (Deere, 1984).

India

The first land reform in India, in 1952, was aimed at bringing to an end the 'zamindar' system. Zamindars had been the tax collectors in the time of the Moguls. During the British colonial period, they gradually gained property title to those lands over which they collected taxes. At the time of independence, they owned about 50 per cent of cultivated land in India (Ladejinsky, 1977). The zamindar tenancy system consisted of a whole chain of rents: the zamindars rented out to tenants who sub-let it to others, and at the end of the chain were sharecroppers who actually worked the land. These people were left with only a fraction of the produce.

In 1950, the sharecropping agricultural labourers became tenants of the State and paid their rent directly to the State. Zamindars were awarded compensation, which the Indian states provided credit for. It was also made possible for tenants to buy their land. During the tenancy reforms, 7 million acres (1 acre = 0.46 hectare) came into the possession of 3 million tenants. By 1961, the zamindar sub-tenanting system had ceased, but sharecropping remained. Although the law limited the maximum rent to one-half of the crop, because of the scarcity of land the landlords usually demand a lot more than this.

In the 1960s, on a recommendation by the Central Committee for Land Reform, the various Indian states set different upper land-holding limits per member of owner families, and compulsorily purchased estates of greater size, redistributing the land.

In 1971 the Land Reform Committee put out another recommendation for the states, advising that the property limit should not apply to family members, but to families. If families had more than five members, they would be entitled to twice the limit. The recommended limits were 10-18 acres on irrigated land and 54 on non-irrigated. Limits were not defined for plantations. Compensation was to be offered for expropriated land.

Different states regulated the upper limits of land that could be kept in differing ways and carried out the expropriations differently. Allocation of land to families should have made more land available for distribution, but many landowning families got round the rule by registering themselves as having split up. The various states' laws left many loopholes in the implementation of the reforms, and many landowners, in connivance with the local official apparatus, used these to their advantage (Land Reform, 1974; Tai, 1974; Sharma, 1984). Despite a series of reforms since independence, then, there are

275

still very large variations in the size of Indian landholdings and the incomes they provide.

Pakistan and Bangladesh

The East Bengal State Land Acquisition and Tenancy Act of 1950 abolished the zamindar system in former East Pakistan and gave rent collection rights to the provincial government. Compensation was paid to the zamindars here too. The law gave permanent, inheritable and transferable occupancy rights to tenants. From 1951 to 1965, 443 large estates were taken over by the government from the zamindars.

The former West Pakistan's land reform decree of 1959 set in train the abolition of the sub-tenanting (jagir) system as well as land reform. The right of rent-collection was taken away without compensation from jagirs who did not own the land, and confiscated from jagirs who held proprietary rights their land in excess of the ceiling that private landowners were allowed to retain. All expropriated lands were then resold to smallholders. (Tai, 1974).

Philippines

The Philippines' legacy from the Spanish Empire was composed of large haciendas, and shareholder and minifundia systems.

The Agricultural Land Reform Code of 1963 set out rights of tenants and established maximum amounts of land which could be rented out. It announced that land above this limit could be expropriated at the request of the tenant. It also included measures to put unused land into private hands.

The 1972 land reform provided for tenanted rice and maize fields to be put into the ownership of the tenants. According to the terms of the Tenant Emancipation Act, the tenant of irrigated land up to 3 hectares, and non-irrigated land up to 5 hectares, was to be regarded as the owner. Land affected by the reform made up only the tenanted 42 per cent of rice and corn land and left a large part of the total farmland untouched (Tai, 1974; Árvai, 1986; Ahmed, 1987). The government which came in after President Marcos' overthrow would like to extend the reforms, but most land is still in the hands of big landowners.

Nepal

The Land Act of 1964 fixed the ceiling for permitted land areas both of ownership holdings and tenant cultivated holdings. Lands and tenancy rights exceeding the ceiling limit could be expropriated by the State and redistributed. Rent was restricted to 25 per cent of produce, and tenants gained inheritable and transferable rights to land (Progress in Land Reform, 1970).

The Near East

Iran

During the rule of the Shah, radical land reforms were carried out. Before the reform, 56 per cent of the estates, covering 82 per cent of the agricultural land, were leases. Most of the great landowners lived far from their estates and did not practice farming. Small tenants only had leases from year to year, a system which lent itself to exploitation of the land.

The core of the 1962 reform was to restrict landowners to the land belonging to one village only. Holdings larger than this were expropriated and distributed among the tenants. Plantations, endowed lands and mechanized farms were exempted from expropriation. Those granted land were obliged to join a cooperative. In the second phase of the reforms, in 1964, the upper limit of properties on non-irrigated land was set at 150 hectares, and on irrigated land 10-20 hectares. Landowners were presented with a range of options of what to do with their excess land: 1) lease it to their tenants for 30 years; 2) sell it to tenants; 3) buy the right of tenancy from the tenants; 4) share their land with their tenants according to the customary produce-sharing proportion; 5) formation of share holding (joint stock) farms with their tenants. Villages which were publicly endowed were to be rented to the local peasants on the basis of 99 year leases. Villages which were privately endowed could be purchased by peasants or could be rented for 30 years.

Most landowners chose the first option, that is they granted their tenants 30 year leases on the land.

The peasants were dissatisfied with this second reform phase, since they did not become owners of their land. In consequence, the 1969 reform law and its implementation, which was completed in 1972, converted all 30-year leases into titles.

In the course of the reforms, more than 3 million families received land and the share-cropping system disappeared. The remaining large estates, and the new properties established as a result of property concentration, became intensive capitalist farms.

From 1970 onwards, farm corporations, agricultural share companies and agrobusiness companies were set up to concentrate farms and modernize them. The merger process sparked off widespread dissatisfaction. Although merger was said to be voluntary, it was not without coercive measures from the central bureaucratic control. The establishment of the large agrobusiness companies covering 20,000 or more hectares was particularly hard on small farmers. This involved destroying many peasant farms, demolishing the villages and resettling the populations in workers' townships, as well as making many agricultural workers redundant without finding them suitable alternative employment. A large proportion of the agrobusiness companies went bankrupt. They were mismanaged, their workers worked grudgingly and production was not properly adapted to the ecological conditions.

Formation of the agrobusiness companies led to many tens of thousands of peasants losing their land and home, so that they became wage-workers, seasonal workers or unemployed. The number of landless multiplied further as a result of farm concentration and mechanization. Despite all this, independent small farmers came out of the reforms as the majority in Iranian villages (Land Reform, 1974; Ehlers, 1979; Katouzian, 1985; Lahsaeizadeh, 1987).

Syria

Before the land reforms, more than three-quarters of land under cultivation belonged to large landowners and hardly 20 per cent to the peasants. Two-thirds of the rural population were landless labourers, who received 20-25 per cent of the produce for their work. Nearly half of the land area was in estates of more than 1,000 hectares, about 40 per cent in middle-size properties of 10-100 hectares and hardly more than 10 per cent smallholdings.

After the unification of Egypt and Syria, one of the first measures to be announced was land reform. The land reform law of 1958 determined the maximum size of land properties. These were 80 hectares on irrigated, and 300 on non-irrigated land. Further land could be kept by the family members: a maximum of 40 hectares on irrigated and 160 on non-irrigated land. Land above this amount could be compulsorily purchased by the state and redistributed at the same price (payment by the new owner could be by instalments). Each family could purchase up to 8 hectares on irrigated and 20 hectares on non-irrigated land.

This radical land-reform law was only partly put into effect. Up to the time when the United Arab Republic broke up in 1961, a total of 3,962 hectares of state-owned land had been distributed to 547 families and another 2,057 sold to 524 families. In addition, 600,000 hectares had been leased to 244,000 peasants.

The government which came to power in 1961 raised the ownership ceiling of holding and although it allowed for free land distribution, it did not implement it.

The Baath Party government announced new land reforms when it came into power in 1963. It amended the property maxima and gave preference in land grants to agricultural labourers. The reform should have been implemented by 1969, but progressed only with difficulty, with 700,000 hectares having been distributed among 362,000 families by the end of that year. In consequence of the reform the land covered by holdings over 100 hectares fell to 13 per cent and that by farms of less than 10 hectares rose from 13 to 35 per cent.

The land reform law of 1980 further reduced the upper land-property limits (to 10 ha on irrigated and 55 ha on non-irrigated land) and made provisions for expropriation and redistribution of holdings above these. With the priority being to grant property rights to as many families as possible, there is a danger of fragmentation of land (Deere, 1984, Al-Dulaimi Faisal, 1986).

Iraq

On coming to power in 1970, the Baath Party drew up the country's most radical land reform law to date. It determined the maximum area landlords could retain at 10 hectares on irrigated and 150 on non-irrigated, although this could be extended, depending on fertility, to 500 hectares. The government expropriated holdings above this limit without compensation and redistributed them without charge. The peasants received lands of between 1 and 50 hectares. The basic condition for a grant of land was that the recipient join an agricultural cooperative. The government considered it of the highest importance to set up production cooperatives and collective farms, which would provide services for the new owners and deal with procurement and marketing. The cooperatives received considerable state funding (Al-Dulaimi Faisal, 1985).

Yemen

The socialist government of South Yemen carried out land reforms in 1972 which after having the land nationalized granted peasants rights of use over lands on which they had previously been share tenants. The law defined various forms of cooperative, from mutual help groups up to completely collectivized production cooperatives. New owners were required to join some kind of cooperative. Production cooperatives were working 70 per cent of the land in 1980 (Deere, 1984). After the unification of North and South Yemen in 1990, the question of differing property relations have remained to be solved.

Egypt

The first land reform law was promulgated after the overthrow of the monarchy in 1952. In the following years, the royal estates were expropriated and sold to the peasants who worked them. Royal estates made up 39 per cent of the total redistributed area. The maximum retainable land holding was fixed in 1952 at 200 feddan (84 hectares), and reduced to 100 feddan (42 ha) in 1961 and 50 feddan in 1964. Redistributed land could be claimed by people not owning more than 5 feddan (2.1 ha). Recipients normally ended up with between 2 and 5 feddan. Holdings of less than 5 feddan thus came to represent 51 per cent of the cultivated land, in 1979. The proportions of the rest were: 5-10 feddan, 11 per cent; 10-50 feddan, 22 per cent; 50-100 feddan, 9 per cent; and above 100 feddan, 7 per cent.

The new owners were required to join an Egyptian-style cooperative. These carried a centrally-prescribed three-year crop rotation. The land of a roughly 1,000 feddan and 300-member production cooperative was divided into several blocks, and each block into 3 parts. The same set of crops were grown on the corresponding parts of each block, with one being left fallow. Every cooperative member had an equal parcel of all three parts. Cooperative members ploughed, applied insecticide and fertilizer, irrigated and flooded commonly, but were individually responsible for planting, sowing, hoeing and doing other labour-intensive work on their own patches. In effect, the members received their share of the produce according to the yield on their parcels of land. The cooperatives handled procurement, selling of produce, and arranging credit, although individual selling was also allowed. The state subsidized the cooperatives and gave free access to irrigation water. In return there was a strict central planning system both for of the sowing and planting and for the compulsory sale of the prescribed crops.

Since the 1970s, and especially since the early and mid-1980s, when the Mubarak government announced its 'Open Door' liberalization policy, state control has relaxed, and the cooperative system has lost its central significance. The State has, in fact, allowed the return of the sharecropping system (Tai, 1974; Al-Dulaimi Faisal, 1985).

Africa

Countries in Africa generally have more abundant land and a lower density of rural population than in Asia. Soil, however is often poor. Communal use of land is widespread, especially in sub-Saharan countries. But it also features in North Africa, usually in nomad regions.

In many countries it is not a basic lack of land that is the problem, so much as the legalization of use or ownership of land already under individual cultivation. Such legality gives farmers security and the opportunity to seek credit, allowing farming to modernize. Experiments in such registration have taken place in many African countries, among them Kenya and Malawi.

There is still a hunger for land in several countries despite its abundance on average across the continent. One reason for this is the tendency for population to concentrate in areas where the land is relatively fertile and there is enough rainfall or irrigation potential. This tendency, aggravated by rapid population growth, causes land to become scarce.

Scarcity of land can often be traced to social and political origins as well. In the present and former white settler countries (South Africa, Namibia, Zimbabwe) the settlers appropriated huge estates (from 1,000 to several hundred thousand hectares) for themselves, while the local population were restricted to infertile or less fertile parts of the country, where farmers worked one or two hectares on common land. With the passing of white rule in most of these countries, the question of land reform has become an active question. Zimbabwe, which has had majority rule since 1980, is still held to be in a preparatory condition in this regard. The latest plans are for 5 million hectares, or one-half of the country's commercial farmland, to be compulsorily purchased from their owners at prices set by the government (The Economist, October 2nd 1993).

North African countries, where farming practices and property relations are closer to those of the rest of the world than in sub-Saharan countries, have for the most part already carried through some land reforms. In most of them this has primarily been a matter of expropriating lands of former white settlers, but in a few, such as Algeria, domestic landowners have also had their lands confiscated.

A similar radical land reform outside North Africa took place in Ethiopia, and in some former settler countries south of the Sahara – such as Angola and Mozambique – former white estates have also been expropriated.

Morocco

Agrarian reform legislation was passed in 1962, 1966 and 1972. Distributed land was firstly obtained from expropriated foreign holdings, but state-owned and communal lands were also included. At independence in 1956, 900,000 hectares were in foreign hands. 300,000 hectares of these had been transferred to Moroccan ownership by 1963. From 1963 on, land expropriated was nationalized. The plantations from that time remained government-controlled or state-owned, and the rest of the nationalized land was shared out. The process of distribution was slow up till 1967, but accelerated after this. By the end of the 1970s, a total of 24,000 families, less than 2 per cent of agricultural families, had received land with an area making up about 6 per cent of the 355,000 hectares of land under cultivation. Trading and production cooperatives were set up to assist the new owners. The number of production cooperatives is tiny (Land Reform, 1974; Al-Dulaimi Faisal, 1984).

Tunisia

In Tunisia, about 600,000 hectares, or 15 per cent, of the agricultural land was in the possession of foreign settlers. These were expropriated and their land nationalized, state farms being set up on 300,000 hectares and production cooperatives on 200,000. Anti-cooperative peasant movements after 1964 led to the abandonment of the former 'systematic collectivization' programme in 1969. After this, the bigger landowners bought up part of the former colonial lands and those of some cooperative members who, lacking all appropriate means, had been unable to work their land. These inconsistent reforms did little to dampen the land-hunger problem (Sinha, 1984; Al-Dulaimi Faisal, 1985).

Algeria

27 per cent, or 2.73 million hectares, of Algerian cultivated land was in the hands of white settlers in 1960. Domestic large landowners owned one-fifth of the land.

In 1963 the government took into its possession the white settlers lands, most of which had been abandoned. In the last year of the war of liberation, much of this land had already been occupied by the rural people under the leadership of the Union Générale des Travailleurs Algériens (UGTA). Self-ruling cooperatives took over the running of the plantations. The cooperatives vigorously protested against nationalization. As a result, the government recognized their self-ruling status, but still took possession of the land. Control was thereafter gradually centralized nonetheless. The State appointed their managers and integrated them into the central planning system.

In 1980 the so-called self-ruling farms accounted for 27 per cent of agricultural land, but 77 per cent of permanent workers and 45 per cent of seasonal agricultural workers.

The 1972 agrarian reform legislation ordered the expropriation of lands belonging to village communities and other organizations, and absentee landlords and private holdings above specified limits. The lesser part of these lands were distributed to private farmers, the greater part made over for use by production cooperatives. Expropriation of the domestic large landowners – according to both the under-use and over-size criteria – was implemented in 1972-73. Ten socialist villages were founded at this time.

The cooperative and the state farm sectors dominated Algerian agriculture in the first part of the 1980s. There were 2,000 production cooperatives and 6,000 state farms working around 60 per cent of the cultivated land. From the mid-1980s, one of the openings of the liberalization policies gave rise to support for individual farming and private initiatives (Etienne, 1979; Árvai, 1983; Deere, 1984).

In the land reform of 1987, state farms were abolished and 25,000 collectives set up in there place. In these collectives, individual households and groups have permanent and heritable rights of cultivation (Binswanger and Elgin, 1989).

Kenya

During British rule, much of the fertile land was taken up by European plantations. Unrest broke out in the Kikuyu areas after the Second World War. The Kikuyu were sharecroppers on the white estates and the land area they could use for subsistence was legally limited to the minimum amount. Neither were they allowed to buy land in the White Highlands. Land hunger led to the breakout of the Mau-Mau revolt in 1952. In addressing the unrest, which persisted for many years, the British authorities drew up a settlement project, repealed the ban on land purchase, gave title to some sharecroppers over the land that they worked, and consolidated fragmented parcels. In practice, however, very few people actually received any land as a result of this process.

The law passed after gaining independence in 1962 gave title to sharecroppers on white settlers' lands and provided for distribution among black farmers of about 400,000 hectares of the 3.1 million formerly occupied by white settlers. The five-year land reform was completed in June 1967, by which time in fact 570,000 hectares had been distributed among 36,000 black settlers. Some of the sugar plantations were purchased by Kenyan Indians, others by Kenyans, and some continued under white management.

New settlers had to pay compensation for their land. Many of them could not keep up their instalments, and were thus or for some other reason, forced to sell their land. This was bought in many cases by local or foreign capitalists who reconstituted the divided plantations. A significant proportion of the former White Highlands are still run by planters of whom quite a large proportion are still white, mainly British (Progress in Land Reform, 1970; Land Reform, 1974; Németh, 1984).

Ethiopia

Agriculture in imperial Ethiopia had a feudal character. 57.6 per cent of holdings were of less than 1 hectare, and took up 18.4 per cent of the land. The sharecropping system was widespread. Many of the large landowners did not live on their estates. In the very fertile area of the administrative region of Hararghe, for example, land belonging to 44 per cent of owners proprietors covered just 3.4 per cent of the area, while 0.2 per cent of them owned 75 per cent. Of the latter, 95 per cent was owned by two people.

After the Emperor was deposed in 1974, the new government nationalized the land and proclaimed land reform in 1975. The proclamation fixed the ceiling of holdings at 10 hectares and prohibited buying and selling of land. Share tenancy was abolished and former tenants were exempted from payment not only of rent but also of any debt or other obligation to the former landowner. The proclamation also outlawed hiring of labour. Land was passed to peasant associations for them to distribute among former tenants, the landless and smallholders.

In 1979 government directives were issued on the setting up of agricultural production cooperatives. These, however, made little headway up to the political changes of 1989 (Abate and Kiros, 1985).

It can be seen from the above discussion that in the last few decades many countries have attempted to alleviate peasant land-hunger through various kinds of land reform. Some of these were radical, many however were not sufficiently consistent and only partly solved the problem of land scarcity. The most consistent reforms – as in Japan, Taiwan and South Korea – would not have reached their goal either had they not been linked to agricultural modernization, raising yields, and had land reform not followed rapid industrial development which absorbed surplus . The example of India shows a less satisfactory situation, where there were a series of land reforms, even if not all of them were consistent, but the result was the fragmentation of land to the extent that viability of many farms is endangered (after the reforms of the 1970s, the average holding had fallen to 1.15 hectares, and farms of over 4 hectares were considered large). And despite all the reforms the India's problems of land unemployment and poverty remain. Peru's strict, socialist-style land reform had no more success in alleviating land hunger and did not prevent social turbulence. The inconsistent reforms in Brazil and other Latin American countries, however, left landlessness and the minifundio system virtually untouched.

In an attempt to avoid the trap of land subdivision, recurrent land hunger and fragmentation which causes inefficiency and narrows opportunity for modernization, many countries set up state farms and production cooperatives. Most of these programmes did not live up to hopes, and in most parts of the world the era of reprivatization has taken hold. This offers something less than a panacea to less developed countries. In contrast to collective agriculture, it offers more incentives and can release energy which can be turned to productive effect for a while – China being a good example – but the momentum can quickly become exhausted in the absence of sufficient investment, and if the economy does not develop sufficiently quickly, the increased expectations can sharpen the effects of land scarcity and aggravate social tension. It is difficult to find an optimal solution, but some promise is offered on the reassertion of the currently-discredited production cooperative in areas where it is by now a tradition with some roots. This will depend on its being voluntary in truth rather than, as hitherto, only in name, and also on freedom from central control and the maintenance of individual ownership and incentives.

284

The time of mass land reforms, it seems, has passed. In countries where large estates prevail these could still serve to alleviate economic and social troubles. In countries where property is already in small units, however, despite persisting and recurrent demands, such reforms could only lead to further fragmentation, further diminishing opportunities for agriculture's modernization. The only real cure is faster overall economic development and assistance for agricultural modernization.

Closing remarks

The last two decades has seen such exceptional changes in the world's economy that agriculture has not been left untouched by them. Some effects have been negative, but there has been a lot of positive too. The first significant changes were those sparked off by the oil price rises of the 1970s. In their wake the apparently permanent and secure economic growth in the developed countries turned to depression and prolonged recession. Most poor countries experienced the breakdown of the economic upswing which had started after the second World War or the winning of their independence. What followed was a permanent food production shortfall, which started with the food crisis of the early 1970s, and an ever-growing demand for food imports. Some oil-producing countries grew very rich, but some of the smaller producers, after an initial boom, fell back into poverty after the decline of oil prices in the 1980s.

Most less developed countries become deeply indebted because of the depression and recession, and were unable to avoid the 'debt-trap' where debt led to more debt and more had to be borrowed for repayments and interest on the original. The effects of the world recession also reached the socialist countries. Economic decline, coupled with the arms race, led to first to the economic, and then the political collapse of the leading socialist country, the Soviet Union and the other European socialist countries.

In the middle of stagnation, we are witnessing a surprisingly rapid rate of development in part of the world: East- and South-East Asia, perhaps also spreading to South Asia. After the 'four little tigers', South Korea, Taiwan, Hong Kong and Singapore, countries now breaking out of the less developed camp include Indonesia, Malaysia and Thailand, which will very likely sooner or later catch up with the developed world. China also looks set to join them, and there are signs that India and perhaps Vietnam are following.

The economic events brought political changes in their wake. Dictatorships fell in the former socialist countries and beyond, in many developing countries. Reeling from the loss of support from their former mentors, the Soviet Union and the United States, many left- and right-wing dictatorships have collapsed or are severely shaken. The United States has no interest in continuing to buttress authoritarian right-wing regimes which in the past helped to balance Soviet influence. Several Latin American dictatorships have also given way, albeit for different reasons.

Charged with keeping indebted countries under control, the IMF, whose experts represent monetarist economic views, have pressured numerous countries with debt problems into following an economic and political liberalizing line. National policies of protectionism, and import-substituting industrialization are giving way to economic openness, and dominant state sectors to privatization. A similar influence has been exerted by the United States on Latin American countries which are allied to, or have close economic ties, with them. The former socialist countries in Europe have also liberalized their economies, partly under foreign influence of and partly from their own desire for reform.

This rapid changeover to free-market economic liberalism has yet to show its beneficial effects on less- and medium-developed countries. Import competition has even further weakened their underdeveloped industry, low-productivity agriculture and weak food industry, and withdrawal of agricultural subsidies and moves towards privatization have increased bankruptcies and unemployment. Abolition of food subsidies and liberalizing prices have multiplied food prices and aggravated mass poverty.

The upcoming Asian countries are also liberalizing, some only economically (like China and Vietnam), and others politically, too. In these cases, however, liberalization is gradual and moderate, and accompanies an economic upswing, in contrast to those weak and stagnating countries where economic liberalization has been enforced.

The position of agriculture has changed along with that of the world economy and of individual countries.

Countries not overburdened with debt, and who recognized that the only way they could avoid hunger and the food-import trap was to develop their agriculture, made great sacrifices after a temporary break caused by the oil crisis to continue to spread the green revolution, and now have significant results to show for it. Such countries are India, Pakistan and the Philippines. In the industrially rapidly developing East- and South-East Asian countries, agricultural development followed general growth, and has become a smaller part of the overall economy, with a smaller workforce but higher production. The richer oil countries have also vigorously developed their agricultural sector and their food-importing capability has risen. Hunger is most seriously threatening those African countries whose economies are stagnating and cannot break out of the debt trap.

In the former socialist countries, the political changes and liberalization of their economies has not led to the expected upturn in economic fortune. Returning the land to its former owners and their descendants and the distribution of wealth of the big farms has not led to the hoped-for formation of family farms, but to the misery of surviving large farms. This is exacerbated by the withdrawal of their subsidies, and the reduction of domestic demand for food and of export opportunities. The end result is that production, which was stagnant before the changes, is now plummeting.

On the other hand, agriculture is prosperous in China and Vietnam, where common farming was abandoned 15 years ago, and individual farming has returned.

Recession forced developed countries to strengthen the protection of their markets. They especially protect one of their weakest sectors, agriculture, with import barriers, and subsidies both internal and for exports. Agricultural protectionism led to mounting overproduction and the fall of world prices. The protectionism practised by developed countries is a burden both to themselves and developing countries: for the former it is a matter of rising budget expenditure and burdens the taxpayers and consumers, the latter suffer from depressed world prices and the difficult access to the developed countries' markets.

The last two decades have, however, seen some reductions of protectionism as well as rises. Under pressure from developing countries, countries with interests in liberalizing trade and international organizations, there was some progress in this area. Trade preferences and trade liberalization agreements have been reached which allow developing and former socialist countries more access than before to developed markets. Price supports are being brought down in the European Community and there are an increasing number of measures to restrain production. Most significant is that subsidies, although their total amount is not falling, are directed towards income support, which causes less disturbance of the market than the hitherto general price supports.

The fall of dictatorships in many countries has revitalized the question of agrarian and land reforms. The mass reforms of the post-war period are not being repeated, but subject of land reform, which was postponed or badly implemented in the past, is finding its way back on to the agenda. In countries where latifundia still hold sway, peasant associations are demanding thorough land reforms. The fall of left-wing dictatorships, on the other hand, is being followed by reprivatization of state farms and production cooperatives.

There are, then, a multitude of processes currently in motion, and it is difficult to foresee what the future holds for a world in such a state of flux. It is beyond doubt that a vigorous economic upturn is the answer to many of the world's troubles. It would raise demand, stimulate exports and imports, could dampen protectionism, reduce the debts of poor countries, give a boost to production and raise the standard of living. Hopefully the multitude of local wars will not spread to international conflict, and the world will experience new prosperity in an era of peace.

Bibliography

Abate, A. and Kiros, F.G. (1985), 'Agrarian Reform, Structural Changes and Rural Development In Ethiopia' in Ghose, A.K. (ed.), *Agrarian Reform in Contemporary Developing Countries*, ILO Study, Croom Helm, London and Sydney, St Martin's Press, New York.

Agricultural Outlook (1992), 'Central Europe: Agriculture in the New Market Economies', *Economic Research Service, USDA*, February.

Agricultural Policies, Markets and Trade. Monitoring and Outlook (1991 and 1992), OECD, Paris.

Agriculture: Toward 2000 (1981), FAO, Rome.

Ahmed, S. (1987), 'Landlessness in Rural Asia. An Overview' in Land Reform, Land Settlement and Cooperatives, no. 1/2 FAO, Rome, pp. 133-151.

Al-Dulaimi, F. (1984), Morocco, *Mezőgazdasági Világjárás,* Agroinform, Budapest.

Al-Dulaimi, F. (1985), Tunisia, *Mezőgazdasági Világjárás,* Agroinform, Budapest.

Al-Dulaimi, F. (1985), Egypt, *Mezőgazdasági Világjárás,* Agroinform, Budapest.

Al-Dulaimi, F. (1985), Iraq, *Mezőgazdasági Világjárás,* Agroinform, Budapest.

Al-Dulaimi, F. (1986), Syria, *Mezőgazdasági Világjárás,* Agroinform, Budapest.

Alexandratos, N. (1990), *European Agriculture; Policy Issues and Options to 2000,* FAO, Rome, Belhaven Press, London and New York.

Anderson, K. and Tyers, R. (1986), 'International Effects of Domestic Agricultural Policies' in Snape, R.H. (ed.), *Issues in World Trade Policy: GATT at the Crossroads*, Macmillan, London.

290

Árvai, L. (1983), Algeria, *Mezőgazdasági Világjárás*, Agroinform, Budapest.

Árvai, L., Éliás, A. and Szarvas, I. (1984), Vietnam, *Mezőgazdasági Világjárás*, Agroinform, Budapest.

Árvai L., (1985), Laos and Cambodia, *Mezőgazdasági Világjárás*, Agroinform, Budapest.

Árvai L. (1986), Philippines, *Mezőgazdasági Világjárás*, Agroinform, Budapest.

Árvai L. (1987), Cuba, *Mezőgazdasági Világjárás*, Agroinform, Budapest.

Aziz, S. (1990), *Agricultural Policies for the 1990s*, OECD Development Centre Studies, Paris.

Baade, F. (1984), *...Denn Sie Sollen Satt Werden'*, Gerhard Stalling Verlag, Oldenburg und Hamburg.

Balassa, B. (1961), *The Theory of Economic Integration*, Allen and Unwin, London

Balázs, D. (1978), *Australia, Oceania and Antarctica*, Gondolat Kiadó, Budapest.

Balázs, P. (1991), 'Miként bővíthető az Európai Közösség?' (In what form can the European Community expand?), Európa Fórum, vol. I, no. 1, Budapest, pp 5-17.

Bastiaensen, J. (1988), 'The Peasantry and Post-Revolutionary Agrarian Policy in Nicaragua: 1979-1986', in Aurio, C (ed.), *Bulletin '88.*, European Association of Development Research and Training Institutes, Executive Secretariat EADI, Geneva, pp. 29-41.

Becker, S.G. (1989), 'Fundamentals of Domestic Farm Programs', *CRS Report for Congress*, Congressional Research Service, The Library of Congress, March 6.

Benedek, E., Karceva, V., Probáld, F. and Szegedi, N. (1988), *Ázsia, Ausztrália, Óceánia gazdaságföldrajza*, (Economic Geography of Asia, Australia and Oceania), Tankönyvkiadó, Budapest.

Benet, I. (1979), *Mezőgazdaság, élelmiszergazdaság, agráripari komplexum* (Agriculture, food industry and agrobusiness), Közgazdasági és Jogi Könyvkiadó, Budapest.

Bernát, T. et. al. (1978), *Általános gazdasági földrajz*, (General Economic Geography), Tankönyvkiadó, Budapest.

Binswanger, H.P. and Elgin, M. (1989), 'What are the Prospects for Land Reform?' in *Agriculture and Governments in an Interdependent World*, Proceedings of the Twentieth International Conference of Agricultural Economists, Dartmouth Publishing Company, pp. 739-752.

Blick durch die Wirtschaft, Frankfurter-Zeitung (1991), 'Die Verhandlungen über eine neue Agrarpolitik in der Gemeinschaft beginnen. July 12.

Borszéki E. and Mészáros, S. (1991), 'A mezőgazdasági termelés és termelők pénzügyi támogatása az Európa Közösségben' (Financial subsidies for agricultural production and producers in the European Community), *Gazdálkodás,* vol. XXXV, no. 6 and 7-8, pp. 13-25 and 1-11.

Boserup, E. (1965), *The Conditions of Agricultural Growth: The Economics of Agrarian Change under Population Pressure,* George Allen and Unwin Ltd, London.

Boserup, E. (1981), *Population and Technological Change,* The University of Chicago Press.

Boserup, E. (1990) *Economic and Demographic Relationships in Development Essays,* Selected and introduced by Schulz, T.P. The Johns Hopkins University Press, Baltimore and London.

Braun, von J. and Kennedy, E. (1986), *Commercialization of Subsistence Agriculture,* Int. Food Policy Research Institute, Washington D.C.

Brown, L.R. (1987), 'Sustaining World Agriculture' in Starke, L. (ed.), *State of the World. A Worldwatch Institute Report on Progress Toward a Sustainable Society,* W.W. Norton and Company, New York, pp. 122-138.

Bukharin, N.I. (1988), *Töprengések a szocializmusról* (Thoughts on socialism), Kossuth Könyvkiadó, Budapest.

Burger, A. (1969), *A mezőgazdaság szerepe a népgazdaság növekedésében,* (The role of agriculture in economic growth), Kossuth Könyvkiadó, Budapest.

Burger, A. (1980), *Az élelmiszer-termelés gazdaságtana,* (The economics of food production), Mezőgazdasági, Közgazdasági és Jogi Könyvkiadó, Budapest.

Burger, A. (1983), 'Hogyan értékeljük a földet? (How is land valued?) *Gazdálkodás,* vol. XXVI, no. 3, Budapest, pp. 31-41.

Burger, A. (1985), *Food Economics,* Akadémiai Könyvkiadó, Budapest.

Burger, A. (1988/a), The Future of Horticulture in Some Socialist Countries. A Case Study of Hungary, *Acta Horticulturae,* no. 223, May, Wageningen, pp. 426-435.

Burger, A. (1988/b), 'Eszmefuttatások a magyar mezőgazdaságról', (Essay on problems of Hungarian agriculture), Közgazdasági Szemle, April, Budapest, pp 426-435.

Burger, A. (1989), 'A mezőgazdasági kistermelők háztartása', (Households of smallholders), *Gazdálkodás,* vol. XXXIII, no. 10, pp. 23-33.

Burger, A., Keszthelyiné, M., Salamin, P. (1990), 'A mezőgazdasági kistermelők jövedelmei és kiadásai', (Incomes and spendings of smallholders households), *Gazdálkodás,* vol. XXXIV, no. 6, pp. 1-12.

Castillo, L and Lehmann, D. (1985), 'Agrarian Reform and Structural Change in Chile, 1965-79' in Ghose, A.K. (ed.), *Agrarian Reform in*

Contemporary Developing Countries, ILO Study, Croom Helm, London and Sydney, St Martin's Press, New York, pp. 240-272.

Chayanov, A.V. (1966), *On the Theory of Peasant Economy*, Richard D. Irwin Inc., Homewood, Illinois.

Ciepielewski, J. et. al. (1985), *A világ gazdaságtörténete* (The economic history of the world), Kossuth Könyvkiadó, Budapest.

Comecon Data, 1990 (1991), Edited by the Vienna Institute for Comparative Economic Studies, Macmillan.

Commodity Review and Outlook 1970-71, 1980-81, 1990-91, FAO, Rome.

Csaba, L. (1990), 'Kelet-Európából Közép Európába' (From Eastern Europe to Central Europe), *Valóság*, no. 11, pp. 18-29.

David, S. (1993), 'Agricultural Reform in Russia', *Agricultural Outlook Economic Research Service*, USDA, June, pp. 23-27.

Deere, C.D (1984), *Agrarian Reform and the Peasantry in the Transition to Socialism in the Third World*, Working paper, Kellogg Institute, USA.

Dezséri, K. (1990), 'Az Európai Közösség társulási szerződései a közösségen kívüli országokkal' (The European Community's associate agreements with outside countries), *Külgazdaság*, vol. XXXIII, no. 9, pp. 66-77.

Dickenson, J.P. et. al. (1985), *A Geography of the Third World*, Methuen, London and New York.

Domar, E.D. (1957), *Essays in the Theory of Economic Growth*, Oxford University Press, New York.

Dunn, H.M. (1988), 'Zu den komparativen Nachteilen der Entwicklungsländer' in Körner, H. (ed.), *Probleme der ländlichen Entwicklung in der dritten Welt*, Duncker und Humblott, Berlin.

Economic Bulletin for Europe 1992 (1993), vol. 44, United Nations, New York.

Economic Survey of Europe 1991-1992 (1992), Economic Commission for Europe, Geneva, New York, 1992.

Ehlers, E (1979), 'Die iranische Agrarreform. Voraussetzungen, Ziele und Ergebnisse' in Elsehans, H. (ed.), *Agrarrefrom in der Dritten Welt*, Campus Verlag, Frankfurt/New York, pp. 433-469.

Ehrlich, É. (1991), *Országok versenye 1937-1986, (Competition between countries 1937-1986)*, Közgazdasági és Jogi Könyvkiadó, Budapest.

Enyedi, Gy. (1971) 'A mezőgazdaság földrajzi tanulmányozása' (Studying the economic geography of agriculture) in Sárfalvi, B. (ed.), *Válogatott tanulmányok a gazdasági földrajzból* (Selected studies in economic geography), Tankönyvkiadó, Budapest.

Epstein, D.B. (1983), *Theoretical and Methodical Problems of State Regulation of Agricultural Production in the Non-Black Earth Zone of the*

Russian Federation, Thesis for the degree of Doctor of Economic Science, St Petersburg-Pushkin, Manuscript.

Etienne, B (1979), 'Die Agrarrevolution in Algerien' in Elsehans, H. (ed.), *Agrarrefrom in der Dritten Welt*, Campus Verlag, Frankfurt/New York, pp. 275-307.

Europe in Figures 1989/90 (1990), Eurostat, Brussels.

Europe: World Partner, 1991. The External Relations of the European Community (1991), Commission of the European Communities, Brussels, Luxembourg.

FAO Production Yearbook 1987 and 1991 (1988 and 1992), FAO, Rome.

Fáyné Péter E. (1990), *Gazdasági reform Vietnamban* (Economic reform in Vietnam), Külgazdaság, no. 10, Budapest, pp. 58-64.

Fleszar, M. (1974), '*A világ gazdaságföldrajza*' (Economic geography of the world), Kossuth Könyvkiadó, Budapest.

Figyelő (1993), 'NAFTA: Erények és Remények' (NAFTA: Virtues and hopes) December 9, Budapest, p. 39.

Food 2000 (1987), *Report to the World Commission on Environment and Development*, Zed Books Ltd., London and New Jersey.

Friedman, M. (1969), 'The Role of Monetary Policy', *American Economic Review*, 58.

Gale, F.H. and Harrington, D.H. (1993), 'US Farms – Diversity and Change', *Agricultural Outlook*, July, Economic Research Service USDA, pp. 3-6.

Gilg, A. (1985), *An Introduction to Rural Geography*, Edward Arnold, London.

Griffin, K. (1987), *World Hunger in the World Economy*, Macmillan, London.

Grigg, D.B. (1974), *The Agricultural Systems of the World. An Evolutionary Approach*, Cambridge University Press, Cambridge.

Haggblade, S., Hazell, P. and Brown, J. (1989), 'Farm-Nonfarm Linkages in Rural Sub-Saharan Africa', *World Development*, vol. 17, no. 8, pp. 1173-1201.

Handelsblatt (1990) 'Präsident Collor de Mello formuliert ein Reformprogramm für die Landwirtschaft', August 27, p. 7.

Handelsblatt (1993), Reyhl, E., 'Schlussdokument/Neue Handelsorganisation MTO', no. 243, 16. 12., p.10.

Harrod, R (1948), *Towards a Dynamic Economics,* Macmillan, London.

Hayami, Y. and Ruttan, V.W. (1971), *Agricultural Development: An International Perspective*, 1st edition, Johns Hopkins University Press, Baltimore.

Hayami, Y., Ruttan, V.W. (1985), *Agricultural Development: An International Perspective*, Revised and expanded edition, The John Hopkins University Press, Baltimore and London.

Hecklau, H. (1989), 'Kenias Landwirtschaft auf dem Weg in die Modern', *Geographische Rundschau Jahrgang*, 41, Heft 11, pp. 620-626.

Heti Világgazdaság (1991), 'Magyarország társulása az EK-val' (Hungary's Association Agreement with the EC), vol. XIII, no. 48, Budapest, pp. 6-8.

Heti Világgazdaság (1992), 'Dánia és az EK' (Denmark and the EC), vol. XIV, no. 24, Budapest, pp. 25-27.

Heti Világgazdaság (1993), 'Ki mint vet és Mégis mozog a föld' (As we sow..., and The earth still moves), vol. XV, no. 40, Budapest, pp. 24-26.

Heti Világgazdaság (1993), 'NAFTA megállapodás' (NAFTA agreement), vol. XV, no. 47, Budapest, pp. 21-23.

Heti Világgazdaság (1993), 'GATT megállapodás' (GATT agreement), vol. XV, no. 52-53, Budapest, pp. 21.

Hobsbawm, E.J. (1988), *A forradalmak kora* (The age of revolution: Europe 1789-1848, Weidenfeld and Nicolson), Kossuth Könyvkiadó, Budapest.

Horváth, G (1993), *Tulajdoni-szervezeti változások a szövetkezeti szektorban és gazdasági hatásaik*, (Changes in ownership and organization in the cooperative sector and their economic effects), MSS.

Időgazdálkodás és Munkatevékenység (1989), (Time management and work), Data from the 1986/87 survey, KSH-MTA Sociological Research Institute, Budapest.

Imfeld, A. (1986/a), 'Die Entkolonialisierung des Mais in Afrika' in Glaeser, B. (ed.), *Die Krise der Landwirtschaft. Zur Renaissance von Agrakulturen*, Campus Verlag, Frankfurt/Main and New York.

Imfeld, A. (1986/b), 'Vom Überfluss zur Dürre im Sahel' in Glaeser, B. (ed.), *Die Kriese der Landwirtschaft. Zur Renaissance von Agrarkulturen* Campus Verlag, Frankfurt/Main and New York.

International Economic Indicators 1993 (1993), Institut der deutschen Wirtschaft, Köln

Jánossy, F. (1963), *A gazdasági fejlettség mérhetősége és új mérési módszere*, (The measurement of economic development and a new method of measurement), Közgazdasági és Jogi Könyvkiadó, Budapest.

Jorgenson, D.W. (1961), 'The Development of a Dual Economy', *Economic Journal*, 71 pp. 309-334.

Kalecki, M. (1986), *Vállalatvezetés, tervezés, gazdasági növekedés,* (Management, planning, and economic growth), Közgazdasági és Jogi Könyvkiadó, Budapest.

Kartali J. (1992), *A volt KGST-térség országainak agrárkereskedelmi helyzete és a jövőbeni együttműködés lehetőségei, Oroszország.* (The agricultural situation of the former CMEA-area countries and the possibilities for future cooperation, Russia), Agrárgazdasági Kutató és Informatikai Intézet, Budapest.

Katouzian, H. (1985), 'The Agrarian Question in Iran' in Ghose, A.K. (ed.), *Agrarian Reform in Contemporary Developing Countries*, ILO Study, Croom Helm, London and Sydney, St Martin's Press, New York, pp. 309-357.

Kautsky, K. (1899), *Die Agrarfrage. Eine Übersicht über die Tendenzen der modernen Landwirtshaft und die Agrarpolitik der Sozialdemokratie*, Dietz Verlag, Stuttgart.

Kay, D. (1985) 'The Agrarian Reform in Peru: an Assessment' in Ghose, A.K. (ed.), *Agrarian Reform in Contemporary Developing Countries*, ILO Study, Croom Helm, London and Sydney, St Martin's Press, New York pp. 185-239.

Keynes, J.M. (1936), *The General Theory of Employment, Interest and Money*, Harcourt, Brace and World, Inc., New York.

Koester, U. and Bale, D.M. (1990), 'The Common Agricultural Policy' *The World Bank Research Observer*, Vol. 5.

Kohlepp, G. (1979), 'Brasiliens probematische Antithese zur Agrarreform: Agrarkolonisation in Amazonien' in Elsehans, H. (ed.), *Agrarrefrom in der Dritten Welt*, Campus Verlag, Frankfurt/New York pp. 471-503.

Konjunkturajelentés 1993/1 (1993), (Conjunctural Report, The state of the world and the Hungarian economy and prospects in Spring 1993), KOPINT-DATORG, Budapest.

Kopeva, D. and Mishev, P. (1993), *Summary of Land Reform*, Ministry of Agricultural Development, Phare Programme: Agricultural Policy Analysis Unit, MSS February, Sofia.

Korán, I. (1980) *Világmodellek* (World models), Közgazdasági és Jogi Könyvkiadó, Budapest.

Kornai, J. (1993), 'Transzformációs visszaesés', (Transformation recession), Közgazdasági Szemle, vol. XL, no. 7-8, Budapest, pp. 569-599.

Krajkó, Gy. (1987), *A Szovjetunió gazdaságföldrajza*, (The economic geography of the Soviet Union), Tankönyvkiadó, Budapest.

Külkereskedelmi statisztikai évkönyv (Statistical yearbook of foreign trade), *1988, 1989, 1990*, KSH.

Kuznets, S. (1966), *Economic Growth and Structure, Selected Essays*, W.W. Norton and Co., New York.

Ladejinsky, W. (1977), 'Indian reforms since Independence' in Walinsky, L.J. (ed.), *The Selected Papers of Wolf Ladejinsky: Agrarian Reforms as Unfinished Business*, Published for the World Bank, Oxford University Press, Oxford, pp. 376-393.

Lahsaeizadeh, A. (1987), 'Land reform and Social Change in Rural Iran' in *Land reform, Land Settlement and Cooperatives,* no. 1/2 FAO, Rome, pp. 22-57.

Land Reform (1974), World Bank Paper, Rural Development Series, July.

Lenin, V.I. (1975), 'A szövetkezetekről' (On Cooperatives), *Collected Works of Lenin,* vol. 45, Kossuth Könyvkiadó, Budapest.

Leontief, W. (1970) *Essays in Economics,* I-II, M.E. Sharpe Inc., New York.

Leontief, W. (1977): *The Future of the World Economy.* Oxford University Press, New York.

Levin, C. and Giordano, M. (1993), 'New Directions for Vietnam's Economy',. *Agricultural Outlook,* March, Economic Research Service, USDA, pp. 28-32.

Lewis, W.A. (1963), *The Theory of Economic Growth,* 6th ed., Allen and Unwin Ltd, London.

Maede, J.E., *Neo-Classical Theory of Economic Growth.* George Allen and Unwin Ltd. London, II edition.

Malthus, T.R. (1933), *Essay on Population,* Dutton, New York.

Mándy, Gy. (1971), *Hogyan jöttek létre a kulturnövényeink?* (What is the origin of our cultivated plants?), Mezőgazdasági Kiadó, Budapest.

Manegold, D. (1993), 'Die landwirtschaftlichen Märkte und der Jahreswende 1992-93', Agrarwirtschaft, vol. 42, no. 1, pp. 1-18.

Márton, J. and Ujhelyi, T. (1986), *Kilépés a világélelmezési válságból,* (The way out of the world food crisis), Közgazdasági és Jogi Könyvkiadó, Budapest.

Marx, K., 1965: Capital vols. I-III. Progress Publishers, Moscow.

Meadows, D.L. and Associates (1972), *The Limits to Growth.* Universe Books, New York.

Meisel, V.S. and Mohácsi, K. (1993) *'A társulási szerződés és a magyar agrárágazat' (The Agreement of Association and Hungarian agriculture),* Európa Forum, April, Budapest, pp. 114-139.

Mellor, J.W. (1967), 'Toward a Theory of Agricultural Development' in Southworth, H.M. and Johnston, B.F. (eds.), *Agricultural Development and Economic Growth,* Cornell University Press, Ithaca, N.Y.

Mertins, G. (1979), 'Konventionelle Agrarreformen – Moderner Agrarsektor in Andinen Südamerika. Die Beispiele Ecuador und Kolumbien' in Elsenhans, H. (ed.), *Agrarreform in der dritten Welt,* Campus Verlag, Frankfurt/New York, pp. 401-431.

Mesarovic, M. and Pestel, E. (1974), *Mankind at the Turning Point,* New York.

Mészáros, R., Probáld, F., Sárfalvi, B. and Szegedi, N. (1987), *Amerika gazdaságföldrajza*, (Economic geography of America), Tankönyvkiadó, Budapest.

Mészáros S. and Spitalszky M. (1991) 'Az Európai Közösség és Magyarország árrendszerének összehasonlítása' (Comparison of the agricultural price systems of Hungary and the European Community), *Gazdálkodás*, vol. XXXV, no. 6, Budapest, pp. 1-12.

Morgan, W.B. and Munton, R.J.C. (1971), *Agricultural Geography*, Methuen Co. Ltd., London.

Morgan, W.B. (1978), *Agriculture in the Third World*, Westview Press, Boulder, Colorado.

Morgan, W.B. (1990), 'Agrarian Structure' in Pacione, M. (ed.), *The Geography of the Third World,* Routledge, London and New York, pp. 77-113.

Moyer, H.W. and Josling, E.T. (1990), *Agricultural Policy Reform.* Harvester Wheatsheaf, New York.

Myrdal, G.K. (1957), *Rich Lands and Poor. The Road to World Prosperity*, Harper, New York.

Myrdal, G.K. (1970), *The Challenge of World Poverty, A World Anti-Poverty Programme in Outline,* Penguin Books, Ltd., England.

Nagy, P. (1990): 'Az emberi fejlődés rangsora' (Human Development Index) in *Figyelő*, vol. XXXIV, no. 38, Sep. 20, Budapest, p. 14

Németh, J. (1984), *Trópusi Kelet-Afrika: Kenya, Uganda* (Tropical East Africa), *Mezőgazdasági Világjárás,* Agroinform, Budapest.

Németh, V. (1987/a), Angola, *Mezőgazdasági Világjárás,* Agroinform, Budapest.

Németh, V. (1987/b), Mozambique, *Mezőgazdasági Világjárás,* Agroinform, Budapest.

Nemzetközi Statisztikai Évkönyv (1989), (International Statistical Yearbook), KSH.

Osteuropas Landwirtschaft 1992 (1993), *Osteuropa Wirtschaft,* 38. Jahrgang, Juni.

Our Common Future (1987), World Commission on Environment and Development, 'Food Security: Sustaining the Potential and Species' and 'Ecosystems: Resources Development', Oxford University Press, Oxford and New York, pp. 118-146 and 147-167.

Parikh, K.S., Fischer, G., Frahberg, K. and Gulhrandsen, O. (1988), *Toward Free Trade in Agriculture*, Austria Food and Agriculture Program, International Institute of Applied Systems Analysis, Laxenburg.

Peek, P. (1985), 'Agrarian Reform and Rural Development in Nicaragua, 1971-81' in Ghose, A.D. (ed.), *Agrarian Reform in Contemporary*

Developing Countries', ILO Study, Croom Helm, London and Sydney - St Martin's Press, New York, pp. 273-308.

Perroux, F. (1950), 'Economic Space: Theory and Applications', *Quarterly Journal of Economics*, 64.

Pfeffer, M.J. (1989), 'Part-time Farming and the Stability of Family Farms in the FRG', *European Review of Agricultural Economics*, vol. 16-4, pp. 425-444.

Pfeffer, M.J. (1989), 'The Feminization of Production on Part-time Farms in the Federal Republic of Germany', *Rural Sociology*, 54 (1), pp. 60-73.

Probáld, F., Sárfalvi, B. and Szegedi, N. (1984), *Az európai tőkés országok gazdaságföldrajza*, (Economic geography of European capitalist countries), Tankönyvkiadó, Budapest.

Production Yearbook 1991 (1992), FAO, Rome.

Progress in Land Reform (1970), Fifth Report, United Nations, New York.

Ranis, G. and Fei, J.C.H. (1961) 'A Theory of Economic Development', *American Economic Review*, 51, pp. 533-565.

Reimund, D. (1991), 'The US Farm Sector in Review. Trends Since the Mid-Seventies', *Agricultural Outlook*, October, Economic Research Service, USDA, pp. 32-34.

Ricardo, D. (1817), *On the Principles of Political Economy and Taxation*, London.

Rostow, W.W. (1960), *The Stages of Economic Growth, A Non-Communist Manifesto*, Cambridge University Press, London.

Rural Industry in Australia (1983), Bureau of Agricultural Economics, Australian Government Publishing Service, Canberra.

Rui-zhen, Y. (1989), 'Changes in the System of Ownership in Rural China' in Longworth, J.W. (ed.), *China's Rural Development Miracle*, IAAE, University of Queensland Press, pp. 11-17.

Sanders, Th.G. (1987), 'The Politics of Agrarian Reform in Brazil' in *Land Reform, Land Settlement and Cooperatives*, no. 1/2, FAO, Rome, pp. 1-21.

Schmitt, G.H. (1989), 'Warum ist Landwirtschaft Überwiegend "bauerliche Familienwirtschaft"?', *Berichte Über Landwirtschaft 67, pp. 161-219.*

Schultz, Th. W. (1953), *The Economic Organization of Agriculture*, McGraw Hill, New York.

Schumpeter, J.A. (1952), *Theorie der wirtschaftlichen Entwicklung*, Duncker und Humblott, Berlin, 5th edition.

Sharma, A.N. (1984), *Economic Structure of Indian Agriculture*, Himalaya Publishing House, Bombay.

Sinha, R. (1984), *Landlessness: A Growing Problem*, FAO, Rome.

Solow, R. (1956), 'A Contribution to Economic Growth', *The Quarterly Journal of Economics*, February.

Statistische Grundzahlen der Gemeinschaft (1990), Eurostat, Brussels.

Stevens, R.D. and Jabara, L.C. (1988), *Agricultural Development Principles,* The Johns Hopkins University Press, Baltimore and London.

Surányi, S. (1992) 'Afrika külgazdasági helyzete a 1990-es ev küszöbén' (Africa's foreign economy at the threshold of 1990), *Külgazdaság*, no. 3, Budapest, pp. 65-76.

Szabó, M. (1992), *A volt KGST-térség országainak agrár kereskedelmi helyzete és a jövőbeni együttmüködés lehetőségei, Ukrajna* (The trade situation of, and opportunities for future cooperation between former countries of the CMEA area, Ukraine), Agrárgazdasági Kutató és Informatikai Intézet, Budapest.

Szűcs, I. (1990), *Verseny és rendszerelmélet a földhasználatban* (Competition and system theory in land use), Közgazdasági és Jogi Könyvkiadó, Budapest.

Tai, H-C. (1974), *Land reform and Politics*, University of California Press, Berkeley.

Tanka, E. (1988), 'Az obcsinától a társasgazdálkodásig. Az orosz földviszonyok fejlődési vázlata' (From obchina to community farming. an outline of developments in Russian land tenure), *Szövetkezeti Kutató Intézet Közlemények,* Budapest.

Terlouw, C.P. (1990), 'Regions of the World System: Between the General and the Specific' in Johnston, R.J., Hauer, J. and Hoekveld, G.A. (eds.), *Regional Geography, Current Developments and Future,* Routledge, London-New York, pp. 50-66.

The Economist (1991), 'The Deal in Maastricht', December 14-20, pp. 29-32.

The Economist Business, Central Europe (1993), 'Ploughman's Crunch', vol. 1, no. 4, September , pp. 24-25.

The Economist (1993), 'Zimbabwe: The Price of Food, Land and Rhetoric', October 2-8, pp. 50-51.

The Economist (1993), 'NAFTA', November 13-20, pp. 21-24.

The Economist (1993), 'GATT Comes Right' and 'Now For Something Completely Different', December 18-25, pp. 11-12 and pp. 59-60.

The 1990 Farm Act (1990), A USDA Staff Briefing, USDA, Washington, D.C., November.

The Sahel Facing the Future (1988), OECD, Paris.

The State of the World in 1987 (1987), A Worldwatch Institute Report on Progress Toward a Sustainable Society, W.W. Norton and Company, New York.

Thünen, J.H. von (1827), Der isolierte Staat in Beziehung auf Landwirtschaft und Nationalökonomie, Pt I, Rostock. Collected Edition, Pts I, II and III, 1876, Berlin

Tiers, R. and Anderson, K. (1987), *Liberalizing OECD Agricultural Policies in the Uruguay Round. Effects on Trade and Welfare*, Australian National University, Working Paper in Trade and Development 87/10, Canberra

Tinbergen, J. (1977), *Reshaping the International Order. The Third Report of the Club of Rome,* German edition: *Wir haben nur eine Zukunft,* Westdeutscher Verlag GmbH, Opladen.

Tracy, M. (1982), *Agriculture in Western Europe. Challenge and Response 1960-1980,* 2nd ed., Granada, New York, London.

Trade Yearbook 1991 (1992), FAO, Rome.

Valdes, A. and Zietz, J. (1980), *Agricultural Protection in OECD Countries: Its Cost to Less Developed Countries,* Research Report 21, International Food Policy Research Institute, Washington, D.C.

Varga, Gy. (1993), 'A mezőgazdaság és a szövetkezetek átalakulása' (Agriculture and the transformation of cooperatives), *Társadalmi Szemle* no 4, Budapest, pp. 32-41.

Vavilov, N.I. (1928), 'Geographische Genzentren unserer Kulturpflanzen', Internationaler Kongress Vererbungs, *Zeitshcrift für Abst. und Vererbungslehre.*

Vavilov, N.I. (1949-50), *The Origin, Variation, Immunity and Breeding of Cultivated Plants,* Chronica Botanica, 13, pp. 1-366.

Vincze, Mária (1993), *Átmeneti-e a román agárgazdasági válság?* (Is the Agrarian Crisis in Romania Transitional?), MSS, University of Babes-Bolyai, Kluj, Romania.

Wagner, H. (1993), *Az agrárgazdaság szerkezetében bekövetkezett változások az EK-hoz történt csatlakozás után a keletnémet tartományok példája alapján*, (Changes in the structure of agriculture after joining the EC, based on the case of the East German Provinces), Agrárgazdasági Kutató és Informatikai Intézet, Budapest.

Wallerstein, I. (1979), *The Capitalist World Economy,* Cambridge University Press, Cambridge.

Wallerstein, I. (1984), *The Politics of the World Economy: The States, the Movements and the Civilizations.* Cambridge University Press, Cambridge.

Webb, S.E. (1993), 'China 2000: A Major Player in the Agricultural Trade Arena', *Agricultural Outlook*, September, Economic Research Service, USDA, pp. 37-42.

Weber, A. (1987-1988), 'Welternährungswirtschaft II', *Internationale Agrarsysteme*, Arbeitsunterlage WS, Kiel.

Woldemeskel, G. (1989), 'Ethiopia's Agrarian Policy and its Effects', *Food Policy,* Nov., vol. 14, no. 4 pp. 308-312.

World Agriculture: Toward 2000 (1988), *An FAO Study*, Alexandratos, N. (ed.), New York University Press, New York.

World Development Report 1992 (1992), World Bank, Oxford University Press, New York.

World Economic Survey 1991 and 1992 (1991 and 1992), United Nations, New York.

Zádor, M. (1986), *Peru, Mezőgazdasági Világjárás,* Agroinform, Budapest.

Index

agrobusiness, 170, 254, 277, 278
animal, livestock
   breeding, 123, 145, 155, 203
   domesticated, 2, 158
   rearing, 54,199, 203, 204, 240
balance of payments, 44,60, 61, 67, 68
balance of trade, 104
bureaucracy, 47, 57, 226, 227, 233
calories, intake of, 39, 43
capitalist economic cycles, 58
capital-labour ratio, 24
capital-output ratio, 21, 22, 25
central control, 52, 223, 226, 227, 238,
239, 265, 284
central planning, 46, 226, 227, 280, 282
climate, 2, 65, 74, 78, 139, 143, 156, 163,
164, 169, 186, 195, 198, 199, 226, 246,
258
climatic change, 157-59
climatic zones, 2, 39, 137, 142-46, 163,
199, 200, 201, 202, 203, 205, 207-9
Club of Rome, 60, 63, 68
Cobb-Douglas function, 26, 27
collectivization, 46, 50, 52, 216, 225,
227, 228, 233, 235, 236, 254, 275, 282
Commodity Credit Corporation (CCC),
123, 124, 125
Common Agricultural Policy, 119, 121,
269
commune, 53, 54, 154, 219, 224, 225,
234, 233-35, 253
Community of Independent States (CIS),
46, 54, 57, 110
compensation vouchers, 228, 229

compulsory delivery, 38, 54, 225
cooperatives, 5, 222-39, 248, 254, 262,
271
core and peripheral areas, 111, 112
Council of Mutual Economic Aid, 9, 50,
51, 104, 106, 108, 110, 130, 131, 170
   Complex Programme, 131
credit, loan, 29, 43, 48, 56, 57, 61, 62,
121, 123, 124, 125, 228, 231, 232, 237,
238, 271, 272, 273, 275, 280
crisis
   debt, 62, 61-63
   food, 44, 60, 161
   oil, 60
crop rotation, 18, 76, 163, 170, 172, 192,
280
cultivation
   extensive, 3, 76, 136, 144, 239, 240,
   241, 258, 262, 270
   intensive, 50, 136, 163, 192, 235, 272
   modern, 172, 196, 218
   shifting, 4, 48, 163, 172, 189, 191,
   192, 193, 218, 219, 220
   traditional, 28, 79, 80
currency
   convertible, 33, 48, 131
   devaluation, 62, 63, 235
   foreign, 30, 32, 33, 124, 125
demand, 21, 47, 58-61, 67, 79, 207, 248
   for agricultural products, 29, 31, 33,
   37, 43, 49, 56, 74, 80, 163, 226, 231,
   241, 244, 252
   for food, 1, 29, 57, 148
   for labour, 30, 243

for services, 15
deregulation, 61, 63
desertification, 3, 145, 159
Domar, E.D., 21, 22, 23, 25
efficiency
    of capitalist farms, 251
    of irrigation, 150
    of means of production, 21-28
    of socialist agriculture, 224, 227, 262, 269, 284
egalitarianism, 48, 226
ejido, 237, 238, 263, 264
employment, 15, 24-25, 48, 56, 60, 69, 231
    in agriculture, 4, 15, 31, 57, 83, 167, 170, 218, 228, 249, 255, 257, 258, 262, 265, 267, 268, 271, 277, 284
Engels, F., 46, 224
environment
    damage, 156-59
    natural, 2, 3, 4, 66, 195, 196, 226
    pollution, 64, 66, 125, 135
    protection, 3, 43, 64, 65, 67, 69, 65, 118, 119, 121, 147, 150, 154, 223
European Community (EC), 87, 94, 100, 104, 106, 108, 109, 112, 116, 117, 118, 119, 120, 122, 123, 125, 127, 128, 129, 130, 169, 170, 198, 255, 118-23, 127-30
European Currency Unit (ECU), 104, 118, 119
European Free Trade Association (EFTA), 106, 108, 127, 130
European Union (EU), 119
famine, 3, 160, 161
FAO, 1, 18, 39, 41, 42, 43, 45, 39, 100, 137, 142, 149, 155, 156, 157, 158, 159, 167, 168, 216, 217, 223
Farm Act, 127
farms
    capitalist, 218, 224, 277
    collective, 51, 236, 264, 269
    common, 224-25
    cooperative, 45, 225-28, 230, 237, 238, 267, 288
    extensive, 4, 218
    family, 47, 74, 154, 161, 167, 215, 216, 230, 260, 288
    individual, 218, 235, 238, 268
    intensive, 217

irrigated, 4, 163
part-time, 169, 230
private, 47, 223, 231, 234, 237, 239-40, 266, 273
state, 5, 45, 49, 52, 57, 223-24, 229, 236, 239, 262, 265, 282, 284, 288
transformation of socialist, 54-58, 228-37
white-run, 154
fertilizer, 3, 18, 30, 36, 39, 41, 43, 49, 56, 125, 135, 136, 147, 154
feudalism, 46, 215, 216, 218, 215, 249, 251, 252, 253, 255, 261, 262, 273, 283
food
    crisis, 44, 60, 161, 286
    demand for, 1, 29, 33, 36, 67, 80, 148, 286, 288
    oversupply, 4
    prices, 38, 49, 63, 287
    processing, 11, 36, 56, 76, 170
    production, 1, 39, 41, 42, 44, 63, 64, 69, 79, 143, 160, 164, 286
    supply, 3, 31, 38, 39, 42, 67, 160, 161
General Agreement on Tariffs and Trade, 111, 112, 116, 117, 122
green revolution, 39, 61, 146, 150, 154, 158, 159, 163
growth
    agricultural, 163, 164
    economic, 9, 18, 20, 21, 23, 27, 28, 30, 32, 37, 44, 59, 60, 61, 63, 64, 65, 66, 67, 167, 286
    indicators, 18, 20, 47
    limits to, 37, 64-65
    models of, 63-69
    slowing of, 44, 58-63
    sustained, 28, 68
    uneven, 19
hacienda, 238, 263, 269, 276
Harrod, R., 21, 22, 23, 25
household
    farm, 49, 57, 85, 230, 231, 258
    plot, 50, 53, 226, 233, 254
    production, 224, 225
    responsibility system, Chinese, 54, 234
income
    distribution, 31, 266

304

farmers', 32, 48, 52, 53, 57, 75, 76, 80, 83, 85, 120, 124, 150, 164, 168, 169, 177, 226, 234, 255, 264, 276
household, 54, 231, 248, 258, 273
national, 9, 18, 43, 45, 150, 151, 161, 162
indebtedness, of countries, 20, 44, 45, 57, 232, 283
industrial
goods, 33, 37, 68, 74, 79, 80, 127, 128, 129, 131, 262
sector, 3, 14, 29, 30, 59, 74
industrialization, 31, 32
input-output model, 27, 67
interest, 61, 62, 121, 123, 124, 128, 228, 232, 258
International Monetary Fund (IMF), 62, 63, 68
investment, 10, 15, 21, 20-28, 48, 64, 67, 128, 130
agricultural, 20, 43, 49, 61, 64, 121, 156, 223, 226, 232, 235, 268, 284
infrastructural, 59
irrigation, 2, 4, 39, 43, 61, 80, 135, 136, 137, 142, 143, 144, 146, 147, 148, 149, 150, 155, 157, 163, 185, 189, 191, 192, 193, 196, 199, 200, 201, 202, 221, 223, 224, 235, 238, 280
Kalecki, M., 24, 25
Kautsky, K., 46, 224
Keynes, J.M., 21, 58
kolkhoz, 57, 225, 226, 232
labour
agricultural, 15, 31, 47, 49, 53, 57, 58, 135, 161, 198, 220, 233, 239, 242, 244, 248, 252, 255, 257, 265, 269, 271, 284
and land reform, 260-84
division of, 18, 74, 79, 86, 111
substitution of, 170-79
urban, 30, 38, 169, 215
land
common, 218, 219, 220, 236, 237, 238, 251, 261, 281
communal, 218, 220, 254, 281
cultivable, 26, 137, 139, 142, 143, 144, 156, 261
diversion, 124

fallow, 18, 76, 123, 136, 159, 162, 170, 172, 185, 192, 218, 251, 267, 280
Land Act, 276
latifundium, 266, 272, 288
Lenin, V.I., 46, 225
levies, 63, 80, 86, 120, 121, 129
location rent, 74, 75, 76, 78, 119, 183, 204
Maastricht Agreement, 119
Malthus, T.R., 160, 161
malthusian, 161, 162
Mansholt Plan, 121
Marx, K., 20, 21, 46, 224, 225
Marxism, 21, 45, 47, 161
mechanization, 59, 257
mixed economy, 58
minifundio, 266, 272, 276, 284
national product
GDP, 9, 10, 11, 13, 14, 15, 44, 118, 122
GNP, 9, 10, 13, 14, 67, 68, 151, 166, 167
NNP, 9, 10
natural vegetation, 2, 195, 198, 200, 203
New Deal, 58
obchina, 219, 233, 254
plantation, 4, 80, 168, 197, 198, 199, 200, 220, 222, 223, 236, 239, 240, 242, 243, 244, 245, 246, 248, 257, 260, 261, 262, 263, 265, 271, 275, 277, 281, 282, 283
plants
cultivated, 2, 158, 186, 187
domesticated, 18, 158, 185, 186-92
natural, 2
population
density, 3, 4, 143, 164, 166, 235, 273
growth, 3, 25, 36, 37, 41, 42, 44, 60, 64, 65, 67, 160, 161, 162, 163, 164, 216, 217, 220, 218, 280
rural, 38, 167, 169, 216, 236, 274, 278, 280
prices
export, 38, 85, 86, 116, 121, 122, 125
fixed, 48, 62, 83
guaranteed, 120, 121, 122, 125
import, 61, 62, 106
liberalization, 52, 56, 57, 62, 232, 287

reference, 121
support, 54, 85, 86, 121, 123, 124, 288
target, 121, 125
privatization, 5, 52, 55, 56, 57, 61, 62, 63, 129, 227, 228, 230, 232, 233, 238, 267, 270
producer subsidy equivalent (PSE), 87, 123
productivity
agricultural, 4, 15, 28, 29, 25, 30, 31, 43, 47, 52, 55, 56, 57, 61, 62, 63, 81, 85, 119, 135, 156, 170-82, 202, 238, 262, 267, 273
of capital, 22
of labour and capital, 26
protectionism, 1, 4, 78, 83, 87, 108, 112, 116
protein intake, 37, 39, 110, 123, 159
purchasing power parity, 11, 13, 14, 32, 33, 57, 62, 83, 130, 231, 237, 273
ranching, 4, 148, 221, 240, 241, 244, 258
reform
agrarian, 264, 266, 267, 271, 272, 281, 282
regulation
overregulation, 48
price, 86
Ricardo, D., 20, 21, 75, 81, 82
Rostow, W.W., 28, 29
Sahel, 41, 142, 143, 159, 161, 200, 220, 248
savannah, 142, 189, 198, 199, 201, 207, 219, 220, 221, 240
seed agriculture, 189, 191, 193
self sufficiency, 51
set-aside, 122, 123, 124
settler countries, 5, 18, 240, 245, 249, 281
share tenants, 5, 266, 271, 273, 279
sharecroppers, 238, 239, 242, 243, 257, 261, 264, 266, 267, 272, 273, 274, 275, 283
Single European Act, 119
slash and burn, 170, 189, 218, 219, 220
smallholding, 5, 215, 231, 239, 265, 278
soil erosion, 3, 147, 156, 157
sovkhoz, 57

species, 3, 157, 158, 159, 186, 187, 189, 195, 196, 223
subsidy, 1, 32, 39, 43, 52, 56, 57, 61, 62, 63, 78, 83, 85, 86, 87, 116, 117, 120, 123, 124, 125, 128, 226, 227, 228, 229, 232, 234, 255
subsistence agriculture, 10, 31, 32, 57, 74, 76, 151, 172, 255, 283
take-off, 28, 29
tariffs, 111, 112, 116, 117, 120, 121, 122, 125, 128, 129, 130
tax, 32, 38, 39, 53, 54, 61, 63, 80, 81, 85, 87, 118, 119, 122, 128, 146, 161, 221, 245, 246, 252, 261, 271, 273, 275
Thünen, J.H. von, 74, 75, 76, 78
trade agreement, 108, 109
traditional cultivation, 81, 154, 159, 163, 164, 195, 199, 202, 218, 252
Uruguay Round, 112, 116, 117
vegeculture, 189, 192, 193, 199
wages, 31, 48, 49, 53, 120, 215, 226, 234, 237, 238, 248
withdrawal, 32, 47, 49, 87, 226, 227, 255
zamindar, 275, 276